The Political Economy of Pakistan 1947-85

The Political Economy of Pakistan 1947-85

Omar Noman

KPI
London and New York

To Latifa, for standing by.

First published in 1988 by KPI Limited
11 New Fetter Lane, London EC4P 4EE

Distributed by
Routledge & Kegan Paul, Associated Book Publishers
(UK) Limited
11 New Fetter Lane, London EC4P 4EE

Methuen Inc., Routledge & Kegan Paul
29 West 35th Street
New York, NY 10001, USA

Produced by Worts-Power Associates

Set in Times New Roman
by Papyrus Limited, Thetford, Norfolk
and printed in Great Britain
by Thetford Press Limited, Thetford, Norfolk

© Omar Noman 1988

No part of this book may be reproduced in any form
without permission from the publisher, except for the
quotation of brief passages in criticism.

ISBN 07103 0211-8

Contents

INTRODUCTION
Preface — vi
Key Social Indicators — ix
Chronology of Major Political Events — x
Map of Pakistan — xiii

PART ONE: FROM PARTITION TO CIVIL WAR, 1947-71
Chapter 1: 1947-1958 . . . The Disenchantment with Freedom — 3
Chapter 2: Military Rule and Civil War — 27

PART TWO: AUTHORITARIAN POPULISM UNDER BHUTTO, 1971-77
Chapter 1: Political Development under the PPP — 57
Chapter 2: Economic Developments and their Consequences — 74
Chapter 3: Populism and Ideology — 101

PART THREE: MILITARY RULE UNDER ZIA, 1977-85
Chapter 1: Strategies for Self-Preservation — 117
Chapter 2: A Military Theocracy — 140
Chapter 3: Economic Developments — 157
Chapter 4: Ethnic Conflict — 180
Chapter 5: The Role of the State — 197

Bibliography — 204
Index — 214

Preface

An attempt has been made, in this introductory analysis, to provide a fairly comprehensive interpretation of Pakistan's development. Since a fair deal of literature covering the 1947-71 period is available, our coverage is biased towards post '71 events. None the less, part one provides a summary analysis of pre-1971 developments. This section has two objectives. First, to outline a general framework within which one can comprehend subsequent developments. Second, to provide basic background information to those not familiar with Pakistan's evolution. A chronology of major political events, and basic economic data, can be found at the beginning of the text.

There are two chapters in part one. The first chapter contains a summary examination of how and why a constitutional movement for the protection of a religious minority escalated into a violent struggle for the creation of a new nation-state. The chapter also includes an explanation for the failure, in Pakistan, to develop the kind of democratic structure established in India. Chapter two deals with the Ayub Khan era. The chapter lays particular emphasis on a broad theme running through the text — that the political dynamics of Pakistan cannot be understood without reference to the form, structure and consequences of economic policies.

Part two, dealing with the Bhutto era, has three chapters. The first deals with the question of civil-military relations. It suggests an explanation for the failure of the PPP to retain power in spite of a number of favourable circumstances. The following chapter examines the reasons for the somewhat chaotic nature of economic policy making under Bhutto. It offers an explanation of why certain economic policies were chosen and their link with subsequent political developments. The third chapter contains an analysis of Bhutto's populism. It discusses the ideological significance of the populist discourse and implicitly suggests an explanation for the continuing popularity of the Bhutto legacy.

Part three, covering the Zia era, is divided into five chapters. The first analyses the three phases that General Zia's regime passed through, up to 1986. The second chapter probes into the scale and nature of the ideological shift under General Zia. It examines its causes and consequences. The third chapter examines economic developments, and chapters four and five ethnicity and the role of the state. Particular emphasis is placed on the political and economic effects of the large-scale migration to the Middle East. In our view, this process has resulted in a structural change within Pakistani society. Not only has it helped to sustain the Zia regime but it has also, simultaneously, altered the traditional pattern of political mobilisation. The urban classes which brought down Ayub and Bhutto were, between 1978 and 1985, the principal beneficiaries of the migratory process and hence could not be relied upon as eager catalysts for political change.

It is worth emphasising that our analysis of the Zia regime covers the period prior to the incorporation of civilians in 1985-86. The liberalisation since 1985 has extended, at least temporarily, the parameters of permitted political activity. This has implied relatively limited recourse to repression to sustain the regime. Various groups have been accommodated within the new structure, breaking the regime's isolation.

An all-embracing analysis of economic and political events has inherent limitations. Complex issues are condensed and summarised. None the less, tracing the broad contours of diverse economic and political processes provides one with the somewhat indulgent opportunity of offering an integrated analysis of Pakistan's development. Any interpretation of this kind is unavoidably normative. Accordingly, our value judgements are explicit and will, one hopes, be accepted as preferences rather than prejudices.

OMAR NOMAN
Oxford, 1986

Pakistan: Key Social Indicators

	Pakistan			Low Income Asia and Pacific	Middle Income Asia and Pacific
	1960	1970	1985		
Per Capita GNP (dollars)	70.0	140.0	380.0	276.7	1,028.6
Population (millions)	45.9	60.4	90.5	.	.
Urban Population (%)	22.1	24.9	28.7	21.5	32.9
Population Density (sq. km.)	57.0	75.2	102.1	161.7	260.7
Annual Growth Rate (%)	2.3	2.8	3.0	1.9	2.3
Annual Urban Growth Rate (%)	4.6	4.0	4.3	4.0	3.9
Crude Birth Rate (per thousand)	51.3	47.4	45.5	29.3	31.3
Crude Death Rate (per thousand)	24.3	19.9	15.8	10.9	9.6
Life Expectancy at Birth (years)	43.3	46.6	50.2	59.6	60.2
Access Safe Water (% population)	.	21.0	29.0	32.9	37.1
Access Excreta Disposal (% population)	.	3.0	6.0	18.1	41.4
Population per Physician	5,400.0	4,300.0	3,480.0	3,506.0	7,771.9
Adult Literacy Rate (% population)	15.4	20.7	24.0	53.5	72.9
Total Labour Force (thousands)	14,448.0	17,364.0	23,375.0	.	.
Female (%)	8.6	9.3	10.3	33.3	33.6
Agriculture (%)	61.0	59.0	57.0	69.0	50.9
Industry (%)	18.0	19.0	20.0	15.8	19.2
Absolute Poverty Income Level (dollars per capita)					
Urban	.	68.0	176.0	133.9	194.5
Rural	.	47.0	122.0	111.6	155.0
Population Below Absolute Poverty Income Level (%)					
Urban	.	42.0	32.0	43.8	24.4
Rural	.	43.0	29.0	51.7	41.1

Source: International Bank for Reconstruction and Development.

Chronology of Major Political Events

1947: Independence from British rule and simultaneous partition of India. The Muslim majority provinces of India formed into a new nation-state, Pakistan.
1948: M.A. Jinnah, leader of Pakistan Movement and the first head of state, dies. Liaquat Ali Khan takes over as Prime Minister.
1951: Liaquat assassinated. Controversy surrounds murder. Suspicion remains that it was plotted by factions within the government. After Liaquat, central government dominated by the Civil Service. Political figures in positions of nominal authority. Real power lies with bureaucrats such as Ghulam Mohammad and Iskander Mirza.
1952: Language riots in East Pakistan, in protest at central government attempts to impose Urdu as the only official language. The first violent manifestation of ethnic tensions. Bengalis, the major ethnic group, constitute 54% of the population but are inadequately represented in government and administration.
1954: Muslim League, the party which led the Pakistan Movement, routed in provincial elections in East Pakistan. Pakistan joins SEATO, a U.S. sponsored military alliance.
1955: The provinces of West Pakistan merged into 'One Unit', a scheme to achieve parity *vis-à-vis* East Pakistan. Provokes considerable resentment among the smaller provinces of West Pakistan. Pakistan joins CENTO, another Western military pact.
1956: Constitution framed after a delay of nine years. Outlines a framework for a parliamentary democracy.
1958: The military intervenes under the command of Field Marshal Ayub Khan. The *coup d'état* is followed by the dissolution of the National Assembly. Parliamentary elections, scheduled for early 1959, are cancelled. Martial law is imposed.
1959: System of 'basic democracies' established, to provide a safe electoral college for the President. Part of a process of creating institutions designed to absorb civilian elites into the structure of military rule.
1961: Reforms of Islamic laws announced under the Family Laws Ordin-

ance. Banned polygamy. Symbolised secular flavour of the Ayub Government.
1962: Martial law replaced by a second constitution. Contains a framework for a centralised, presidential system underwritten by military sanction.
1964: Ayub 'wins' presidential election, defeating Miss F. Jinnah, sister of the Quaid-e-Azam (title of 'great leader' given to the founder of Pakistan).
1965: War with India. Kashmir, the only Muslim majority province remaining in India, was the source of conflict. The unsatisfactory outcome of the war weakens Ayub's hold on the army.
1966: East Pakistan's major political party, Awami League, puts forward a six-point platform which proposes a confederation of the two regions. Mujib, leader of the Awami League, is subsequently charged with treason.
1968: Growing class conflict and regional tensions provide an explosive base for a national mass movement against the Ayub regime.
1969: Ayub resigns in the face of continuing violence. General Yahya Khan takes over.
1970: Yahya honours his pledge to hold free elections. Awami League sweeps East Pakistan. A more surprising result in West Pakistan, where Z. A. Bhutto's Pakistan People's Party emerges as the dominant political force.
1971: The army refuses to transfer power to the Awami League, fearing implementation of the six points. The army launches a military offensive against the Bengalis. The latter, assisted by India, secede from Pakistan to form Bangladesh. The army transfers power to Zulfiqar Ali Bhutto in the truncated Pakistan.
1972: PPP Government nationalises large industries. Land reforms announced.
1973: Pakistan's third constitution, but the first to have the support of all political parties. Ethnic divisions continue to plague Pakistan. The Baluchistan Provincial Government is dismissed. The consequent armed insurrection, and protest resignation of the provincial government in Frontier Province (NWFP), undermines civilian structure outlined in the 1973 Constitution.
1974: Islamic Summit held at Lahore. This gathering of Muslim heads of state is symbolic of Pakistan's closer association with the Islamic world.
1977: PPP Government rigs parliamentary elections. The army takes advantage of resulting protest movement. General Zia-ul-Haq promises fresh elections within ninety days of the *coup.* Deposed Prime Minister Bhutto charged with murder.
1978: The army turns to Islam. Measures introduced to convert Pakistan

into a military theocracy. The process, referred to as Islamisation, includes 'religiously sanctioned' punitive measures such as hand amputation and public floggings.

1979: Bhutto executed. Army removes major political threat. Soviet Union invades Afghanistan. Consequent American support for Zia's government breaks regime's isolation, due to revulsion at Bhutto's hanging. Political parties are banned. Political activity declared a punishable offence.

1983: Army eventually contains violent revolt in Sind Province; an uprising against military rule and for greater provincial autonomy.

1984: Assembly elected on a non-party basis. Provides civilian buffer for military rule. Zia declares himself 'elected' as President after referendum on Islamisation. Law of Evidence gives female testimony, in certain cases, half the weight of male evidence.

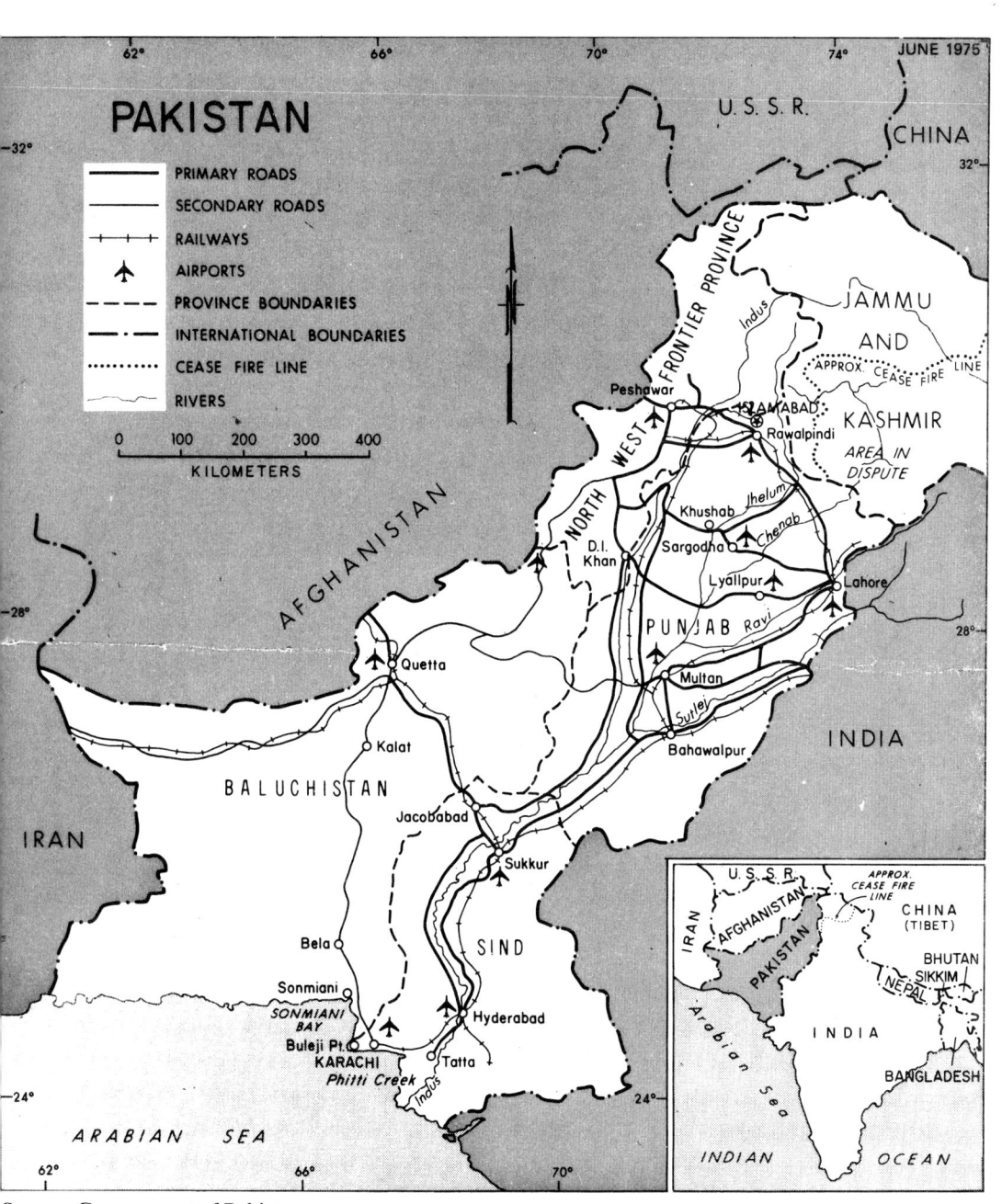

Source: Government of Pakistan

Part One
FROM PARTITION TO CIVIL WAR. 1947-1971

"Suppose this was a realistic novel! Just think what else I might have to put in . . . the longago Deputy Speaker who was killed in the National Assembly when the furniture was flung at him by elected representatives . . . or about the issue of Time magazine (or was it Newsweek) which never got into the country because it carried an article about President Ayub Khan's alleged Swiss bank account . . . or about genocide in Baluchistan . . . or about the attempt to declare the sari an obscene garment; or about the extra hangings — the first for twenty years — that were ordered purely to legitimise the execution of Mr Zulfiqar Ali Bhutto; or about why Bhutto's hangman has vanished into thin air . . . or about smuggling, the boom in heroin exports, military dictators, venal civilians, corrupt civil servants, bought judges, newspapers of whose stories the only thing that can be confidently said is that they are lies; or about the apportioning of the national budget, with special reference to the percentages set aside for defence (huge) and for education (not huge) . . . Realism can break a writer's heart. Fortunately, however, I am only telling a sort of modern fairy tale, so that's all right; nobody need get upset, or take anything I say too seriously. No drastic action need be taken either. What a relief!"

Salman Rushdie, *Shame*

Chapter One

1947 — 1958 . . . The Disenchantment With Freedom.

It is ironic that Pakistan continues to be plagued by a controversy regarding the precise role for religion in its politics. The country is haunted by the ideological schizophrenia permeating the Pakistan Movement. The demand for the partition of Indian territory into two nation-states was based upon the notion that Muslims and Hindus constituted two distinct nations. This communal division implied a theologically determined divergence in social structure. Muslims could refer to a holistic conception of society outlined in the Quran. Economic, political and legal institutions delineate vectors within a comprehensive ideological matrix. Jinnah's rhetoric often conformed to this vision: "Islam is our guide and complete code of life".[1]

Rhetoric apart, Jinnah, in common with most of the Muslim League leadership, had only tangential contact with religion. Secular, liberal thought had exercised a strong influence on Jinnah, who was a leading advocate for the separation of religion and politics.[2] Indeed, Jinnah categorically refused to commit the Muslim League to basing the Constitution of Pakistan on Islamic principles.[3] Such ambivalence regarding the precise form a separate Muslim state will take was also reflected in public pronouncements of Iqbal, the philosopher most closely associated with the Pakistan Movement. Addressing the Muslim League at Allahabad, he tried to reassure Hindus and Sikhs with the promise that they should not fear "that the creation of autonomous Muslim states will mean the introduction of a kind of religious rule in such states".[4]

It is not surprising, therefore, that the creation of Pakistan was opposed by a large section of India's Muslim religious leaders.[5] Maududi, the leading Muslim theologian in India, raised the obvious question: if the intention was to create a secular state in Pakistan, then what was the harm in a united India? Why should Muslims pay a heavy price in terms of life and property for the establishment of another secular state?[6] These religious leaders had two interrelated reservations regarding Pakistan. One was the fear that the 'westernised'élite had no intention of creating a theocracy. Secondly, the religious leaders would have no political authority in Pakistan, and therefore had little to gain by supporting the partition of India.

There were obvious contradictions in the demand for a separate, but *secular*, Muslim state. However, the protection of the Muslim élite's interests did not require the creation of a theocracy. The subtle, but important, distinction was emphasised by the penetrating observation, "The Pakistan Resolution (1940) can be explained *without reference to Islam*, though not without reference to Muslims".[7]

The demand for Pakistan had grown out of an environment in which the British were extending indigenous élite participation in the administration of India. The Muslim component of this élite, comprising mostly landlords and professional groups such as lawyers, sought positive discrimination through provisions such as a reserved quota in the public services and the legislature.[8] It is, however, important to emphasise that the Muslim élite did not consist of a homogenous bloc. Ninety-five million Muslims, 25% of the population, were spread across India. Of considerable significance to the nature of the Pakistan Movement was the division between those Muslims who lived in Muslim majority provinces and those who lived in areas where Muslims were in a minority. The core of the Muslim League leadership came from the latter group [9] — Muslims from the northern United Provinces (UP). They feared marginalisation by the numerically dominant Hindus at the centre of a unitary structure of government advocated by the Congress Party.[10] There were two reasons for the disproportionate power and influence exercised by this section of the Muslim élite. The first was the legitimacy, conferred by their historical pedigree, as descendants of the Mughal administration which was governing India at the time of the British conquest. The second related to their physical proximity to the central government, a position which gave them an advantage over provincially based leaders. Pakistan appealed more to the insecure UP Muslims than it did to those who lived in Muslim majority areas, a tendency recognised by the penultimate viceroy, Wavell: "The Pakistan idea is stronger in the Muslim minority provinces than in the Pakistan provinces".[11]

The reason for the difference in perspective, within the Muslim élite, was obvious. In some of the Muslim majority provinces, such as the NWFP, Hindu domination was not a serious threat, since the Muslims had an overwhelming majority.[12] The bulk of the Muslim population, however, lived in the provinces of Bengal and Punjab, both containing a substantial Hindu or Sikh population. The Muslim élite of these provinces was well represented in the state governments formed after the 1937 provincial elections.[13] In their majority provinces, Muslims were "already well on top and with a little forbearance could easily placate the minorities ... they would gain little or nothing by Pakistan".[14] Indeed, the Muslim élite of Punjab and Bengal was initially hostile to the division of their provinces on the basis of religion.[15] In order to get the support of these regional élites, the UP Muslims at the centre had to make substantial concessions regarding provincial autonomy. Consequently, the Muslim League's proposals for grouping the Muslim majority provinces were heavily weighted in favour of state governments. Similarly, it was not surprising that the Pakistan Resolution committed itself to 'sovereign and autonomous' states vesting limited powers to a weak centre. This provincial bias is ironic in view of subsequent developments in Pakistan. Eventually, both Punjab and Bengal had to be divided when India was partitioned. The relatively prosperous areas of each province remained in India. The Punjabi Muslims were subsequently compensated by a share in political power. For the Bengalis, the partition of their province was an unmitigated disaster. The part of Bengal which Pakistan inherited consisted of overpopulated rural areas with a bleak economic future.[16] Such an unfavourable demarcation was not offset by political power for Bengali Muslims. Indeed, the denial of a share in government to the Bengalis led to the dismemberment of Pakistan in 1971.

The partition of India along communal lines was not the only option pursued by the Muslim League. On the contrary, there was a great deal of ambiguity surrounding the Muslim demand for representational parity. Even up to 1946, Jinnah had not abandoned his quest for a constitutional structure which could accommodate Muslim interests within a united India. In this context it is worth noting that the Muslim League accepted the Cabinet Mission Plan for a confederal India, just a year before Partition.[17] Jinnah's acceptance of the principle of a united India provoked anxiety amongst his followers regarding the Muslim League's true intentions *vis-à-vis* Pakistan.[18] The Congress Party, however, refused to accept the Plan's provisions for a weak and impotent centre. Neither Nehru nor Gandhi was willing to preserve the unity of India at the expense of accepting what to them appeared to be a chaotic, fissiparous and unworkable political structure.

The Muslim League had pushed itself into a tight corner. Jinnah was a staunch constitutionalist who had been forced into mass politics, a role which he did not relish.[19] The Muslim League had required a demonstration of popular Muslim support to strengthen its negotiating position. The rallying of mass support, however, had a dynamic of its own. It had two consequences. First, religious passions had to be aroused if communalism was to form the basis of mobilisation. The operational logic of such a scheme encouraged and nurtured communal hatred. The brutal and violent consequences could not be controlled by secular constitutionalists. Second, for the Muslim masses, the goal of Pakistan acquired the symbol of a promised land. Its creation was to be a source of liberation for the underprivileged. The Muslim League promised a just, egalitarian economic and social order.[20] The expectations generated by such pledges explains, to a large extent, mass support for the Pakistan Movement. In a rigidly repressive society, Muslim underprivileged classes saw the prospect of economic and social liberation in Pakistan.

The appeal to liberty was, however, perverted through its adulteration with rhetoric which portrayed another religious community as the barrier to this freedom. To suggest a sinister equation between repression and communal division was provocative. It was a dangerous game and one over which Jinnah and the Muslim League had lost control. The outcome of the passions that were unleashed is unfortunately only too familiar to bear repetition. Thus, what had started as a constitutional struggle for the protection of the Muslim élite had culminated in a mass movement for a separate nation-state. In 1947 Pakistan was propelled into existence, its leaders uncertain of what lay ahead, its followers clinging to visions of a just social order.

To what extent religion would determine politics remained, as we argued earlier, undefined. However, once the territorial truncation along religious boundaries was completed, the Ulema (religious leaders) seized the opportunity to exercise pressure on the secular rulers of the new country. Their demand for a Muslim theocratic state was, after all, perfectly logical for a nation-state created on the basis of religion. In early 1948, the Ulema drafted a detailed proposal for the establishment of a Ministry of Religious Affairs. The ministry would not only regulate and encourage religious institutions but would also function as a body which monitored the conduct of Civil Servants. The views of the Ulema, regarding the form of a theocratic state, were summarised in the report of the Board of Talimat-e-islamia.[21] Their conception of an Islamic state was based on the model of the classical Muslim Caliphate. Since God was the ultimate sovereign, the legitimacy of temporal rulers rested upon their claim as implementors of divine will. Accordingly it was required that the head of state, a Muslim male to be elected for life, be well versed in the laws of the Sharia derived from the Quran and Sunnah.[22] Similarly since God, not the people, was the sovereign, legislation was circumscribed by the requirement of conformity with the Sharia. A committee of theologians was to be the final arbiter on whether particular laws were consistent with the Sharia,[23] thus ensuring that legislation would be controlled by the Ulema.

Maududi distrusted both the westernised political leaders and the other theologians, with whom he had long-standing doctrinal quarrels. He emphasised the incongruity of creating a secular state in Pakistan: "The case of Pakistan is different from other Muslim countries . . . this is so because it has been achieved exclusively with the object of becoming the homeland of Islam".[24] Maududi classified the population into three categories. The first subset consisted of the vast majority of poor, uneducated Muslims who were deeply devoted to Islam, but grossly ignorant of its cardinal doctrines. Their love of religion had been exploited by the Muslim League. The second

1947-1958 The Disenchantment with Freedom

category consisted of a small but powerful minority of westernised Muslims who favoured a secular state. The third group, containing a small fraction of the total population, comprised serious and knowledgeable practitioners of religion. Maududi's theocratic state was to be governed by a religious dictator emanating from the category of informed Muslims. He would exert supreme authority, derived from his piety, over legislative, judicial and executive functions.

Confronted with specific proposals for an Islamic state, the Muslim League Leaders had to tread carefully. They had no intention of conceding to the demands for a theocratic state. However, they did not want to give an opportunity to the religious leaders to utilise this issue in order to mobilise mass support against the Muslim League government. Their capacity to create trouble was evident in the widespread rioting that took place in 1952. The civil disturbances were part of a campaign demanding the expulsion of the Qadiani sect from the fold of Islam.

The Qadiani community maintain that their leader, Mirza Ahmed, was a prophet. This outraged fundamentalist groups, who felt that the claim questioned their passionate belief in the Khatim-e-Nabuat, i.e. prophet Mohammad was the last messenger of God. It is important to emphasise that the demand was not conceded. Twenty-five years later, Z. A. Bhutto's government declared the Qadianis to be a non-Muslim sect. In 1952, the disturbances were quelled through the use of martial law.[25]

None the less, the government had to respond to the proposals for a theocratic state. It did so by issuing a statement of intent regarding the future constitution. This declaration, known as the Objectives Resolution, was deliberately vague. It reiterated the need to build an Islamic state without attempting to define the form of such a state. Indeed, the concept of a Muslim state based on the Sharia was not even mentioned in the Resolution. Prime Minister Liaquat Ali Khan stressed the fact that the Objectives Resolution did not imply a theocracy.[26] The Resolution achieved its objective of outmanoeuvring the religious parties. By issuing a vague pledge to incorporate Islamic principles in the future constitution, the government was able to assert its commitment to Islam without binding itself to specific provisions. The point was not lost on certain commentators: "This Resolution, though grandiloquent in words phrases and clauses is nothing but a hoax ... not only does it not contain even the semblance of the embryo of an Islamic state but its provisions, particularly those relating to fundamental rights, are directly opposed to the principles of an Islamic state".[27] The Muslim League leaders were skating on thin ice. It was a dilemma from which they had to extricate themselves without engaging in an embarrassing public debate about the *raison d'être* of Pakistan. This task was, however, much easier than it may appear since there was no popular support for a theocracy. The lack of popular enthusiasm for a theocracy confirmed the Ulema's suspicions that mass appeal for Pakistan was based less on a desire to observe a strict religious code and more to do with expectations of social and economic advancement.

The alienation of religion from the institutions of government reflected the ideological preferences of the dominant political groups. Jinnah's much quoted inaugural speech to the Constituent Assembly was uncompromising in its commitment to a secular state.[28] Jinnah would define a set of desirable properties for a form of government and then assert that these properties were compatible with Islam. Since Islam was "everything that is good and decent",[29] there was no need to present a rigorous analysis of precisely which aspect of the religion supported various claims of compatibility. In the same vein, Liaquat equated British parliamentarianism with Islam as far as the Constitution of Pakistan was concerned, implying thereby that secularism was compatible with Islam.[30] After Liaquat's death the Civil Service emerged as the dominant political institution. The secular traditions of the Indian Civil Service were reflected in the views of the two most powerful Civil Servants in the 1947-58 period. Ghulam Mohammad declared that "Pakistan is a secular, democratic and not a theocratic state".[31] Iskander Mirza warned that "if the learned maulanas try to dabble in politics there will be trouble . . . religion and politics should be kept apart otherwise there will be chaos".[32] Thus, those elements who had hoped that Pakistan would establish governmental institutions bound by religious authority had suffered a decisive defeat.[33] The issue of an Islamic state was revived, two decades later, by the military government of General Zia-ul-Haq.

The Political Structure: 1947-1958

The political process was shaped by four interrelated developments. The first was the failure of the Muslim League to develop as a national, democratic party. Second was the retention of a highly centralised system of executive government, inherited from the colonial era, rather than the anticipated adoption of legislative supremacy. Third, a tiny mahajjir-Punjabi élite acquired control over the key decision-making posts at the apex of centralised state power. Finally, the period witnessed an explosive growth in regional tension as the primary source of political conflict.

The creation of Pakistan was accompanied by the establishment of a national governmental structure over territory which was not only physically splintered into two geographic units but also contained powerful ethnic divisions. The western wing consisted of four major ethnic groups — Punjabis, Sindhis, Pathans and Baluchis. A fifth important category comprised of mahajjirs (refugees) from India, principally migrants from UP and Bombay.[34] In direct contrast to the ethnic diversity of West Pakistan was the homogeneity of the eastern wing. Containing 54% of the total Pakistani population, East Pakistan was almost exclusively Bengali. The Muslim League was one political force capable of welding together such ethnic diversity within a structure which could accommodate the aspirations of respective ethnic élites. The Muslim League was expected to play a role similar to that performed by the Congress Party in India, i.e. the formation of a national government through parliamentary elections which would ensure a degree of mass participation in the political structure.

The Muslim League's inability to perform this role was conditioned, to a large extent, by the imbalances and hierarchies of power within the Muslim élite of India. As emphasised previously, the core leadership of the Muslim League came from the Muslim minority provinces in North India. During the Pakistan Movement, they had controlled the key Muslim positions. Their supremacy at the centre was not challenged by leaders from Muslim majority provinces, such as Bengal. The support base of regional leaders was confined to their provinces. After Partition, the migrants from Muslim minority provinces dominated the Pakistani Central Government. In addition, both Jinnah and Liaquat, who took over after the former's death in 1948, relied extensively on the bureaucracy in the formulation and execution of policy. The ethnic background of the senior Civil Servants was similar to that of the central Muslim League leadership. The only other ethnic group to be well represented at the centre were the Punjabis, primarily on account of their dominance of the military. The insecurity of this élite regarding Pakistan's ability to survive as a nation-state [35] had two consequences. Externally, Pakistan joined military alliances under the American umbrella as protection against Indian military intervention. Internally, Jinnah accumulated power at the centre. A powerful central government would bind diverse elements into a national framework. However, the power of the central government was divorced from any representative base. Particularly after Liaquat's assassination in 1951, the Civil Service dominated the decision-making process. The growth of bureaucratic power could have been curbed if the Muslim League had called an election and sought a popular mandate, which would have re-established political dominance over the administrators. The reluctance of the central League leadership to resort to parliamentary democracy was inextricably linked with ethnic divisions.

For the League to have developed as an integrative force required an extension of its representative base across the nation. However, the political arithmetic was awkward for the League's central élite. If an election was called, East Pakistan would emerge as the determinant of power at the centre, on account of its majority. This would involve a shift in power away from the mahajjir-Punjabi élite to the Bengalis. None of the leaders in command at the centre, including Liaquat, had a political base in East Pakistan. Elections, would therefore, have altered the hierarchies of power within the national élite, with Bengalis emerging at the helm of the central government.

The refusal to accept such a shift prevented the Muslim League from developing into a national representative force.

Thus, although the Muslim League repeatedly proclaimed its role as a unifying national party, it did little to cultivate such a position. On the one hand, the League promoted a tendency to equate the party with the nation, "If you destroy the League you destroy Pakistan".[36] Indeed, Jinnah went so far as to suggest that there was no need for any party other than the Muslim League.[37] However, in the absence of a representative institutional framework, the party was inevitably smothered by the Civil Servants, on whom it had become so dangerously dependent.

The reluctance of the power bloc at the centre to share power with Bengalis was also the primary cause for the delay in constitution-making. India had a constitution by early 1950. In contrast, the Muslim League dragged its feet on constitutional issues, a performance which contributed to its decline. Between 1948 and 1954 the Constituent Assembly met, on average, a paltry sixteen days a year to frame a constitution.[38] The average attendance consisted of forty-six members,[39] hardly an indication of urgency. Underlying the constitutional delays was the escalating friction between West Pakistani bureaucrats and Bengali politicians. In 1952, for example, Chaudhri Mohammad Ali (Finance Minister) and Gurmani (Interior Minister) objected to Khwaja Nazimuddin's constitutional proposals, embodied in the Basic Principles Committee Report, on the grounds that they were detrimental to the interests of the Punjab.[40] Some of the Punjabi leaders, such as Daultana, were even against parity for East Pakistan,[41] let alone giving them representation in accordance with their population share.

It was ironic that the Muslim League élite was engaged in a quest for an arrangement to reduce the voting power of the Bengalis. The leaders from the Muslim minority provinces of India were thus back to square one. Before Partition they had sought constitutional safeguards against Hindu majority rule. Now they sought protection from a group of Bengali Muslims. A plan was devised whereby some form of parity could be achieved *vis-à-vis* East Pakistan. Accordingly, the four provinces of the western wing were amalgamated into a single province, West Pakistan. Through this merger two provinces were created: East Pakistan and West Pakistan. Both were given equal representational power, thus reducing the aggregate Bengali majority. The central government steamrollered the provincial governments of the western wing into the notorious one-unit scheme. In November 1954, Governor General Ghulam Mohammad dismissed Pirzada's Sind ministry due to its opposition to the one-unit plan. A similar fate befell the NWFP ministry. Indeed, the Governor General intervened in the Punjab when Noon's ministry opposed certain aspects of the scheme. Thus the 'one unit' was created with great haste. The draft bill of the constitution was brought before the Constituent Assembly just three months after the creation of West Pakistan as a single provincial unit. The 1956 Constitution was adopted in March of that year amidst considerable dissatisfaction, particularly from East Pakistan.

It had taken Pakistan nine years to frame a constitution. Moreover, the 1956 Constitution was not a symbol of legislative dominance. On the contrary, the true architects of the document were Civil Servants. Their dominance, and the implied eclipse of the Muslim League, was the logical outcome of the structure favoured by Jinnah. He had chosen to rely on the strong bureaucratic machinery and had thus reinforced the inherited imbalance of power within the institutions of government. In order to develop representative institutions, the Muslim League had to assert the supremacy of the legislature. The shift towards cabinet government required the cultivation of an electoral system. Both Jinnah and Liaquat assigned a higher priority to the development of a strong central government. By the time Liaquat died, the die had been cast. The Civil Service, not the Muslim League, was in charge. Under the circumstances, the disintegration of the League came as no surprise. It had not only failed to institutionalise its mass base, but had also withdrawn from its commitment to reform the economic and social structure. Between 1947 and 1954, the Muslim League was in power at the central and provincial level. From '54 onwards, the party lost control over both levels of government.

The pattern of centre-state relations, as well as that of executive dominance, was set by the dismissal of Khan Sahib's provincial government in NWFP by the Governor General M. A. Jinnah. Thus, within a fortnight of Pakistan's creation, the central government had toppled a provincial administration. Seven months later, Jinnah dismissed Sind's Chief Minister M. A. Khuro.[42] On 25 January 1949, the Punjab Provincial Government was superseded, the Provincial Legislative Assembly dissolved and administration handed over to the Governor. The central government had dismissed a provincial ministry which still enjoyed the confidence of the legislature and commanded a majority in the house.[43] Although Section 51 of the Government of India Act (1935) gave the Governor General power to replace provincial governments, central dominance was strengthened further by subsequent legislation. Under Jinnah, Section 92a was introduced to facilitate implementation of direct rule by the centre. Accordingly, governments were dismissed in Punjab and Sind under the enlarged scope of central intervention.[44] The erosion of any semblance of provincial autonomy further strengthened the Civil Servants who "effectively controlled the entire administration in the provinces and the politicians there were kept in power subject to their willingness to obey central government directives".[45]

The first public exposure of who was effectively in control of Pakistan's political system, behind the facade of parliamentary institutions, came with the Governor General's dismissal of the Prime Minister in April 1953. Ghulam Mohammad, a bureaucrat, had taken over as Governor General after Liaquat's assassination. His dismissal of Prime Minister Nazimuddin's cabinet impugned the role of the legislature as the maker and sustainer of government.[46] The significance of this action lay in how it served to demonstrate the absence of an effective link between the Prime Minister and the institutions of party and parliament.

Had such a framework existed, the Governor General would have found it politically impossible to toy with the legislature. This feature was confirmed when, following the April dismissal, the new regime imposed by the Governor General proceeded painlessly to establish its authority over the Muslim League — the party nominally in command of the legislature. Instead of developing into a mass organisation, the League had reverted back to its pre-Pakistan Movement phase of decorative élite politics. None the less, the shoddy manner in which the Prime Minister was dismissed provoked a belated response from the politicians. In 1954, the Assembly attempted to curb the power of the Governor General by introducing legislation which made it impossible for him to dismiss a prime minister. The Assembly also repealed the PRODA legislation (1949) which had been used to investigate charges of corruption against politicians. In effect it had provided Civil Servants with considerable regulatory power over the conduct of political leaders. The response of the Civil Service was swift. The Governor General dissolved the Constituent Assembly on 24 October 1954.[47] The turmoil within the institutions of the central government had culminated in an act which effectively terminated the institutional arrangement which had accompanied Partition.

From 1954 to 1958, Pakistan's political system degenerated into a farce. The Civil Service, assisted by the military, controlled the key decision-making process. In 1956, Iskander Mirza, another bureaucrat, took over as head of state from Ghulam Mohammad. The one-unit plan was expedited. Khan Sahib was appointed Chief Minister of the province of West Pakistan. Sections of the Muslim League leadership did not approve of the appointment on the grounds that this ex-Congress leader had opposed the creation of Pakistan. In response, President Mirza encouraged Khan Sahib to form a new party, the Republican Party. The formation was followed by defections from members of the Muslim League, eager to cross over to a party which had the blessing of the Civil Service. Within a few months, the Republican Party ousted the Muslim League at the centre, forming an alliance with Suhrawardy's Awami League. Later, there was a Republican-Muslim League alliance against the Awami League. Thus, a series of short-lived governments was formed. The legislature continued to operate, but its primary function was that of validating decisions taken outside the Assembly. Political parties, deprived of real power in the legislature, were reduced to the status of bickering factions controlled by the executive. The military *coup* of 1958 merely formalised the dominance of the military-bureaucratic complex. It also entailed the abolition of institutions which were redundant.

Accordingly the legislature was dispensed with, as were political parties in nominal control of government.

The establishment of a system of central executive rule, rather than of cabinet government based on a representative legislature, encouraged the concentration of power in a group of officials divorced from mass politics. After Liaquat's assassination, the country's two most powerful political positions — Governor General and Prime Minister — were occupied by men whose roots of power lay in the administrative apparatus rather than in the forums of party and parliament. As previously argued, the institutions of party and assembly were no more than the legitimising mechanism for decisions arrived at in the central executive.[48] It is, however, important to emphasise that the ethnic composition of the bureaucratic élite had an extremely important bearing on political developments in Pakistan. Men in command of the centre were either refugees from Muslim minority provinces or from Punjab. Excluded from power were members of the respective élites of Bengal, Sind, Baluchistan and the Frontier Province.[49] A political structure incapable of accomodating four of the five provincial élites could not have been expected to provide stable government.

It has often been suggested that the Muslim League did not hold an election because it did not have a national base, such as Congress in India, and therefore feared losing an election. This is not a particularly convincing argument. In the immediate aftermath of Partition there is little doubt that the Muslim League would have swept national polls. The problem lay not in the lack of ability to win an election but in the weight that East Pakistan would carry in the electoral process. Since Eastern Bengal contained 54% of Pakistan's population, majority rule would entail a shift in power towards the Bengalis. In order to prevent such an outcome, the political élite of Western Pakistan spent the better part of the first decade devising arrangements which would guarantee parity with Eastern Pakistan. Consequently, the initial reluctance of the Muslim League leadership to develop participatory institutions promoted the emergence of the bureaucracy to a position of dominance at the central government. The subsequent stranglehold established by the non-representative executive institutionalised ethnic discrimination, since the positions of power within the military and the bureaucracy were monopolised by the Punjabi-mahajjir axis.

Dominance by an unrepresentative centre inevitably provoked dissension from the regions. Antagonised by the denial of heterogeneity inherent in a multi-ethnic state, regional élites mobilised popular support for greater provincial autonomy. Centre-state relations became the principal forum for political conflict. We have already referred to the resentment of the three smaller provinces in Western Pakistan at the one-unit scheme. However, the primary source of political tension was the relationship between the Punjabi-mahajjir centre and the majority province of East Pakistan. In 1952, language riots broke out in East Bengal when the central government insisted that Urdu would be the only official language,[50] a measure which would have discriminated against Bengali-speaking aspirants for administrative posts. The United Front, a coalition of anti-Muslim League parties, fought the 1954 provincial elections on the basis of a manifesto demanding a relatively weak centre, in charge mainly of defence, currency and foreign affairs.[51] The platform was, ironically, reiterating the federal structure envisaged in the Pakistan Resolution (1940); the provisions contained therein regarding regional autonomy had successfully mobilised Muslim Bengali opinion in favour of Partition. The overwhelming support for the United Front programme, reflected in Table 1 below, was the first indicator of Bengali frustration with the political structure established by the mahajjir-Punjabi élite. The failure of the central government to heed the warning signals, and accommodate Bengalis, meant that the events of 1952 and 1954 marked the first stage of the process leading to Bangladesh.

Table 1: *Provincial Elections in East Pakistan. 1954.*

Party:	Seats:
United Front	233
Muslim League	10
Congress	24
Scheduled Caste Federation	27
Others	15
Total	309

The Muslim League was stunned by the magnitude of its defeat. It was not long, however, before the centre responded to the growth in regional tension. On 30 May 1954, the United Front Government was dismissed and Iskander Mirza was appointed Governor of East Pakistan.[52]

On the international front, Pakistan could not simultaneously achieve its two foreign policy objectives — military security in relation to India and associating Pakistan with the wider Muslim community. The former objective led to military alliances with the U. S. These alliances angered a number of Muslim Arab countries, including Saudi Arabia. Egypt, under Nasser, was a particularly fierce critic of Pakistan's subservience to the West. Along with Nehru, Nasser's primary foreign policy concern was the development of the non-aligned movement. Thus, for Pakistan, being shunned by the Arab Muslim world was a price it had to pay for joining SEATO and CENTO.[53] Two decades later, Pakistan's Islamic credentials were revived by the governments of Bhutto and Zia.

Under the 1956 Constitution, national elections were to be held in February 1959.[54] The electoral process would have entailed a shift in power from the mahajjir-Punjabi executive to a Bengali-dominated legislative government. To circumvent the transfer of power the Civil Service asked the army to take over. This was the second occasion on which such a request was made to the army.[55] By the time of Ayub's *coup* two critical issues had been settled. First, parliamentary democracy would not be allowed to function in Pakistan. Second, a strong central executive would dominate the provinces. Pakistani politics have never recovered from these twin setbacks.

Economic Development

The first decade of economic policy making was characterised by three features. First, the emphasis was on the establishment of import-substituting industries. Although consumer goods were being substituted by domestic production, all the machinery for the capital-intensive industrialisation drive had to be imported, due to the absence of a capital goods sector in Pakistan. Second, the agricultural sector suffered serious problems on account of official neglect in resource allocation. Growth performance was hampered by a stagnant agriculture. Finally, miserly allocations for education and health established a pattern of governmental negligence of social sector provisions, particularly for the poor. Allocations for social services were squeezed by heavy defence expenditure for military security against India.[56].

At the time of Partition large-scale industry was virtually non-existent in the areas comprising Pakistan. The initial phase of industrialisation under the colonial government had concentrated around the large ports. Expansion into the hinterland had been a function of proximity to natural resources such as coal and iron. The areas constituting post-Partition India retained the industrial base. Pakistani territory had played a complementary role in the integrated Indian economy. These areas provided raw materials for the industrial units located in Indian territory. For example, East Bengal supplied jute to the jute industry situated in West Bengal. Similarly, cotton-producing areas of West Pakistan supplied the raw material to the textile industry. To compensate for the loss of these industrial units, the Industrial Policy Document (1947) emphasised the need for import-substituting industrialisation.[57]

The prominence given to industrialisation was symbolised by the controversial decision of not devaluing the rupee in 1949. The devaluation of the pound had been followed by a similar readjustment of the Indian rupee.[58] Pakistan's decision was principally motivated by the favourable impact of an overvalued exchange rate on the industrial sector — the cost of importing machinery would have been higher had Pakistan devalued.[59]

15

Heavy tariff protection was also given to 'infant' industries. The industrialisation drive was also supported by fiscal policy. Profits of new undertakings in approved areas were exempted from direct taxes for a number of years.[60] The government's role went further than providing incentives and protection. In many cases it initiated investment in sectors where the private sector was unable, or unwilling, to enter. The state-run Pakistan Industrial Development Corporation (PIDC) raised capital and developed projects to the stage of operation. These projects were then handed over to the private sector, either through a public issue of shares or a partnership arrangement. The PIDC established a number of jute mills in East Pakistan and a variety of industrial units in West Pakistan, which were subsequently handed over to the private sector.

The industrialisation drive was given a considerable boost by the outbreak of war in Korea. The Korean war led to a boom in raw material prices, particularly between 1950 and early 1952. During this period, Pakistani traders accumulated substantial surpluses through the export of jute and cotton. This fortuitous growth in export revenues supported government policy, which had been geared towards channelling merchant capital into the industrial sector. The end of the Korean boom was accompanied by the imposition of severe controls on the import of consumer goods.[61] This provided erstwhile traders with the ideal opportunity to produce consumer goods domestically, importing machines for the purpose from the surpluses that had been accumulated during the Korean boom.

Rapid growth during the initial phase of import-substituting industrialisation is reflected in Table 2 below. The spectacular growth rates of large-scale manufacturing are somewhat misleading, since the starting base was extremely low. None the less, the first phase of accumulation of industrial capital ran out of steam by the mid-fifties. The market for substituting previously imported consumer goods by domestic production had been exhausted. Further growth was restricted by the poor performance of the agricultural sector. The stagnation of incomes in the major commodity-producing sector of the economy, reflected in Table 2, meant that the domestic market for the manufacturing sector's output was not expanding. In its pursuit of rapid industrialisation, the government had neglected agricultural development, relegating responsibility for its performance to the inadequately endowed provincial governments. The prices of agricultural goods had been maintained at a low level to provide cheap raw materials and cheap food for urban consumers. This disincentive for agricultural growth was compounded by the high price farmers had to pay for the goods produced by the protected industrial sector. Official indifference towards the agricultural sector underestimated the extent to which the industrialisation drive could be hampered by agricultural stagnation. Not only was the stagnation restricting the growth of the domestic market, but the rising food deficits were also absorbing an increasing share of foreign exchange

Table 2: *Growth Performance. 1949-58.*

Growth rate:	1950-51	1951-52	1952-53	1953-54	1954-55	1955-56	1956-57	1957-58	1949-58
Per capita income	1.4	4.4	−0.9	6.8	0.6	0.8	0.5	0.3	1.7
Agriculture	2.6	−9.1	0.18	13.6	−0.8	2.1	2.3	1.9	1.4
Large-scale Manufacturing	23.5	18.7	23.6	28.7	24.1	17.5	8.1	4.9	19.1

Figures refer to the growth performance of West Pakistan.
Source: Government Of Pakistan 'Twenty-five years of Pakistan in statistics'.

resources. Scarce foreign exchange was going into importing food, thus limiting the amount available for the import of capital goods.

The bottlenecks generated by the contradictions inherent in the development strategy were later acknowledged in the third five-year plan (1965-70). The plan reflected on the "considerable transfer of income from the agricultural to the industrial sector during the fifties as terms of trade were *deliberately* turned against agriculture through such policies as licensing of scarce foreign exchange earned primarily by agriculture to the industrial sector . . . the rural areas were transferring savings to the fast modernising urban capitalist sector".[62] According to one study, agriculture transferred 15% of its gross output annually to the urban sector.[63] Not more than 15-37% of the amount transferred from agriculture was turned into investments, and the remaining 63-85% dissipated in higher consumption by the richer urban classes.[64] An over-valued exchange rate was the mechanism through which resources were transferred from agriculture to industry. Since the major exports of the country were agricultural products, the rural sector was the source of foreign exchange earnings. The over-valuation of the rupee meant that a farmer was being paid less than would be his due at the free market rate of exchange. The difference between potential earnings under the conditions of a competitive rupee, and the actual earnings at the official rate, constituted a sort of tax on agriculture. In the same manner, the sale of import licences at the official rate of exchange to traders constituted a corresponding subsidy to the capitalists. These import licences were used for acquiring capital goods and industrial raw materials. These goods were thus underpriced, which reduced industrial costs and encouraged the use of capital intensive techniques.[65]

The transfer of resources from agriculture to industry had important political connotations. The resource transfer provided the material ammunition for the growth of regionalism in East Pakistan. The transfer of foreign exchange revenues, earned by jute exports of the eastern wing, to West Pakistani industrialists, became a symbol of regional exploitation.[66]

The economic policy framework, adopted in the fifties, did not concern itself directly with measures to alleviate mass poverty. Popular aspirations for a better economic future in Pakistan were frustrated by the refusal of the Muslim League to implement its pledges for economic reforms. Partition provided an ideal opportunity to redistribute assets, but the dominance of landed interests over the political structure ensured that even mild reforms were not introduced.[67] The lack of concern for welfare provisions for the poor was reflected in the allocation of the government's resources. Barely 4% of government expenditure was allocated annually for education, health and social services. Moreover, when one considers that most of this expenditure was targeted towards the urban middle class, there was virtually no provision for the education or health of the largely illiterate and malnourished population. Social sector provisions were squeezed particularly hard by the diversion of resources for defence; an indication of the latter's magnitude is provided by Table 3 below.

Table 3: *Defence Expenditure. 1949-58. (Rs. million)*

	1949-50	1954-55	1957-58
Defence Expenditure as % of			
(i) Total development expenditure	193.0	114.8	60.7
(ii) Central government revenues	63.7	46.6	48.0

Source: *The Budget 1959-60.* Ministry of Finance, Government of Pakistan.

In 1949, the expenditure on defence was nearly twice that of the total amount spent on development projects. Nearly two-thirds of central government revenue receipts were consumed by the military. Although the share of defence came down in subsequent years, this unfortunate pattern of resource allocation has persisted since Partition. Its effects have been obvious. Pakistan has a powerful army and a literacy ratio which is one of the worst in the world.

The sluggish aggregate performance of the Pakistani economy, during the first decade, is reflected in Table 4 below.

Table 4: *Incomes per head. 1949-58.*

	GNP per capita *(Rs.)*	*Rural Incomes* per capita *(Rs.)*
1949	311	207
1950	312	205
1951	313	204
1952	314	202
1953	315	202
1954	316	201
1955	316	199
1956	316	198
1957	317	195
1958	317	195

Source: Griffin, K.: *Financing Development Plans in Pakistan.*

There was a decline in *per capita* rural incomes during the decade. The increase in average incomes was negligible. The aggregate stagnation was accompanied by a decline in the wages of industrial workers. As Table 5 demonstrates, incomes of workers fell in both East and West Pakistan.

Table 5: *Real wages of industrial workers. (Rs. per year per worker).*

	East Pakistan	West Pakistan
1954	794.5	966.2
1955	702.3	911.5
1956	726.5	909.4
1957	743.3	933.6
1958	737.5	936.7

Source: Khan, A. R.: 'What has been happening to real wages in Pakistan?' *Pakistan Development Review.* Autumn 1967.

Two classes did, however, benefit from the economic policies pursued in the fifties. The primary beneficiaries were the migrant traders, who were provided with inducements to channel their merchant capital into the industrial sector. Protection for domestic industries ensured high prices for locally produced consumer goods. Simultaneously, costs of the industrial enterprises were reduced by artificially low import prices of capital goods as well as price ceilings on urban wage goods. Consequently, profit margins were high and encouraged industrial capital. The other beneficiary class was large landowners. Although their incomes may not have risen during this phase,[68] they were able to obstruct proposals for redistributing land.

The ethnic composition of the emerging industrial élite reinforced political tensions. Pakistan's economic development has been shaped by a mixture of historical accident and a few critical policy decisions made in the early fifties. Muslim merchants and traders from North India had migrated to Karachi, a destination determined by the fact that Karachi was the capital. These small merchant communities dominated the import trade, accumulating substantial surpluses during the Korean boom of 1951-52. The end of the boom led to severe foreign exchange shortages, in response to which the government introduced tight import quotas. The administrative nature of the import control system had a strong influence on the subsequent development of the manufacturing industry. In particular, it determined the *location* of industry, a process which had sensitive regional connotations.

Most of the industrial sanctions went to Karachi or Punjab. These allocative decisions were influenced by the proximity, access and market power of the traders who had migrated to Karachi. The merchant communities possessed the advantage of familiarity with the bureaucracy, which was critical for success under the ethos of administrative controls. Of no small importance must have been the fact that key Civil Servants dealing with licensing allocations were migrants too.[69] By 1959, migrants from India controlled over half of Pakistan's industrial assets.[70] Indeed, nearly 70% of the workers employed in Karachi's industrial sector were refugees, not local Sindhis.[71] The consequent tensions in Sind are discussed in greater detail in part two.

National resentment against this cosy network of bureaucrats and merchants sharing a common ethnic background led, in the sixties, to political convulsions which were to undermine the economic strategy pursued since Partition.

Footnotes:

1 Sharif-ul-Mujahid: *Jinnah* p. 236.
2 See Hector Bolitho: *Jinnah* pp. 8-12. The liberal influences are evident in Jinnah's speech to the Indian Legislative Assembly, 7.2.1935. See Jinnah's *Speeches and Writings* Volume 1, p. 5, for his early views on politics and religion.
3 A resolution, drafted by Dr. Kazi at the Muslim League's Delhi Session in April 1943, called for Pakistan's future constitution to be based on the Quran, and the principles of government established by the first four caliphs. Jinnah insisted that the resolution be withdrawn. See Pirzada (ed): *Foundations of Pakistan* Volume 2, pp. 425 and 440.
4 Quoted in A. H. Syed: *Pakistan, Islam Politics and National Solidarity* p. 48. Such assurances were necessary to placate non-Muslim communities in Muslim majority areas, such as Punjab and Bengal.
5 The Ulema organised under the Jamiat-al-ulama-e-hind, belonged mostly to the Deobandi school of religious conservatism. They co-operated with the Congress and opposed the Muslim League right up to Partition. See Binder: *Religion and Politics in Pakistan* pp. 25-30 for details. The Ahrar also opposed Pakistan as did the Jamaat-e-Islami.
6 Maududi: *Islamic Law and Constitution* pp. 5-6.
7 Binder: op cit p. 63. Until 1935 the Muslim League did not attempt to woo the Ulema. Subsequently, the League used Pirs and Sajjada Nashins to mobilise mass support. Indeed, some League leaders were given false religious titles when they were presented at mass meetings. For details see K. B. Sayeed: *Pakistan: The Formative Phase* pp. 218-240.
8 The colonial government granted separate electorates for Muslims in 1909. This measure was announced in the wake of the Minto-Morley reforms.
9 For example, three of the four Muslim League representatives at Simla to discuss the Cabinet Mission Plan in May 1946, were from Muslim minority provinces. The four representatives were

Liaquat, Jinnah, Nawab Ismail Khan and Sardar Nishtar. For further discussion on the Pakistan Movement see A. Jalal: *The Sole Spokesman* and Phillips and Wainwright (eds): *The Partition of India.*
10. The Congress Party favoured a strong centre, which was subsequently implemented in India.
11. Letter from Wavell to Secretary of State Pethick-Lawrence 20.8.1945. R/3/1/105 p. 43 India Office Library, London.
12. Similar sentiments prevailed in the Baluchi areas. These areas, ruled by tribal chiefs, were later merged into Pakistan as the Province of Baluchistan.
13. In the Punjab, the '37 provincial government was formed by Sikander Hayat, a Muslim leader of the Unionist Party. The Unionists, a landlord-based party cutting across communal lines, retained control over the Punjabi Administration. The Muslim League won just one seat. The poor League performance provoked an outburst from Jinnah: "I will never come to the Punjab again. It is such a hopeless place". In Bengal, the Muslim League formed a government through a tenuous coalition with Haq's Praja Party. Even though the Congress had emerged as the single largest party in Bengal, it could not come to an agreement with the Praja Party, enabling the League to fill the vacuum. For details see S. Sen: *Muslim Politics in Bengal 1937-47* and S. Oren: "Sikhs, Congress and Unionists in British Punjab", *Modern Asian Studies* 8.3.1974.
14. Wavell's letter to Pethick-Lawrence, op cit.
15. The desire to preserve the unity of Bengal and Punjab was evident in the meetings of Muslim leaders with Viceroy Wavell and the Cabinet Mission. For example, the Bengali Muslim League leader Suhrawardy emphasised the cultural and linguistic solidarity among Bengalis which cut across religion. Similarly, the Nawab of Mamdot, the President of the Punjab Muslim League, pleaded to the mission that Pakistan must get an undivided Punjab. For details, see Jalal, op cit pp. 175-185.
16. Almost all of the industry was located in West Bengal. East Pakistan produced one useful cash crop: jute. However, in recent years synthetic substitutes have replaced jute in most applications.
17. The Cabinet Mission Plan, initiated by the newly elected Labour Government, proposed establishment of two constituent assemblies, one each for the Hindu and Muslim majority provinces. The plan opted for a weak centre, which was inherent in the logic of grouping provinces on a communal basis.
18. On 6 June 1946, the Muslim League passed its momentous

resolution accepting the Cabinet Mission Plan. Jinnah's letter, of 12 May 1946, to Pethick-Lawrence, member of the mission, accepted the need for a union government. Some of Jinnah's followers were bewildered by his acceptance of a plan which explicitly rejected Pakistan in its preamble. See All India Muslim League, File # 142 (Working Committee's meetings 1943-47).

19. Jinnah was comfortable only in English, which posed obvious problems. Quite apart from communication difficulties, Jinnah was wary of mass politics. This was reflected in his comment on the civil disobedience movement: ". . . it has struck the imagination mostly of the inexperienced youth, the ignorant and the illiterate. All this means complete disorganisation and chaos".

20. The '37 Lucknow session of the Muslim League promised a guaranteed minimum wage and elimination of usury. The League's manifesto of 1944 included a provision for land reforms. In Bengal, Abul Hashim developed peasant support for the League on the basis of socialist promises. A League member reported to Jinnah that in a province like Bengal, "any mass movement is bound to become egalitarian or socialistic in outlook and character. And naturally the Bengal League is more and more becoming imbued with socialistic and anti-capitalistic outlook". Letter of Raghib Ahsan to Jinnah. 15.11.44. AIML/ Syed Shamsul Hasan Collection/3. Bengal volume 1V.

21. An advisory committee set up by the government in 1949.

22. Report on Constitution Appendix l: "Views of the Board of Talimat-e-Islamia".

23. ibid. p. 59. The head of state was not bound to accept the advice of ministers unless the issue related to the Sharia. Such disputes were to be referred to and settled by the Sharia Committee.

24. Maududi: *Islamic Law and Constitution.* p. 4.

25. The Provincial Government of Punjab, where most of the rioting took place, initially appears to have encouraged the movement against the Ahmedis. This was related to factional intrigues in the Muslim League, with contending groups seeking to gain advantage from the civil disturbances.

26. L. Binder: op cit p. 198. Liaquat, while presenting the Objectives Resolution, made it clear that a theocracy was not intended. Later, he re-affirmed, in his speech at the White House, that the resolution did not imply a theocracy.

27. The Munir Report on civil disturbances in the Punjab during the Ahmadya movement. (Government of Pakistan) p. 203.

28. The speech contained the famous phrase, "you may belong to any religion or caste —— that has nothing to do with the business

of the state", which continued to haunt fundamentalists under the Zia regime who were keen to distort Jinnah's preferences for a secular state.

29 A. H. Syed: op cit pp. 57-59.
30 L. Binder: op cit p. 190.
31 *Dawn.* 9.10.47. Also see his statements in *Dawn*, 1.1.53 and 13.2.53.
32 *Dawn.* 31.10.54.
33 Some politicians had also favoured a more religious orientation of the state. In December '52, K. Nazimuddin presented recommendations of the Basic Principles Committee to the Constituent Assembly, specifically providing for Ulema boards at both central and provincial levels to review legislation with regard to Islamic principles. Proposal for a board of Ulema was dropped in 1953. By 1954 the two politicians in favour of a religious state, Nazimuddin and Abdur Rab Nishtar, had been removed from positions of authority. With their departure evaporated much of the official support for the Ulema.
34 The most substantial migration occurred within Punjab, but the mahajjir category referred to here does not include migrants within Punjab.
35 Such insecurity was not pacified by statements by some Congress leaders which created doubts as to whether the Indian Government had accepted Partition as irreversible.
36 Miss Jinnah quoted in K. B. Sayeed, op cit p. 83. In 1954, the Constituent Assembly debated a motion calling for a ban on all parties, except the Muslim League, for 21 years.
37 ibid, p. 82.
38 K. K. Aziz: *Party Politics in Pakistan, 1947-58* p. 86.
39 ibid, p. 89.
40 I. Hussain: *Political Development, 1947-54.* (unpublished Ph.D. thesis, Oxford) p. 72.
41 Aziz, op cit p. 62.
42 ibid, pp. 2-3.
43 ibid, p. 4.
44 K. B. Sayeed, op cit pp. 346-7.
45 ibid, p. 329.
46 K. Callard: *Pakistan: a Political Study* discusses these aspects in some detail. See in particular pp. 130-60.
47 Gazette of Pakistan (extraordinary) 24.10.54 stated, ironically in view of the Prime Minister's dismissal: "The ultimate authority vests in the people who will decide all issues, including constitutional ones, through their representatives to be elected afresh".

48 For details, see I. Hussain's thesis referred to above.
49 The case of Pathans was slightly more complex. Pathan representation in the army ensured that some Pathan generals had a stake in central power. None the less, the civilian Pathan elite was not only underrepresented at the centre, but was positively hostile to it.
50 Urdu was the court language of the Mughals. It was the first language only of mahajjirs from North India. All the five provinces had different languages. Bengali is spoken in what was then East Pakistan.
51 For a discussion, see R. Jahan: *Pakistan; Failure in National Integration.*
52 The excuse for central intervention was provided by the somewhat irresponsible antics of Fazlul Haq, the leader of the United Front Government. During a visit to India, he spoke against Partition at the Sarat Bose Academy. He also suggested the unification of Bengal. For details see S. Maron, *Pacific Affairs.* June 1955.
53 SEATO stood for the South East Asian Treaty Organisation, and consisted of Pakistan, Phillipines, Thailand, Australia, New Zealand, U.K. and U.S. CENTO stood for Central Treaty Organisation, consisting of U.K., Pakistan, Turkey and Iraq. (The latter left in 1958)
54 Initially scheduled for November 1958.
55 Ghulam Mohammad had asked Ayub to take over in 1954.
56 One must of course bear in mind that official resources were stretched in the immediate aftermath of Partition. Seven million refugees were resettled and a new government structure established. Both were considerable achievements.
57 Industrial development was a provincial subject under the Government of India Act (1935). The Industries Federal Control Act (1949) made it a central subject.
58 Pakistan's decision not to devalue led to a trade embargo being imposed by India. India refused to import Pakistani raw material at such a high exchange rate.
59 Pakistan Government's decision seems to have been based partly on the premise that its exports were relatively price inelastic. See the Finance Minister's budget speech in Dawn, 14.3.1950.
60 Investment in approved projects was tax-free up to a certain percentage of personal income. For details of fiscal incentives see Andrus and Mohammad: *The Economy of Pakistan*, pp. 150-70.
61 During the Korean boom, the Pakistan Government followed a fairly liberal import policy, having dismantled the highly

regulated system imposed in the aftermath of the non-devaluation in 1949. Severe controls were reintroduced at the end of the Korean boom. This led to a rise in prices of consumer goods, providing the appropriate incentive for private capital to invest in import substituting consumer goods industries.

62 *Third Five-Year Plan*, p. 7. June 1965, Government of Pakistan, Islamabad.
63 Griffin & Khan: *Growth and Inequality in Pakistan.* p. 44.
64 ibid, p. 45.
65 For further discussion see Bhatia: *Pakistan's Economic Development.*
66 Belated measures were taken to mitigate the effects of urban bias. Some of the controls on food prices were removed, in the mid-fifties, to encourage agricultural production. The rupee was eventually devalued by 30% in 1956. Although the first five-year plan (1955-60) emphasised the need for agricultural development, it allocated an insubstantial amount for the sector, thus attempting to raise agricultural productivity with too modest capital investment.
67 Mian Iftikharuddin, a liberal Punjabi politician, proposed a redistribution of evacuee property among landless peasants. Not surprisingly, the Muslim League leadership rejected his proposals.
68 Due to the fall in agriculture's terms of trade, a number of farmers suffered a fall in incomes.
69 For details see S. R. Lewis: *Pakistan: Industrialisation and Trade Policies.* pp. 45-55.
70 ibid.
71 For details see M. I. Khan: "Industrial Labour in Karachi". *Pakistan Development Review*, Winter 1963.

Chapter Two

Military Rule and Civil War

The epilogue to Ayub's rule contained another painful division in South Asia. Ethnicity, rather than religion, formed the basis of the second rupture. The Ayub regime could not be held responsible for creating the ethnic imbalances which it inherited. It was guilty of a far more serious crime. It had pursued policies which had consciously exacerbated the explosive schisms within Pakistan. It had done so by brazenly pursuing other objectives, dismissing sensitive equity issues as costs to be contained ultimately by force. This neglect was particularly serious in view of Pakistan's geographical structure and historical evolution. The Bengalis were separated, by a 1,000 miles of Indian territory, from the central government based in West Pakistan. India could be expected to take advantage of a serious revolt in the eastern wing. Simple military strategy, let alone political sagacity, necessitated the integration of the major ethnic community within the national political framework. We shall begin our analysis by outlining the institutional structure, adopted by the Ayub regime, which led to a civil war.

The military coup of 1958 was followed by a peculiar form of representational dictatorship. A system of basic democracies was introduced in October 1959. The country was divided into 80,000 geographical units; these constituencies contained an average electorate of 1,000. Each constituency elected, on the basis of universal suffrage, a representative called a basic democrat.[1] The system served two primary functions. First, the basic democrats formed a safe electoral college for the election of a president. In February 1960, basic democrats were asked to say yes or no to a simple question: "Have you confidence in President Ayub Khan?". Ayub was "elected" president by a 95.6% yes vote, an exercise which made East European elections look glamorous. The second function was to develop a direct relationship between the bureaucracy and the rural élite, thus cultivating a network of allies for the government, based on access to the state's resources. The Civil Servants were responsible for selecting candidates, thereby extending detailed administrative control over political issues, even at the local level.[2]

Two features of Ayub's political structure were evident not only in the basic democracies but also in subsequent constitutional developments. Power was concentrated in the hands of Ayub who, none the less, relied extensively on the bureaucracy for the effective functioning of the governmental machinery. Most of the routine decision-making powers were delegated to Civil Servants, with the army maintaining a relatively low profile as far as day-to-day administration was concerned. Indeed, it bore a striking similarity to the structure of colonial rule.[3] The role played by the viceroy in the British viceregal system was now played by Ayub as the supreme martial law administrator. Similarly, the viceroy's reliance on the "steel frame" of the Imperial Civil Service was duplicated with minor adjustments. Accordingly, the constitution, framed in 1962, incorporated these features. Ayub had modestly suggested that "resolution and courage would be provided by the top leadership — me",[4] going on to specify the requirement of creating a strong central government with a dominant executive independent of the "whims of the legislature". To avoid such whims, members of the National Assembly were chosen on "personal merit", since the 1962 Constitution did not recognise political parties.[5]

As indicated by the above, Ayub was not content with undiluted military rule. Under his regime, considerable emphasis had been placed on setting up an institutional framework for presidential rule, based on the '62 Constitution and the structure of basic democracy. However, the regime made the error of confusing the establishment of institutions with the process of political institutionalisation. The latter implies legitimacy for the formal structures of public authority. Such approval integrates a political system, playing a critical role in the process of nation building. The establishment of public institutions without consent, on the other hand, is counter-productive. Instead of neutralising political tensions, these institutions become a symbol of mass alienation. In these circumstances, their significance lies not in their ability to incorporate specific groups but in their capacity to exclude critical sections of the population. This is precisely what happened to Ayub's institutional framework. The only groups it incorporated were those who directly benefited from governmental patronage. It failed to provide the central element for an effective political structure — it had no mechanism for accommodating opposition. It was an institutional structure which forced groups with political grievances into mobilising for violent confrontation. As a result, those who argued that "more than any other political leader in a modernising country after World War Two, Ayub Khan came close to filling the role of a Solon or Lycurgus or great legislator on the Platonic or Rousseauien model",[6] seem to have missed the point altogether.

Before we analyse the effects of Ayub's political structure on specific sectors, we shall briefly document the other aspects of the Ayub regime which contributed towards the political eruptions of the late sixties.

The Ayub era was marked by considerable efficiency in the *execution* of policy. This was only appropriate for a period which witnessed the unrivalled dominance of the bureaucracy. This administrative efficacy had obvious merits, especially in the economic sphere. Once a policy was decided, it was well executed. These superior management skills did not, however, imply prudence in policy *formulation*. This was nowhere more evident than in the manner in which the regime suffocated all forms of social, political and cultural expression. Pakistan has yet to dismantle the structures of regimentation and control imposed by the Ayub regime. On 16 April 1959, a Martial Law Ordinance empowered the government to take over newspapers which "in the opinion of the government, published or contained matters likely to endanger the defence, external affairs or security of Pakistan". Subsequently the Pakistan Times and Imroze, the largest and most influential English and Urdu dailies, were seized by the government.[7] The Progressive Papers Limited were taken over on the grounds of left wing bias. On 28 March 1963, the government promulgated a Press Ordinance banning the publication of any news relating to strikes or industrial unrest. In September of the same year, another ordinance ordered newspapers to publish all the press notes distributed by the central or provincial governments. The repression of independent newspapers was only the first stage in the process of establishing official ideological control. The second step consisted of creating an official body to monitor and smother any traces of independent thought. A National Press Trust (NPT), financed by twenty-four industrialists,[8] was entrusted with the task of stifling dissent.

In addition to journalists, who were curbed by the press laws, two other critical sources of independent opinion were decimated. Law reforms[9] gave the administration absolute control over the legal profession, with judicial appointments being subjected to thorough political scrutiny. Indeed, judges were interviewed by provincial governors and the President to ensure excision of illusions of judicial independence. Finally, academics were contained with considerable ease. They could neither publish works of any substance nor would they be employed by universities, all of whom were owned by the state, if there was any public manifestation of dissent. These measures collectively cordoned off and tamed the intelligentsia, which has had profound implications for cultural and social development in Pakistan. A society not allowed to analyse or express itself suffocated in silence, stunted by ideological imprisonment and deformed by sustained repression. To rub salt in the wound, the military was referred to, among official Western circles, as the most progressive modern institution in society.[10]

The latent dissent which erupted across the nation in the late sixties contained important regional variations. In particular, the nature of the revolt in East Pakistan was different, in certain critical aspects, from the agitation in

West Pakistan. Accordingly, we shall first consider the effects of Ayub's policies on the eastern wing. Pakistan's political problems were rooted, as we noted in chapter l, in the structural imbalance between a Bengali majority and a power bloc representing Punjabi-mahajjir dominance. The danger signals were evident as early as 1952 when language riots erupted in East Pakistan. Nevertheless, the fifties was a period in which the Bengalis were negotiating the terms on which they would participate in the central government. Delayed and imperfect though it was, the 1956 Constitution did provide a framework for incorporating Bengalis within a national political system. There were signs of Bengali frustration, but not of despair. The elections, which were to be held in 1959, would have provided acceptable representation in the central government. Ayub's *coup* undermined this process, reinforcing the dominance of the bureaucracy and the military. Bengali representation in these institutions, particularly the latter, was negligible. In view of its serious implications, the Ayub regime may have been expected to respond to Bengali aspirations through an accommodatory stance. However, instead of placating the Bengalis, Ayub's posture betrayed a deep contempt for the major ethnic group: "East Bengalis probably belong to the very original Indian races . . . until the creation of Pakistan they had not known any real freedom or sovereignty . . . In addition they have been, and still are, under considerable Hindu cultural and linguistic influence. As such they have all the inhibitions of downtrodden races and have not yet found it possible to adjust psychologically to the requirements of the newborn freedom".[11] This passage, written by Ayub as the Head of State, is symptomatic of the perceived hierarchies within the Muslims of the Indian subcontinent. It is also a useful indicator of why the West Pakistani power bloc would not contemplate a transfer of power to the Bengalis. It combines racial and religious prejudice, implicitly contrasting Muslim Aryan breeds with the inferior Hindu, Dravidian races. Like many aspects of Ayub's era, the ghosts of colonial rule were evident. Ayub's racism was reminiscent of Macaulay's descriptions of Bengalis as a people whose "mind is weak" and who have been historically "trampled upon by men of bolder and more hardy breeds".[12]

The formal manifestation of regional subjugation was contained in the 1962 Constitution, which embodied the dominance of an unrepresentative central government. The framers of the constitution officially described the country as "a form of federation with the provinces enjoying such autonomy as is consistent with the unity and interests of Pakistan as a whole".[13] In practice the 'interests of Pakistan' had a peculiar habit of coinciding with the interests of the power bloc. Article 131 gave sanction to any action the central government took, as long as it was taken in the 'national interest'. Article 133 entitled the judiciary to decide on conflicts of jurisdiction between the centre and the provinces. But the judiciary had no control over the central legislature when it crossed its legislative domain in the name of national interest, a power guaranteed to the centre under Article 131.[14] Under judicial challenge the Dacca High Court, for example, admitted its impotence in the face of central power.[15] In effect, provincial administrations performed functions similar to those of local government in a unitary state. Instead of playing the role of integrating local ethnic groups, regional government became an extension of much resented central power. Thus, the three principal features of Ayub's political structure — his personal dominance, the reliance on the bureaucracy and centralisation of power — seriously aggravated the basic political problem facing Pakistan. It increased Bengali alienation, setting in motion a process of violent confrontation.

The extent to which Ayub's regime mishandled East Pakistan was evident in the Bengali response.[16] By 1966 the mainstream political parties of East Bengal had adopted a platform which effectively represented the partition of Pakistan into two nation-states. The proposals for a confederation between the two geographic units were summarised in the six-point demand of the Awami League. The six points, listed below, were originally put forward in 1966 and later amended and incorporated in the 1970 election manifesto of the Awami League.

1. The character of the government shall be federal and parliamentary.
2. The federal government shall be responsible for only defence and foreign affairs.
3. There shall be two separate currencies mutually or freely convertible in each wing.
4. Fiscal policy shall be the responsibility of the federating unit.
5. Separate accounts shall be maintained of the foreign exchange earnings of each of the federating units.
6. Federating units shall be empowered to maintain a militia or parliamentary force.

The demands for a confederation had emerged from an environment of violent protest against the Ayub regime. As Table 1 indicates (see p. 32), the Ayub era was marked by sustained conflict in East Pakistan. On average, there were 4,946 riots a year in East Pakistan from the year of Ayub's *coup* up to 1966, when the six-point demand was made.

The six points evoked a swift response from the central government. Within three months of programme's announcement, Sheikh Mujibur Rahman, the leader of the Awami League, was arrested. Two years later, the party's leaders[17] were charged with conspiring with India for the break-up of Pakistan. The consequent Agartala Conspiracy case was destined to be, given the circumstances, one of those treason trials which makes martyrs of the accused. Although Mujib was not in the initial list of the accused,[18] his latter inclusion ensured that, among the Bengalis at least, it was the central government which was on trial.

Ayub was forced to transfer power, which he did in 1969 to General Yahya Khan, by a series of mass demonstrations against his regime.[19] At this

Table 1: *Riots in East and West Pakistan.*

Year	West	East
1958	1,356	4,550
1959	913	3,232
1960	1,114	4,499
1961	1,681	4,777
1962	609	4,792
1963	758	5,182
1964	1,086	5,723
1965	995	5,626
1966	967	6,135

Source: Pakistan Statistical Yearbook, 1967.

stage, the secession of East Pakistan was by no means a foregone conclusion. It could still have been prevented by a process of accommodation. None the less, the policies of Ayub regime had made a substantial and critical contribution towards Pakistan's political disintegration. As we shall see below, the government's economic policies had exacerbated regional disparities. Although economic issues were important and some, such as the transfer of jute export revenues from East Pakistan for capital imports in West Pakistan, acquired value as symbols of exploitation, the Bengali struggle was essentially political. Their share in the central government, the citadel of power, was negligible.[20] Ayub's political structure, far from rectifying ethnic imbalances, had maintained the supremacy of the Punjabi-mahajjir élite. To be described as an inferior breed was not the kind of privilege Bengalis had in mind when they had opted for Pakistan in 1947.

Whereas East Pakistan represented a cohesive, ethnic-based confrontation with the power bloc, the response in West Pakistan to Ayub's political structure was more diverse. A disaggregated analysis of the western wing revealed some similarities with the eastern wing, but contained important differences as well. Resentment against the one unit and forced centralisation was strong in rural Sind, NWFP and Baluchistan. In the latter there was intermittent armed conflict between Baluch tribal groups and the army. Although sentiment in Baluchistan towards the Punjabi-mahajjir dominance was similar to East Pakistan, the logistics were quite different. Baluchistan was sparsely populated, fragmented and in physical proximity to the army's headquarters. Its politics were dominated by the struggle against the central government, with the National Awami Party (NAP) emerging as the principal spokesman of Baluch opinion. The situation in the Frontier Province (NWFP) was more complex. On the one hand, there was substantial representation of Pathans, the primary ethnic group in NWFP, in the army. On the other hand, there was strong opposition to the central government among civilian groups. It was among these groups that the Congress Party had been particularly strong in pre-Partition India. There were serious misgivings, at the time, about the frontier's decision to join Pakistan.[21] These doubts were not eased by the subsequent accumulation of power by the centre. Again, as in Baluchistan, the left-of-centre NAP had emerged as the leading political party.[22] Resentment against inadequate representation for their ethnic group was also growing in Sind Province, particularly in the rural areas. At the same time, the industrialisation programme was generating tensions of a different nature. The inequalities it bred led to the articulation of class-based demands for distributional justice. These 'modern' urban groups, as well as the traditional rural forces, were mobilised by the Pakistan People's Party (PPP). The party, led by the former foreign minister in Ayub's cabinet, also emerged as the primary political force in the army's heartland, Punjab. Its support was based on articulating the antagonisms of the dominated classes against Ayub's economic policies. Z. A. Bhutto also gained support in the Punjab for his strong nationalist views against India, a position which earned him respect within factions of the army high command.

Collectively, three strands of the opposition movement against Ayub were to topple his regime in 1969. The first component was the situation in East Pakistan, where a united Bengali opposition highlighted the failure of the Ayub regime to rectify the ethnic contradictions permeating Pakistan's power structure. Second was the growth of opposition in Punjab and Sind, primarily on the basis of class tensions bred by Ayub's economic policies, emphasising the costs of neglecting equity issues in formulating an economic strategy. The third feature was the increasing resentment expressed by the smaller provinces of West Pakistan against the dominance of the Punjabi-mahajjir power bloc. We shall recount the consequences of this three-pronged attack on the Ayub regime later in the chapter. Before we do so, we shall summarise the developments with regard to religion and economic policy.

Islam

As we noted in chapter 1, the question of the role to be played by religion in politics had been settled, at least temporarily, with the dominance of a bureaucracy wedded to a secular government. The coup in 1958 did not alter this official disposition. The Ayub government was quite firm in its resolve of not permitting a role for Islam in determining institutional development or governmental policies. The official position was evident in both symbolic and substantive measures. Of symbolic significance was the characterisation of Pakistan as a republic in the 1962 Constitution. There was no reference to Islam. Although the government had to pass a constitutional amendment to change the official title to Islamic Republic of Pakistan, the initial characterisation was representative of government sentiment. The more substantive measure was the Muslim Family Laws Ordinance (1961). Under the terms of the ordinance polygamy was banned and women's rights in divorce cases were strengthened. The government also stressed the need for establishing minimum educational qualifications for religious functionaries, such as Imams. The official measures incurred the wrath of the Ulema; they felt particularly threatened by the power given to basic democrats to solemnise marriages and prohibit or arrange divorces.[23] This encroachment upon their traditional domain undermined the status and security of the Ulema. Although they failed to emerge as a leading element in the anti-Ayub movement, their contribution was by no means insignificant.

The Ayub regime has often been criticised for not undertaking more fundamental reforms in the religious sphere. This appears to be a rather harsh and rash judgement. The regime's caution was understandable. Had it tried to push the pace of reform, it may well have provoked a reaction. Its strategy of modest adjustments was perhaps the best that could be hoped for under the circumstances. It is none the less worth noting that official secularism in Pakistan, as under the Shah in Iran, was largely superficial. It had no deep effect on transforming the traditional role played by religion. This inability to affect desired changes was due partly to the indirect effects of the government's external allegiances. It became a symbol of much resented Western political influence, which was so unabashedly supportive of a military dictatorship. Secularism was unfortunately associated with an unpopular, unrepresentative government. The regime's allocative priorities did not help either. The education sector received less than 1% of the GNP, that, too, going disproportionately to urban higher education institutions. The lack of basic educational facilities for the vast majority of the population maintained the hold of traditional beliefs and customs. Thus, in practice, the reform of religious laws had little effect on the lives of target groups, such as women.

In spite of its secular orientation, the government could not resist the temptation of using religion to control dissent. The revival of political parties in 1962, for example, was conditional on their adherence to Islamic ideology. Since parties had to adhere to an undefined concept, it provided the government with a flexible instrument for suppressing political opposition. It was used on a number of occasions, particularly when left wing or communist forces were attacked.[24] At the same time, religious sanction for Ayub's centralisation and executive control over the legislature was sought by reference to historical parallels during the early days of Islam.[25] Ayub also argued that "without centralisation, unity and solidarity no system can claim to be an Islamic system",[26] implying that his was an Islamic structure. However, such references were of minor importance and represented unavoidable lip service. The tone of the regime remained distinctly secular; ironic in the case of Pakistan but welcome none the less.

The secular orientation of Ayub's regime was, like many aspects of his rule, firmly embedded in the colonial inheritance in the sense that the ideological complexion of the military had been determined by British attitudes and training. The dominance of the military after Independence was aided in Pakistan, as elsewhere in the developing world, by the support given by the United States. An authoritative survey of American foreign policy argued that "In many of the countries to which we extend foreign aid, the army is the best organisation in the country and frequently one of the most forward looking. In my own experience, this is conspicuously so in Pakistan . . . The American military assistance programme is increasingly aware of these possibilities and . . . had tended to bring military and economic elements in closer contact."[27] In a similar vein, an American president's committee concluded that "the military officer corps is a major rallying point in the defence against communist expansion and penetration."[28] The external linkages are worth emphasising, since they determined the manner in which the Ayub regime justified its role in society. The self-perception of the government was provided by the ideological constructs of the modernisation theory.[29] The military was projected as modernisers of traditional society. In common with most self-images, it was a flattering view. The self-delusion was shattered, in the late sixties, by the violent affirmation of political realities.

Economic Development

The Ayub Khan era is remembered for the regime's professional competence in its approach to economic management. There was a clarity of objectives and considerable efficiency in implementation. However, the efficiency and clarity were marred by fundamental flaws in the choice of objectives. In the end, the failures of the sixties were far more significant than its achievements. Since the government was successful in meeting its economic objectives, the inadequacies and failures were the consequence of what it chose to ignore. In a sense, all Pakistani governments have been on trial. Pakistan was, after all, an entirely artificial geographical enterprise. There was no historical basis for engendering loyalty to Pakistan among the various regions. An excessive emphasis on religion as the common bond faced the inevitable danger of drifting into an argument for a theocracy, a position diametrically opposed to the secular orientation of the regime. National integration had to be constructed, therefore, solely on the basis of contemporary structures and policies. Ayub's economic policies seriously hampered this process of national unification. The root of the failure in the economic sphere lay in the government's concentration on promoting economic growth, with a deliberate disregard for equity issues. This neglect of sensitive regional and class inequalities represented a serious failure in the choice of objectives. The Bengalis viewed this choice as inextricably linked with the ethnic composition of the military bureaucratic élite. It was, perhaps, not a coincidence that the main beneficiaries of the growth strategy were mahajjirs and Punjabis. This may not have been the product of conscious design, but the outcome was inherent in the structure of the chosen development strategy. We shall begin our examination of the adopted framework by recounting the impressive aggregate growth performance of the economy.

The Ayub era was a period of substantial economic development. As distinct from the stagnant fifties, there was a significant increase in *per capita* income. The rapid growth in GNP was based on impressive aggregate performance by both the industrial and agricultural sectors. The overall framework of development was outlined in five-year plans. The second (1960-65) and third (1965-70) plans provided the required economic discipline, based on a clarity of objectives and firm control over economic management. In addition to the clear specification of targets and instruments in the plans, the stability of the economic environment was aided by monetary discipline and tight control over budget deficits. The impressive growth performance is reflected in Table 2. GNP grew annually at around 5.5% through both the second and the third plan periods. *Per capita* GNP growth was nearly 3% throughout the sixties. The growth in manufacturing output was particularly impressive between 1960 and 1965. Towards the end of the sixties there was a rapid introduction of new types of seed and fertilisers in the agricultural sector. Along with better water management, the new varieties of inputs led to a substantial boom in crop production. The high agricultural growth rate generated by the 'green revolution' is reflected in Table 2.

Although the economy maintained its striking growth momentum throughout the sixties, the decade can be divided into two phases. The first phase, corresponding to the second plan period 1960-65, was marked by a spurt of activity in the large-scale manufacturing sector. As indicated in Table 2, large-scale manufacturing grew at an annual rate of approximately 17% during the first half of the decade. The period was also characterised by substantial inflows of foreign capital as the government sought to supplement inadequate domestic resources to achieve the ambitious growth targets. Indeed, all sectors grew faster than targets aspired to under the plan. The second phase coincides with the outbreak of the 1965 war and the start of the third five-year plan. Apart from a temporary setback in the immediate aftermath of the war, the economy maintained its growth momentum. Indeed, *per capita* incomes grew slightly faster, as indicated in Table 2. None the less, the large-scale manufacturing sector began to lose some of its frenetic pace, partly on account of the fall in aid inflows after the 1965 war. The real success of the second half of the decade was the 'green revolution', which led to a spurt in the growth of agricultural output. Figure 1 (p. 38), which charts the annual growth process during the sixties, illustrates the acceleration in agricultural performance due to the adoption of the 'green revolution' technology. The figure also illustrates the relative decline in the growth performance of large-scale manufacturing.

Table 2: *Average annual growth rates of key sectors. 1960-70. (%).*

Growth rates	1959-60 to 1964-5	1964-65 to 1969-70
Per-capita income	3.5	3.7
Agriculture	3.7	6.3
Large-scale manufacturing	16.9	9.9

Source: Pakistan Economic Survey, 1979-80.

The growth of the industrial sector was, in large measure, due to the gradual liberalisation of the economy. The excessive bureaucratic controls of the fifties were replaced by a more market oriented approach. The greater reliance on the price mechanism entailed relaxation of controls over industrial investment and trade, as well as a reduction in price 'distortions' caused by official intervention in markets. Accordingly, soon after the second plan was announced, the government removed controls on profit margins and prices imposed in the fifties. In addition, controls over industrial investments were relaxed. For example, no official sanction was required for investment in sectors listed in the Industrial Investment Schedule, thus removing some of the cumbersome procedures of the fifties. There was an immediate response from the private sector to this liberalisation of investment controls. Between 1958 and 1963, Pakistan's industrial growth performance was considerably above the average for Asia. Industrial production in Pakistan grew by 72% over the period, compared with an average of 55% for Asian countries.[30] The World Bank, closely associated with economic policy formulation during the Ayub era, noted the effects of policies with some satisfaction: "Pakistan's economic policy has had an impact on industrial growth in many different ways and has generally been *highly favourable* to such growth".[31]

Easing of investment procedures was accompanied by trade liberalisation which involved relaxation of restrictions on both imports and exports. Previously, official licences were required before goods could be imported into the country. The Ayub regime placed a number of items on the 'free list', so called because the commodities listed therein did not require official clearance. In addition, there was relatively wider availability and easier access to import licences, especially as rewards for those involved in the export of commodities. However, the trend towards import liberalisation

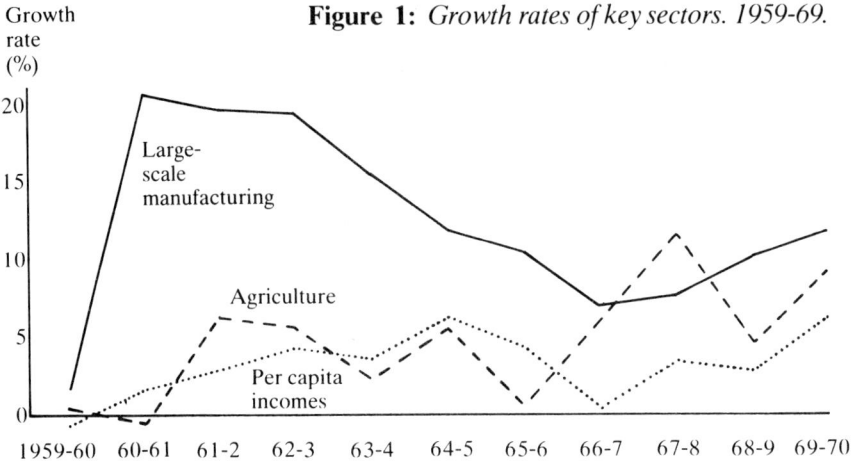

Figure 1: *Growth rates of key sectors. 1959-69.*

Source: Pakistan Economic Survey, 1979-80.

was reversed in 1965. A sudden cancellation of the Aid-to-Pakistan Consortium meeting of 3 July 1965, at the insistence of the United States, was followed by an American aid embargo in response to the Indo-Pak war in September. The cooling of relations with the U.S. and the fickleness of aid flows, made the Ayub government re-evaluate its policy of import liberalisation, which was contingent on easy access to foreign loans to ease any balance of payments difficulties.[32] The latter had been exacerbated by American military sanctions against Pakistan. As a consequence, the import liberalisation policy was abandoned temporarily. The resumption of the liberalisation process was due to American pressure after it revived its commodity aid programme.[33] By 1968, 90% of Pakistani imports had been freed from direct administrative controls,[34] with the government preferring to rely on tariff controls to restrict demand.

Earlier the government had taken measures to increase foreign exchange earnings by encouraging exports. The overvaluation of the domestic currency, however, was favourable to importers, while exporters suffered. A straightforward devaluation, which would eliminate the bias against exports, was not acceptable to the industrialists since this would raise their costs of importing capital goods and raw materials. It would have involved a reduction in the net transfer of resources to them from the rest of the economy.[35] As a consequence, a complicated system of multiple exchange rates was established to promote exports without offending powerful sections of industrial capital. A bonus voucher scheme was introduced in 1959, under which exporters of certain raw materials and manufactured commodities received import permits equivalent to 10-40% of the value of exported goods. These bonus vouchers were transferable, which meant that they could be sold by the exporters who had earned them to others who wanted to import goods. There was strong demand for these vouchers, enabling holders to command a premium of approximately 150%.[36] Thus, the net effect of these vouchers was a boost in the earnings of exporters who, by selling their import permits at a premium, received additional income equal to 30-40% of the value of exports. The scheme had the desired effect, especially in the early years, when there was a substantial rise in the export of cotton and jute products. Exports falling under the export bonus scheme grew at an annual compound rate of 12% as compared to 4% for exports outside the scheme.[37] None the less, it was cumbersome to operate and required continuous adjustments. It was finally discarded by the Bhutto regime in 1972, one of the few acts of that government to receive wholehearted endorsement from the IMF.[38]

The liberalisation of the economy under Ayub was not quite the neoclassical paradise that it appeared to be. The industrialisation programme was as much a product of profit incentives created by government distortions as a response to price signals originating in market transactions.[39] Domestic industries were protected from foreign competition. This boosted profit margins and attracted industrial investment, but also led to the establishment of a number of uncompetitive and inefficient industrial units. In a study of forty-eight manufacturing units, Soligo and Stern found that the value added of twenty-three units was negative, when measured at world prices.[40] In other words, the net subsidy received through tariff protection was greater than the value added by these units, i.e. the value of the goods produced was less than the cost of the inputs if manufacturers had been required to buy and sell all goods at world market prices. Other studies, such as R. Mallon (1967), Nurul Islam (1967) and M. Scott (1969) confirmed Soligo and Stern's conclusions. State protection had inhibited the development of an internationally competitive industrial sector.

The second, post-'65, phase of economic development under Ayub is associated with the achievements of the agricultural sector. The stagnation in crop output, due to the neglect of agriculture, had led to serious problems, as we noted in chapter one. Measures to rectify the imbalance were aided by the development and availability of high yielding varieties (HYV) of seeds and fertilisers. The adoption of the productive seed-fertiliser-water package led to a dramatic revival of the agricultural sector. The HYV package was accompanied by increased mechanisation. The number of tractors increased from just 2,000 in 1959 to nearly 19,000 in 1968.[41] The process led to the emergence of a new 'Kulak' class of enterprising capitalist farmers, responding to market incentives and technological developments.[42] Direct benefits from the 'green revolution' were, however, confined to the Punjab. Moreover, the welfare of the increasingly prosperous Punjabi rural élite had not been adversely affected by the Ayub regime's half-hearted dabble in institutional reform. In 1959, land reforms had fixed the ceiling on private ownership of land at 500 acres irrigated and 1,000 acres unirrigated. The ceiling on ownership was fixed in terms of individual, rather than family, holdings. In addition, there were generous productivity exemptions[43] as well as provisions for orchards. As a consequence, the land reforms represented little more than a token cosmetic exercise, with the landed élite largely unaffected by the measures taken. Indeed, some landlords did rather well from the exercise, receiving generous 'compensation' for surrendering uncultivated land.[44] Barely 35% of the excess land declared by landlords was actually resumed by the government, which suggests a degree of administrative slackness, notably absent when the Ayub regime was serious in implementing any policy.[45]

The lack of concern over distributional issues proved to be the Achilles' heel of the Ayub Government. The mass revolt which brought down the regime was based on two sources of distributional conflict; regional disparity and class inequalities. In view of the government's stated priorities, it was not altogether surprising that political eruptions were rooted in the neglect of distributional issues. In its public pronouncements, the government had made it clear that it was not concerned with mass welfare. These honest declarations of disdain gave a fair indication of how assiduous was the government's desire to cultivate popular goodwill. Indeed, the model of economic development adopted in the sixties consciously promoted inequalities as a necessary precondition for successful economic growth. The doctrine of functional inequality was based on the premise that the initial stages of capitalist development required a high degree of inequality. This was due to the necessity of channelling resources to those classes which have a high savings rate. These high savings would be converted into investment, which would raise the rate of economic growth. This model implied a diversion of resources towards industrialists in an effort to raise their incomes and, consequently, their savings. The model, associated with the works of G. Papanek and Mahbub-ul-Haq,[46] was explicit in its distributional implications. The second five-year plan warned that "It will be necessary to tolerate some initial *growth in income inequalities* to reach high levels of savings and investment".[47] This echoed Haq's argument that developing countries can 'shelve to the distant future' any aspirations for reducing inequalities.[48] G. Papanek, chief of the Harvard advisory group, paraphrased Adam Smith by suggesting the 'social utility of greed', whereby individual greed of the 'robber barons' of industry leads to a larger national cake and therefore eventually benefits society.

The second component of the economic development model referred to the role to be played by foreign capital. Policies designed to divert resources to the high savers within the community were to be supplemented by measures to raise the pool of national savings. A higher level of investment resources was possible through the import of capital. Accordingly, Pakistan's development targets were based on its ability to attract foreign loans, which was facilitated by Pakistan's participation in the network of American sponsored military and political alliances. Although private foreign investment was negligible, Pakistan was able to rely, until 1965 at least, on a steady flow of foreign capital through public institutions. For example, the foreign component of total expenditure accounted for 35% and 50% of the first and second five-year plans respectively.

The major flaw of the development strategy was its implication for both regional and class inequalities. The adopted policy framework concentrated on diverting resources to industrial capital in West Pakistan.[49] The allocative bias against East Pakistan was particularly serious in view of Pakistan's political structure. As we argued in chapter 1, Pakistan's political evolution had been distorted by the reluctance of the West Pakistani élite to accept the logic of majority rule. Deprived of political control, the Bengalis were inclined to view the development strategy as another illustration of West Pakistani dominance. Bengali resentment was fuelled by the growing disparity between the two regions. At the time of Ayub's *coup*, there was a difference of 30% in the *per capita* incomes of the two regions. By the end of the second five-year plan (1965), the disparity of *per capita* income had risen to 45%. By the time of Ayub's departure, the gap had risen to 61%.[50] The tilt towards the western wing was reinforced by development institutions such as the World Bank, "since it usually selected those projects which promised the highest rates of return and they tended to be in West Pakistan".[51] Although there is considerable controversy over the precise magnitude of the intra-regional resource transfer,[52] there is no dispute about the relative decline of East Pakistan under the Ayub regime.

The second source of discontent over the development strategy was the class polarisation generated by the economic élitism with which the regime was associated. The public advocacy of the desirability of greater inequality was followed by disclosures of concentration of wealth within a tiny economic élite. It was revealed that twenty-two families between them owned 66% of industry, 97% of insurance and 80% of banking.[53] In contrast to the pampering of a corporate military-industrial élite was the neglect of basic social services for the public. In terms of the percentage of national expenditure devoted to education, Pakistan's performance under Ayub was the worst in Asia.[54] Similarly, the regime showed little concern for the provision of basic health care and sanitation facilities. The neglect of social services contributed towards the increase in the annual population growth rate from 2.3% to 2.8% during the sixties. The rise in the growth rate was accompanied by a fall in living standards for substantial sections of the population. Pakistan was by no means unique in adopting a development strategy which ignored equity issues. None the less, the policy was pursued with such vigour that the standard of living of important segments actually fell, despite a consistent rise in *per capita* national income. The wages of industrial workers, for example, fell by nearly 12% in West Pakistan, between 1954 and 1967. In certain key industries, such as cotton textiles, real wages fell by as much as

23%. This decline is indicated in Table 3 below, which demonstrates the decline of living standards for workers during the boom years of industrial expansion.

Table 3: *Index of real wages of industrial workers. 1967-8.*
(Base year 1954 = 100).

West Pakistan		
	All industries	88.8
	Cotton textiles	76.9
East Pakistan		
	All industries	101.1
	Jute textiles	94.6
	Cotton textiles	81.7

Source: Griffin and Khan: *Growth and inequality in Pakistan.*

Although there is some controversy regarding the aggregate trend in income distribution under Ayub,[55] there is little doubt about the sharp polarisation produced by the regime's policies. The conflict, between the targeted beneficiaries of government policies and those whom the regime considered dispensable, was to erupt into violent confrontation in the late sixties. The beneficiaries could be divided into three classes. The first category consisted of extremely wealthy urban groups. The concentration of industrial and financial capital became a symbol of the regime's promotion of economic élitism. The second category were the large farmers of West Pakistan, particularly Punjab. Farmers who owned land in excess of twenty-five acres were the principal beneficiaries of the 'green revolution'. The final, more amorphous, set comprised of middle class groups such as senior civil and military officials as well as urban white collar workers. In contrast to this small fraction of the population, the vast majority perceived themselves as dispensable in the government's pursuit of economic growth. Since ideas of equitable distribution were "luxuries which only developed countries can afford",[56] it followed that the poor should resign themselves to the signals emanating from official quarters i.e., national prosperity depends on diverting resources to the rich. The refusal to accept such a fate was mobilised by political parties led, in West Pakistan, by Z. A. Bhutto's PPP. The deficiencies of the policies pursued by the Ayub regime were acknowledged by the government in the fourth five-year plan: "The development strategy has to change fundamentally . . . income distribution has become fairly skewed in the process of economic development. Real wages declined by about a third during the 1960's. . . . The landless labour increased and there was little gain in the real farm income per head for the small farmer. The inequalities between various income groups not only increased but also became more vivid by the growing awareness of the masses . . .".[57] The plan also conceded that due to the resentment towards the regime's economic élitism, the stage was set for the social and economic confrontations which took place in early 1969.[58]

The central role in mass demonstrations was played by student and labour unions. In March 1969, for example, a workers' strike paralysed Karachi,[59] which contained 40% of Pakistan's industrial capacity. Similar action was taken by student and labour unions across Pakistan. Political demands for democratic rule and the removal of censorship were combined with an eight-point demand put forward by the workers. These included a right to strike, minimum wages and the provision of basic social services. Details of the demands for political rights and distributive justice have been documented elsewhere.[60] We can summarise the three main causes for Ayub's downfall. His government's neglect of the equity dimensions of development provoked a backlash from adversely affected regions and classes. In addition, Ayub's position within the junta had suffered as a result of the 1965 war. Factions within his own administration felt that the cease-fire agreement, signed at Tashkent through Soviet mediation, had been excessively generous towards India. Thus an impression was created that Ayub had lost on the negotiating table what the army had won on the battle-field. This was an unfair and incorrect assessment of the Tashkent declaration. None the less, it weakened Ayub's position and made his regime that much more vulnerable to the assault from disadvantaged regions and suppressed classes. Ayub resigned in March 1969, transferring power to another general, Yahya Khan.

The Yahya interregnum: 1969-71

The national revolt against military rule had forced Ayub Khan to concede, on 21 February 1969, to the demand for parliamentary elections.[61] Next month he transferred power to General Yahya Khan, who began his constitutional quest for a settlement to Pakistan's political crisis. Yahya announced a Legal Framework Order under which elections were to be held in December 1970. Yahya earned the respect of all the participants by adhering to his promise of impartiality and honesty. The 1970 national elections have been the only instance, to this day, of a free, untampered exercise of democratic rights in Pakistan.

The results of the national and provincial elections are summarised in Table 4 (p. 45). In East Pakistan, the Awami League won all but two of the 153 seats to the National Assembly. The League's victory was never in doubt, although its overwhelming magnitude came as a surprise. The result in West Pakistan was far more complex. Bhutto's PPP emerged as the major party, winning eighty-one out of the 148 seats. The PPP's significance far exceeded the 54% of seats captured by it. The other parties in West Pakistan were in total disarray, with the Qayyum Muslim League emerging as the second largest party, with just nine seats. Although the collective vote for other parties exceeded that of the PPP in Punjab, Bhutto's party won 75% of the National Assembly seats in this critical province. The splintered pattern of electoral support in Punjab is indicated in Table 5 (p. 47). Although other parties received 46% of the votes, compared with the PPP's 41%,[62] this support was split among ten parties. No party, other than the PPP, managed to get into double figures in either Punjab or Sind. It is also worth noting that the PPP won 14% of votes cast in the North West Frontier Province (NWFP). The National Awami Party (NAP) emerged as the main force in the provincial assemblies of NWFP and Baluchistan. The main feature of the election result was the mutually exclusive regional base of the two major parties. Mujib's Awami League won 151 seats in East Pakistan. Bhutto's PPP had support only in West Pakistan. In fact, no political party was able to win a National Assembly seat in both the regions. Only the relatively minor parties, the NAP, the PDP and the Jamaat-e-Islami, were able to win a few provincial assembly seats in both regions (see Table 4).

Controversy still surrounds the army's motives in holding these elections. One common view holds that Yahya had no intention of surrendering complete power to civilians, hoping to retain a permanent role for the army in a new constitutional structure. The hypothesis that the army hoped to control the victors, rather than fix the ballot, only partially explains the untampered freedom of choice permitted in 1970. Indeed, if one wishes to manipulate the outcome of the electoral process, one does not do so by allowing a free and fair ballot. The conventional, and well tried, method is to ensure the desired result. It would not have been too difficult for the army to bend the electoral mechanism. Further, contrary to popular belief that the army was surprised by the Awami League's victory, official intelligence reports had predicted a large majority for Mujib.[63] Accordingly, in determining the army's motives for holding an unrestricted election, particular emphasis needs to be placed on the sequence of events to which the army was responding. In the wake of the mass revolt against Ayub, the army appeared to have resigned itself to the inevitability of transferring power to civilians.[64] At this stage, the army expected the polls to produce a splintered outcome, with no single party able to command an absolute majority. None the less, the army's primary focus of concern was Mujib's Awami League. Consequently, the Legal Framework Order (LFO), under which the 1970 elections were held, provided a *conditional* framework for the transfer of power. The elected National Assembly had to frame a constitution within 120 days of its first meeting. This constitution required the approval of the President,

Table 4: Results of the elections held in December 1970 to National and Provincial Assemblies

Parties	East Pakistan		Punjab		Sind		NWFP		Baluchistan		Provincial Total 600	National Total 300
	Provincial	National	Provincial	National	Provincial	National	Provincial	National	Provincial	National		
PPP	–	–	113	62	32	18	3	1	–	–	148	81
Awami League	268	151	–	–	–	–	–	–	–	–	268	151
Independents	6	1	28	5	10	3	6	7	5	–	55	16
Pakistan Muslim League (Qayyum)	–	–	6	1	5	1	10	7	3	–	24	9
NAP (Wali)	1	–	–	–	–	–	13	3	8	3	22	6
Council Muslim League	–	–	15	7	4	–	1	–	–	–	20	7
JUP	–	–	4	4	7	3	–	–	–	–	11	7
Pakistan Muslim League (Convention)	–	–	6	2	–	–	2	–	–	–	8	2
JUI (Hazarvi)	–	–	2	–	–	–	4	6	2	1	8	7
PDP	2	1	4	–	–	–	–	–	–	–	6	1
Jamaat-e-Islami	1	–	1	1	1	2	1	–	–	–	4	4
Jamiat (Hadith)	–	–	1	–	–	–	–	–	–	–	1	–
NAP (Pakhtoon)	–	–	–	–	–	–	–	–	1	–	1	–
Baluchistan United Front	–	–	–	–	–	–	–	–	1	–	1	–
Sind United	–	–	–	–	1	–	–	–	–	–	1	–
Pathan Punjabi Front	–	–	–	–	–	–	–	–	–	–	–	–

45

i.e. the army. This measure was designed to give the army the leverage to exercise a veto over the Awami League's six points being incorporated into a constitution. As we have indicated elsewhere, the six points, which included a proposal for two separate currencies, would have created a confederation.[65]

As the polling day approached, the army was aware of the likelihood of an overwhelming victory for the Awami League. However, by this stage it was too late to tamper with the electoral mechanism to prevent such an outcome. Once the elections were held Yahya, armed with the LFO, appeared to be confident of his ability to mediate successfully as far as the Awami League's six points were concerned. Mujib's meetings with Yahya's aides had assured the general that the Awami League leader would modify the six-point demand to the extent that Pakistan would be a federal state, and not a confederation between two regions.[66] The cordiality of Yahya's initial contacts with Mujib suggested his confidence in having reached an understanding for a federal Pakistan. Indeed, Yahya referred to Mujib as Pakistan's next prime minister, whereas the latter is reported to have offered Yahya the post of constitutional head of state.[67]

However, as the time approached for the transfer of power, the divergent pressures on the participants became apparent. Yahya saw his role of arbiter as involving commitments from the Awami League to tone down the six points. Pressed by factions within the army, he sought reassurance for this by demanding to see a draft constitution before transferring power to the Awami League. Mujib became wary of Yahya's conditions, demanding that an immediate announcement be made to call a session of the newly elected National Assembly. Mujib had previously voiced public concern at factions in the army who were conspiring to undo the election results and prevent a transfer of power.[68] The strain between Yahya and Mujib was seized upon by the more hawkish figures in the army. They were not convinced about Mujib's ability to tone down the Awami League's platform for a confederation, especially in view of such an overwhelming mandate for the six points. The position of the hawks was strengthened by the posture adopted by Z. A. Bhutto. The PPP manifesto had criticised the Awami League's demands for a separate currency and a separate militia on the grounds that this implied an effective partition into two nation-states. The PPP's emergence as the main party in West Pakistan, particulary Punjab, lent greater authority to their criticisms. Bhutto took a strident view of the importance of his party, declaring that the question of the six points had to be settled before the convening of the National Assembly. Since the Awami League had a majority in the legislature, Bhutto sought a constitutional accord prior to a meeting of the National Assembly. To this end, he allied himself with the hawks in the army,[69] threatening to 'break the legs' of party members who dared to attend the inaugural session of the National Assembly, scheduled for 3 March 1971. The failure of the Mujib-Bhutto talks to thrash out a broad consensus on the future constitution, had convinced Bhutto that Mujib could not back down from implementing a confederation. Confident of support from within the army, Bhutto pressed Yahya for a postponement of the National Assembly.

Table 5: *Voting Percentage National Assembly Elections.*

Party	Punjab		Sind		NWFP		Baluchistan	
PPP	41.66		44.95		14.25		2.38	
CML	12.66		6.84		4.06		10.99	
PML (Convention)	5.11	23.19	1.79	19.33	0.57	27.27	–	21.93
PML (Qayyum)	5.42		10.70		22.64		10.94	
Jamaat-e-Islami	4.74		10.31		7.22		1.16	
JUP	9.96	19.89	6.94	22.1	0.02	32.69	–	21.16
JUI (H)	5.19		4.85		25.45		20.0	
NAP (W)	–		0.37		18.40		45.23	
PDP	2.26		0.08		0.32		0.37	
Other Parties	1.35		2.16		0.93		2.12	
Independents	11.65		11.71		6.01		6.81	

Two days before the scheduled inaugural session, the convening of the National Assembly was postponed indefinitely. Yahya did not personally announce the postponement, a distance which has been interpreted as demonstrating his reluctance to follow this course. In any case, Yahya's constitutional quest had failed, as the junta prepared for a military crackdown. In East Pakistan, there was little illusion regarding Yahya's appeals for further talks with the Awami League to resolve the deadlock. Mujib was to predict correctly the precise sequence of events leading to the clampdown.[70] As far as Bhutto was concerned, he seemed somewhat ambivalent, even about the outcome of the army action: "A separation of East Pakistan might not be an undivided disaster after all, because we are a very unwieldy country now and the only way to keep together would be to have a type of loose constitutional arrangement that would provide a dangerous precedent for West Pakistan, where the Baluch would demand the same thing. *We might be better off with a smaller but more manageable and more compact Pakistan*".[71] In the same interview, he warned the Baluchis not to take the precedent of Bengal too seriously, displaying a predilection for a military solution to ethnic conflict in West Pakistan. (Later, when Bhutto came to power in a truncated Pakistan, the military clampdown on Baluchistan was to seriously damage his regime.) In East Pakistan, the military offensive led to the creation of a new nation-state, Bangladesh. Perhaps this is the only instance in which the majority of the population had broken away to form a new country.

Conflict between the centre and regional units is inherent in the structure of post colonial nation-states; several of these countries have been carved out of artificial and arbitrary boundaries. Separatist movements are therefore not uncommon. What is universal, however, is their lack of success in meeting their objectives. Modern armies have proved themselves to be quite capable of forcing reluctant regional groups to stay within national boundaries. This supremacy of military power has been evident in separatist movements in Asia, Latin America and Africa. The only factor which seems capable of ensuring success for a regional movement is military assistance and intervention by a foreign power. It is self-evident that Bangladesh could not have been created without Indian military intervention. What is surprising, however, is not the fact that India meddled, but the failure of the Pakistan army to anticipate the consequences of Indian military intervention. On the one hand, Pakistan's entire foreign policy was determined by the fear of India. On the other, insufficient measures were taken to protect the most vulnerable region of Pakistan, perhaps under the delusion that China and/or the United States would prevent an Indian military offensive on East Pakistan. In the event, when the carnage was over, the Muslims of the Indian subcontinent were spread across three nation-states.

Footnotes:

1 The term 'basic democrat' adequately reflected Ayub's arrogance: "This system will give everyone the opportunity to have his say in level with his horizon and power of understanding". See Ayub Khan: *Outlines of our Constitution* (March 1959), a detailed draft for a future constitution prepared within six months of the *coup.*
2 For details of the operation of basic democracies see Government of Pakistan, Bureau of National Construction: *Four Studies in Basic Democracies. 1964.*
3 For a discussion of these issues see K. B. Sayeed: *Political System of Pakistan.* Also see K. B. Sayeed: "The Role of the Military in Pakistan" in Von Vorys (ed): *Armed Forces and Society.*
4 Ayub Khan: op cit, p. 14.
5 In July 1962, Ayub yielded to demands from his own assembly and legitimised the formation of political parties. In May 1963, Ayub joined the Muslim League, an action which split the party with groups opposed to Ayub forming a separate Muslim League.
6 S. Huntington: *Political Order in Changing Societies* p. 251.
7 The Pakistan Times, in particular, was noted for its independence.

8 See K. B. Sayeed: op cit, pp. 123-4.
9 For details of reforms and their effects see *All Pakistan Legal Decisions* (PLD) 1963, xv. Also see Singhal: *Pakistan*.
10 Such views are reflected in E. Mason: *Foreign Aid and Foreign Policy*.
11 Ayub Khan: *Friends Not Masters*, p. 187.
12 Macaulay: *Critical, Historical and Miscellaneous Essays*, v. pp. 19-20.
13 From the preamble of the *Constitution of Republic of Pakistan, 1962*.
14 ibid, Article 131, clause 2.
15 *All Pakistan Legal Decisions* (PLD), 1963, xv, p. 860.
16 As a consequence, organised political activity revolved increasingly around regional issues. The 9-point programme of the Combined Opposition Party, an alliance formed to fight the 1964 presidential elections against Ayub, included an explicit commitment for the removal of economic disparity between the two regions within 10 years. The opposition candidate was Miss Fatima Jinnah, sister of M. A. Jinnah. Despite the manipulative character of basic democracy-based indirect elections, Miss Jinnah got 46.6% of the vote in East Pakistan as opposed to 53.1% for Ayub.
17 Along with some Bengali members of the Civil Service and the army.
18 According to A. Gauhar, Ayub's information minister, Mujib was included at Yahya's insistence. See, "Ayub Khan's abdication". *Third World Quarterly*, Jan. 1985.
19 An event of considerable importance was the success of the general strike called by the East Pakistani political parties on 14 December 1968. The strike brought the provincial capital, Dacca, to a standstill, paralysing all forms of official and economic activities. This was Awami League's decisive encounter with its own organisational strength, political support and potency.
20 For details of poor Bengali representation see R. Jahan: *Pakistan-Failure in National Integration*. M. Ahmed: *Bangladesh — Constitutional Quest for Autonomy, 1950-71*.
21 See A. Jalal: *Jinnah, the Sole Spokesman*, for details.
22 Apart from NAP, the province gave substantial support to the religious party, Jamiat-e-ulema-e-Islam (JUI) and to Qayyum Muslim League. NAP also had a mass base, particularly among peasants, in East Pakistan. In this region it was led by the progressive maulana, Bhasani. But the NAP in East Pakistan was marginalised, as Bengali opinion rallied around Mujib's Awami

League.
23 For details see Singhal: op cit, pp. 110-20.
24 An eloquent justification for government repression of left wing groups can be seen in the Pakistan Times, Lahore, 19.8.62. (editorial). For other examples see T. Ali: *Military Rule or People's Power?* pp. 110-20.
25 A reference was made to the central state structure under the Caliph Omar (634-644) to justify executive control over the legislature. See, for example, the Pakistan Times, Lahore, 21.3.63.
26 Quoted in Sayeed: op cit, p. 104.
27 E. Mason: op cit, p. 115.
28 Supplement to the composite report of the *President's Committee to Study the United States Military Assistance Programme.* Volume 11, p. 79 (1959).
29 For detailed account of modernisation theories, see D. Apter: *The Politics of Modernisation*; M. Janowitz: *The Military in the Political Development of New Nations.*
30 Japan is not included in the calculations for Asian countries. For details see IBRD: *Industrial Development of Pakistan.* International Bank for Reconstruction and Development, report — AS 118, 1966.
31 ibid, p. 4.
32 The removal on restrictions on imports in 1964, of commodities such as non-ferrous metals and iron and steel products, had been underwritten by the U.S. Government. For details see G. Papanek: *Pakistan's Development: Social Goals and Private Incentives,* pp. 120-40.
33 Brecher and Abbas: *Foreign Aid and Industrial Development in Pakistan,* p. 151.
34 ibid, p. 152.
35 For details, see Griffin and Khan (eds): *Growth and Inequality in Pakistan.* pp. 125-130.
36 Demand was inflated partly by groups wanting to import luxury goods which were under severe import restrictions.
37 N. Islam: *Foreign Trade and Economic Controls in Development.* p. 97.
38 This uncertain and cumbersome multiple exchange rate system was eventually dismantled by the massive 130% devaluation undertaken by the PPP regime in 1972.
39 For further discussion see, Griffin and Khan: op cit, pp. 60-70.
40 Soligo and Stern: "Tariff Protection, Import Substitution and Investment Efficiency". *Pakistan Development Review,* 1965.
41 *Report of the Farm Mechanisation Committee,* Ministry of

Agriculture & Works, Government of Pakistan, 1970.
42 There is some controversy over which class of farmer benefited most from the 'green revolution'. Alavi, for example, has argued that the principal beneficiaries were the very large farmers, with the growth of landless labour mitigating the beneficial effects. Burki, on the other hand, has suggested that the medium sized landlords were the main recipients of the privileges. He has also suggested that the increased demand for labour raised real wages, thus benefiting the landless labour. See Alavi et al: *Rural Development in Bangladesh and Pakistan*, which contains articles by both authors.
43 For example, an individual could retain land in excess of stipulated ceilings as long as his holding did not exceed 36,000 produce index units (PIU). PIU was a measure of land productivity, but figures were based on pre-Partition data, which enabled landlords to retain most of their holdings. For details, see M. H. Khan: *Underdevelopment and Agrarian Structure in Pakistan*, chapter 5.
44 ibid.
45 This low proportion of resumed land also reflected the poor quality of the excess land declared by the landlords.
46 M. Haq: *The Strategy of Economic Planning*, and G. Papanek: op cit.
47 *The Second Five Year Plan, (1960-65)*, p. 49.
48 M. Haq: op cit, p. 9.
49 Even within West Pakistan, there was considerable disparity in regional allocations, with Punjab and Sind attracting the bulk of the resources. Baluchistan in particular remained largely unaffected by the 'development decade'.
50 M. Haq: op cit, p. 266.
51 Asher and Mason: *The World Bank since Bretton Woods*, p. 674.
52 Not surprisingly, the two sides of the debate were divided on regional lines. The estimates of regional disparity were much higher among East Pakistani economists. For the divergent views on the growth of regional inequalities, see reports of East Pakistani and West Pakistani economists in "Income Inequalities in Pakistan", *Pakistan Economic and Social Review*, special issue, 1976.
53 Data on the 22 families was released initially by the chief economist of the Planning Commision, M. Haq.
54 For details, see World Bank: *Education Sector Working Paper*, 1974.
55 According to T. E. Nulty: *Income Distribution and Savings in Pakistan*, (Ph.D. thesis, Cambridge University), there was a clear

trend towards increasing income inequalities during 1962-63, 1963-64 and 1966-67. A recent study by Z. Mahmood, *Income Inequality in Pakistan: an Analysis of Existing Evidence*, (1984) suggests, however, that there was a marginal improvement in income distribution. A study by Guisinger and Hicks, "Long term trends in income distribution in Pakistan", *World Development*, Volume 6, 1978, also argued that coarse macro data did not support the view that income distribution had worsened in the sixties.

56 M. Haq: op cit, p. 30.
57 *Fourth Five Year Plan, July, 1970*, pp. 12-14.
58 ibid.
59 For details see Z. Shaheed: *Organisation and Leadership of Industrial Labour in Karachi*. (Ph.D. thesis, University of Leeds, 1977).
60 ibid. Also see K. B. Sayeed: *Nature and Direction of Political Change in Pakistan*.
61 At the round table conference held between Ayub and the opposition parties, the latter had pressed for direct, universal adult franchise for the establishment of a federal parliamentary system.
62 Rest of the votes went to independent candidates. See Table 5.
63 Intelligence reports, particularly that of General Akbar, had clearly anticipated Awami League's total victory in East Pakistan.
64 Yahya is reported to have responded to a question regarding his sincerity by answering: "Am I such a fool as not to be able to see the writing on the wall? . . . the urge for democracy demonstrated in the anti-Ayub movement was too strong for any general to ignore". Quoted in G. W. Choudhry: *Last Days of United Pakistan*, p. 96.
65 Although its proponents often reject this interpretation, it is difficult to see how a country's regions can have two currencies, separate militias, separate foreign exchange accounts, engage in trade relations independently of one another and be called anything other than a confederation.
66 Yahya, referring to his aides, stated that "Ahsan (Governor of East Pakistan) and Peerzada had long sessions with Sheikh Mujib and they assured me, as Mujib assured me himself, that he would modify his six-point plan. Inshalla, Pakistan will be saved". Quoted in Choudhry, op cit, p. 128. Also see S. Salek: *Witness to Surrender*, pp. 16-30. Although the details of Salek's account differ from Choudhry's, both stress Yahya's perception that he had reached an implicit understanding with Sheikh Mujib

regarding modifications to the six-point programme. Both Salek and Choudhry were involved, in an official capacity, with the events of 1970-71.
67 S. Salek: op cit, pp. 16-17. This claim made by Pakistani sources, is vehemently denied by Awami League leaders.
68 See Mujib's statement in the *Pakistan Observer*, 4.1.71. In the same statement, Mujib had thanked Yahya for honouring his pledge to hold elections, but suggested that he was not in full command of the army.
69 Bhutto's talks with General Peerzada were crucial. The army faction which sought Bhutto's support included General Gul Hasan, General Hamid and Major-General Omar.
70 In the first week of March 1971, Mujib had made a precise forecast regarding the course of events leading to a military crackdown. Conversation quoted by Asghar Khan, leading West Pakistani politician, in *Generals and Politics*, p. 30.
71 Interview with Selig Harrison, on 23 March 1971, two days before the army clampdown. Quoted in S. Harrison: *In Afghanistan's Shadow*, p. 155.

Part Two
AUTHORITARIAN POPULISM UNDER BHUTTO 1971-77

"Looking into the future, if we messed it up, if we didn't make the parliamentary system work, if our constitution breaks down, then there is a possibility of the army stepping in again."

Z. A. Bhutto, 1972

Chapter One

Political Development under the PPP

By 1972, a civil war had exhausted what remained of Pakistan. None the less, the fatigue and despair were mitigated by a transfer of power pregnant with possibilities. The military debacle had forced the army into transferring power to the majority party in the truncated Pakistan. For the Pakistan People's Party (PPP), the situation was not entirely unpromising. Although recent events imposed certain constraints, they had simultaneously offered opportunities to undertake structural reforms against an élite haunted by its failure to retain East Pakistan. The radical election pledges of the PPP bred optimism for the emergence of a democratic and liberal Pakistan. Indeed, even the East Pakistan tragedy was being perceived as a welcome political circumcision. The 'new Pakistan' could look forward to a future containing the prospect of a more physically viable nation-state with democratic institutions and a strong economic base. In the event, this optimism was replaced by a feeling of betrayal as the PPP's rule became increasingly repressive. The bitterness and anger were provoked by the violation of the promise to introduce progressive, participatory government in Pakistan. The sense of betrayal was manifested in the spontaneous outbreak of a popular movement in 1977, as the PPP's brief rule culminated in an act which symbolised its corruption . . . the rigging of parliamentary elections. Z. A. Bhutto, the leader of the PPP, was personally to pay a grave price for converting a mandate for democracy into a charter for a civilian dictatorship. In the following chapters we shall examine the multiple causes which led to the abrupt downfall of the PPP government.

    The failure of civilian élites to develop participatory institutions has led to the proliferation of military rule in developing countries. Factors which have facilitated military intervention have been examined elsewhere.[1] In the case of Pakistan, one needs to note two stages of the process whereby the military has come to dominate the political structure. This sequential demarcation is useful, since it emphasises the difference between the initial and subsequent military interventions. Ayub Khan's *coup*, in 1958, was linked to the failure of the Muslim League to accommodate ethnic divisions. Unlike India, Pakistan did not develop a democratic framework since the resultant participatory institutions would have transferred power to the Bengalis. The dominance of the Punjabi-mahajjir élite, which would have been subverted by democracy, was ensured by the military. The consequence of military rule ... the creation of Bangladesh ... was responsible for the reluctant withdrawal of the army. The armed forces were by no means united in their decision to hand over power to the PPP.[2] Indeed, some military officers were reluctant to accept civilian supremacy even after the PPP had assumed office. In just over a year after coming to power, the PPP regime had to confront an abortive *coup* plan involving approximately forty officers.[3] Friction with the military also arose, in 1972, over the refusal of a general to supply troops to quell striking policemen engaged in a pay dispute in Punjab.[4]

The military regained power in 1977, taking advantage of the first opportunity provided by a political crisis. This second intervention revealed how political structures are often persistently impaired by the precedent set by previous military rule. Again, the parallel with India is illustrative. Mrs. Gandhi's emergency was followed by an election which restored the parliamentary process. Thus India was able to rebuild its democratic structure, because the military did not use the emergency as an excuse to intervene. As we argue below, there is strong evidence to suggest that the PPP and the opposition parties had agreed to hold fresh elections in 1977. The military *coup* prevented a restoration of the principle of elected government.

In the event, the PPP failed to prevent a *coup*. None the less, like any government taking over from the military, it tried to establish its authority over praetorian institutions. The apparent restlessness within the military in Pakistan, noted above, lent urgency to the PPP's actions in this regard. The measures taken can be divided into three categories: constitutional safeguards, creation of a para-military alternative and appeasement.

The issue of Bengali representation had meant a delay of nine years for the Constituent Assembly to frame Pakistan's first constitution in 1956.[5] This delay created a political vacuum which was filled by the military. In contrast, the civilian leaders in post-Bangladesh Pakistan took just one year to draft a constitution. Th 1973 Constitution outlined the framework of a federal, democratic structure. Article 271 of the constitution prescribed the death penalty for its subversion. A military *coup* constituted one such violation. However, the value of such a deterrent is inherently limited, since the enforcement of prescribed punishment is hardly possible in the event of a *coup*. But the value of the constitution lay not in the efficacy of the punitive measures, but in the formalisation of a representative federal structure. As shall be documented below, the PPP failed to abide by the framework of legitimate civilian rule, and thereby underwrote its own demise.

Political Development under the PPP

The second component in the PPP's relationship with the military was related to practical concerns. The PPP created a para-military force, the Federal Security Force (FSF), with the objective of minimising the role of the military in the political system. It was envisaged that the FSF would be used to quell rioting, in the event of a serious civil disturbance which the police could not handle. Consequently a civilian government would not need to rely on the army to contain civil disorder. In a memo to his chief security adviser, Bhutto expressed fears of political mobilisation against the regime and consequent involvement of the military: "People come out on the streets on the least pretext. They violently defy established authority . . . the situation deteriorates so much that it becomes necessary to call upon the armed forces to intervene. *Once the armed forces intervene they play the game according to their own rules. It is necessary for a civilian government to avoid seeking the assistance of the armed forces in dealing with its responsibilities and problems* . . . generally the police and the other law enforcing agencies fail to control a really serious agitation. *We must make provisions for a first class force*".[6] The outcome was the FSF, the nucleus of which was created in October 1972 with the headquarters at Lahore. In June 1973 the FSF was given legislative sanction through an act of parliament. The army reacted sharply to the FSF proposal.[7] It refused to undertake training.[8] It successfully blocked the acquisition of tanks and other heavy armour by the FSF.[9]

Deprived of the technical instruments required to act as a substitute for the army, the FSF became an *additional* coercive force. The diminution of its scale also entailed a change in function. Instead of a reserve force, it became an active organism through which the PPP intimidated the parliamentary opposition. In May 1973, for example, the FSF disrupted meetings and rallies of political parties opposed to the PPP.[10] Two years later, members of the National Assembly were forcibly ejected from the premises by members of the FSF. Ironically, this action was taken in response to the opposition's protests against a PPP-proposed constitutional amendment limiting dissent.[11] The degeneration of the FSF into a group of official thugs was acknowledged by the Prime Minister.[12] The use of the FSF as a partisan force to repress civilian leaders undermined the development of democratic institutions. Thus, ironically, a force created ostensibly to minimise praetorian intervention, accentuated its likelihood by undermining the participatory institutions needed to prevent a *coup*. The environment of intimidation generated by the use of the FSF contributed to the widespread feeling of betrayal and anger which galvanised the opposition into forming a united front against Bhutto in 1977.

The third component of the PPP's strategy, relating to the army, consisted of measures to appease the military high command. Accordingly military expenditure, as a percentage of GNP, grew under the PPP, as indicated in Table 1 below. The size of the armed forces also increased, in spite of the territorial loss of East Pakistan. In addition, Bhutto exempted holdings of military officers from the Land Reform Programme. Perhaps more significant than the financial concessions to the military élite was the embargo on a public discussion of the military debacle in East Pakistan. The government did establish a commission to inquire into the disaster. The report of the Hamood-ur-Rahman Commission was, however, never made public, because of the severe criticisms it made of the military's conduct. Thus, instead of utilising the East Pakistan crisis to sustain an environment hostile to military rule on the grounds of past incompetence, the PPP chose to protect the military by not permitting a public discussion on the most serious crisis in Pakistan's history.[13] The reason for doing so cannot simply be attributed to a desire for avoiding a debate on painful national wounds. A factor which was perhaps decisive in the PPP not utilising the horrors of East Pakistan as a symbol of military rule was Bhutto's nebulous role in the '71 crisis.[14] Thus Bhutto's relationship with the military was ambiguous; he had to accommodate the military élite in view of his past association with them. The protection that this involved had to be reconciled with the requirement of retaining civilian supremacy by exposing the consequences of military rule.

Table 1: *Military Expenditure and Size. 1969-75.*

Year	Military Expenditure Amount ($m)	As % of GNP	As % of Budget	Size of the Armed Forces (in thousands)
1969	350	5.0	55.52	365
1970	372	4.8	53.91	370
1971	436	5.6	56.17	404
1972	522	6.7	59.10	350
1973	522	6.6	58.10	466
1974	572	5.7	53.22	500
1975	569	6.3	53.41	502

Sources: U.S. Arms Control and Disarmament Agency; *World Military Expenditures and Arms Transfers, 1966-1975.*[1]
Hussain, A., *Elite Politics in an Ideological State*, p. 139.
Rashid, J., 'Pakistan in the Debt Trap — A Mortgaged Economy', *Viewpoint*, 10/12/76, p. 21.

Finally, Bhutto's attempts to dominate the military élite relied on the mistaken assumption that personal loyalty to a civilian leader could prevent military intervention. The most potent symbol of rewards for personal trust was the appointment of a relatively junior officer as Army Chief of Staff.[15]

The propulsion of Zia-ul-Haq to this post was in recognition of his role as prosecutor of the military officers who had planned a *coup* in 1972. If patrimonial ties operated as effective restraints, the ubiquitous phenomena of palace intrigues and *coups* would be rare. Events in Pakistan in 1977 did little to disprove the theory that institutional development, not personal ties, is the only effective deterrent against military intervention.

The PPP Government was far more successful in its attempts to reform the other component of the military-bureaucratic complex, which had dominated Pakistan's politics since 1947. The supremacy of the Civil Service was deflated through a series of measures designed to curb its influence. The initial phase of this process was heralded by the dismissal of 1,300 Civil Servants in 1972, under a martial law ordinance. Three principal, though often overlapping, categories were the subject of dismissals: too close an association with the previous regime, officials with excessive power and influence who were likely to prove 'troublesome', and those officials who were accused of over extravagance in their corruption.[16]

The purges were followed by wide-ranging reforms. A vital blow to the senior and powerful bureaucrats was the abolition of the élite Civil Service of Pakistan (CSP) cadre on 20 August 1973. Recruitment procedures and the restrictions on selection to this service were similar to those employed by the colonial government. In practice this ensured that selection to the top echelons of the Civil Service remained under the control of a few entrenched families. Approximately 500 bureaucrats of the CSP cadre had stood at the helm of an administrative machinery of over 500,000 members.[17] The annual intake to the élite corps was restricted to around twenty individuals.[18] The system incorporating the élite status of the CSP was replaced by the linear All Pakistan Unified Grades structure. The entire bureaucratic machinery was amalgamated into a hierarchical, but mobile, framework of twenty-two pay scales. Separate provision for entry into an élite corps was terminated.[19]

The senior officials were weakened further by withdrawal of life tenure. Previously they were provided with special constitutional privileges, which virtually guaranteed permanence of service. The new procedures of dismissal accentuated the insecurity of the bureaucrats and further undermined their authority. Bhutto, who never publicly attacked the army after coming to power, felt no such restraint in the case of the Civil Service: "No institution in the country has so lowered the quality of our national life as what is called 'naukershahi'. It has created a class of brahmins or mandarins unrivalled in its snobbery and arrogance, insulated from the life of the people and incapable of identifying itself with them".[20] Accordingly, it is not surprising that non-CSP officials emerged as the more powerful of Bhutto's bureaucratic advisers.[21]

The most significant implication of the reforms was the diminution of the bureaucracy's role as *formulator* of policy. The reforms effectively curbed the autonomy and supremacy of the Civil Service. Policies were now being outlined by elected representatives. These policies involved an extension of the role of the public sector in the economy. Ironically, the process enlarged the functions and duties performed by the Civil Service. None the less, there was a shift in the Civil Service's role from that of decision maker to that of executioner of policy. This conventional bureaucratic function represented, in the context of Pakistan's political development, a significant demotion for the Civil Service.

The reform of the Civil Service was necessary and welcome. The changes had been suggested long before the PPP took over. A number of government-appointed studies in the fifties and the sixties had suggested similar reforms, including the abolition of the CSP.[22] The PPP reforms sought not only to dismantle the élite structure, but also to replace it with a more technocratic and efficient public service. In keeping with such enhanced productivity considerations, a system of 'lateral entry' was introduced, in order to induce technical specialists from professions outside the Civil Service. Theoretically, these measures were designed to replace the 'generalist' élite by technically competent specialists, who would be better equipped to handle the burdens imposed on the administrative machinery of an expanding public sector.

The administrative reform programme was marred, however, by a wide discrepancy between its objectives and achievements. There were serious flaws and shortcomings in the administrative structure established by the PPP. The lateral entry system was used not to attract talent from the private sector, but as an instrument for the distribution of political patronage. Between 1973 and 1977, the Establishment Division[23] accepted 1,374 officers into the Civil Service, approximately three times as much as would have been possible under the rigid scrutiny of the old system. This increase was inevitable in view of the expansion of the public sector. None the less, a large proportion of the senior level recruits were identified as relatives or close friends of members of the central cabinet.[24] Some of the beneficiaries of such flagrant nepotism perceived jobs in the public sector as a source of personal enrichment. The dynamics of greed and corruption are difficult to contain, especially when the public sector is expanding and recruitment is a function of patronage. The opportunities for graft increased, as did its practice. Corruption undermines the authority of state institutions. The healthy development of a political system requires respect for public institutions. Citizens willingly accept the authority of state institutions only when the power they exercise is seen not to be arbitrary and corruptible. In the absence of such consent, citizens heed public directives through fear of the state's coercive powers. This mixture of fear and cynicism had characterised popular perceptions of the Ayub administration. Hence the PPP reforms were initially supported by considerable public enthusiasm. However, the prevalence and growth of corruption undermined faith in the new administrative structure. The explicitly partisan bias in official appointments, and the resulting close association of the PPP with widespread corruption, shook confidence in public institutions under the new government. The line between the party and the state was further blurred in 1977, as members of the Civil Service actively participated in the rigging of parliamentary elections.

Thus, although the PPP was successful in curbing the power and influence of the élitist CSP, it could not establish an efficient alternative. There was considerable popular support for measures to curtail the role of arrogant CSP officers. As we noted above, the senior Civil Servants had adopted a high profile under Ayub and were associated with the repression and failures of his rule. They were a primary target for public scorn and anger during the opposition movements in the late sixties. However, the administrative structure which replaced the previous one was marred by nepotism, inefficiency and corruption. This was particularly unfortunate since the expansion of the public sector and the efficient implementation of the regime's policies required an effective and organised Civil Service.

In order to establish a viable alternative to military rule, the PPP had to operate at two levels. The somewhat negative function, which we discussed above, was the enactment of reforms to curb the power of the hitherto dominant military-bureaucratic oligarchy. The second, more positive, objective was the establishment of civilian democratic institutions. The responsibility for creating the institutional base for a democratic structure rested firmly with the majority party, the PPP. In the Pakistani context, they had to create a structure which met two objectives. First, it had to integrate the minority ethnic groups into the framework of state power. Baluchis, Sindhis and Pathans had to be assimilated into the political system. Second, representative institutions had to be encouraged and developed at all levels of society. Mass integration would occur through the cohesive role played by elections to local, provincial and national government. Needless to say, gross inequalities in wealth and income distort the representative nature of elected bodies, but in spite of such imbalances, the appeal of electoral mechanisms legitimises state authority. Such a structure generates particularly strong support from the middle and lower middle classes, who tend numerically to be the principal beneficiaries of local elected office. These classes tend to mobilise grass roots support for the system. In this manner, the representative structure filters through society. This creates mass support for the institutional framework of participatory democracy. It is a task with which Nehru and the Congress had considerable success. The PPP faced a similar challenge. In both cases the stakes were high . . . the price of failure was military intervention.

Initially, the conditions seemed to be favourable. At the provincial level, two regions had PPP governments, whereas Baluchistan and NWFP were ruled by the NAP-JUI coalition. This outcome ensured participation of the minority provinces as well as providing the basis for extending representative institutions across the nation. However, both objectives, national integration and democratic institution building, were subverted almost casually and with apparent disregard for the serious implications. We shall first deal with the PPP's actions regarding the objective of integrating a multi-ethnic nation.

On 27 April 1972 a tripartite accord was signed between the PPP and the two major opposition parties in Baluchistan and NWFP, whereby the NAP-JUI coalition was allowed to form the government with a guarantee. This was, that the centre would not appoint provincial governors without the approval and consent of the majority parties of the concerned province.[25] In Baluchistan, G. B. Bizenjo was appointed Governor and A. Mengal the Chief Minister. Both were senior members of the National Awami Party (NAP). Similar to the holding of free elections in 1970, the optimism over the accord was to be overshadowed by the horror of subsequent events. On 14 February 1973, less than a year after the accord, the Baluchi Provincial Government was dismissed. The NAP-JUI Government in the Frontier Province resigned in protest. Military operations against the consequent revolt in Baluchistan began in May 1973, barely a month after the National Assembly had passed the new constitution. Ironically, the '73 Constitution, for which there was unanimous support among all the political parties,[26] had granted considerable autonomy for provincial government. With the clampdown in Baluchistan, these provisions became quite meaningless. Most leaders of the NAP were arrested two days after the '73 Constitution had become legally operational.

Much had been expected of the NAP Administration, which had formed the government in Baluchistan in 1972. It had to contend with a legacy of unbalanced regional growth, use of the region's natural resources without adequate reward for the province and the virtual exclusion of the Baluchis from any semblance of state power. Baluchistan is the most impoverished province in Pakistan. This is reflected in all the indicators of modernisation and development. Its literacy rate is barely 6%, compared to a national average of 18%. At $54 its *per capita* income is barely 60% of that enjoyed by Punjab, the richest province. Its share in industrialisation is a paltry 0.7%. This poor share exists in spite of a favourable mineral resource endowment. The question was, however, not so much about higher relative poverty in Baluchistan; it was concerned more with what little had been done to develop Baluchistan, relative to other provinces, since 1947. Indeed, the sense of grievance in Baluchistan over use of its gas and other mineral resources for the development of other provinces, was not dissimilar to sentiments regarding the jute trade in East Pakistan, during the fifties and the sixties. Sui gas fields, for example, provide 80% of Pakistan's gas production and save an estimated $275 million per year in foreign exchange. Yet royalties to the Baluchistan state treasury totalled just $1.2 million in 1980.[27] The share of revenue going to provinces from mineral resources is much higher in other parts of the world.[28] Indeed, the manner in which the central government tends to put back resources into Baluchistan aggravates political tensions. The building of infrastructure and exploration for minerals has been undertaken by the central government in collaboration with foreign firms. The Baluchis derive little benefit from the process, increasing their sense of alienation and resentment.

Economic deprivation is accompanied by poor Baluchi representation in government service, even at the provincial level. Out of 830 higher civil posts in Baluchistan, only 181 were held by Baluchis, almost all in minor posts.[29] In 1972, only one of the twenty heads of department in the provincial administration was a Baluchi. The NAP Administration, which took over in 1972, was naturally expected to rectify these imbalances. Accordingly, it announced plans to repatriate Punjabi, Sindhi and Pushtun bureaucrats stationed in Baluchistan. The decision to do so had been taken at a governor's conference presided over by Bhutto. Although there was some disagreement about how swiftly this should be done, all parties agreed in principle to the proposals. In addition, the NAP Administration announced plans to industrialise the province, utilising its resource endowment to propose the establishment of cement and slaked lime factories.

The NAP's programme, however, went beyond the uncontroversial issues of promoting Baluchi representation and industrialisation. The party's commitment to social and economic reform provoked opposition from within Baluchistan. The government nationalised marble and coal mines. In addition, measures were taken to abolish the Sardari System, under which tribal chiefs had exercised extensive control over their subjects. These proposals provoked a violent reaction among affected groups, such as the Jam of Lasbella and the Zehri tribe. The federal government sent army contingents to end the tribal conflict led by the Jam of Lasbella. The troops were sent in response to an appeal by the NAP Administration.[30] The tense situation was aggravated by attacks against Punjabi migrants in the Pat Feeder area. Nevertheless, although conditions were unsettled, they were by no means beyond the control of the provincial administration. In any case, the central government did not question the efficacy with which the NAP was governing Baluchistan. It accused the party of something far more serious . . . planning to secede from Pakistan.

The centre-piece of the smear campaign against NAP was publication, in all the government-owned newspapers, of the alleged 'London Plan' to further dismember Pakistan. According to stories of the plot, Wali Khan, leader of the opposition and chairman of NAP, had met the Bangladeshi President Sheikh Mujib in London, to plan a secessionist uprising. A. T. Mengal, Chief Minister of Baluchistan, was also accused of participation in the conspiracy. On 10 February 1973, a cache of Russian manufactured arms was discovered in a raid on the Iraqi embassy, in Islamabad. The central government linked these arms to the 'London Plan' for secession of Baluchistan and the NWFP. The discovery of the arms cache provided the pretext for dismissing the NAP Government. There is, however, no proof nor reason to believe that the NAP leadership was aware of the flow of arms through the Iraqi embassy.[31] According to Western intelligence sources, the arms were destined primarily for Irani Baluch areas, since the Iraqi Government was supporting Baluch insurgents in Iran, in retaliation to the Shah's encouragement for the Kurdish rebellion in Iraq. It also appears likely that part of the arms cache was to be received by guerrilla groups in Baluchistan led by Sher Mohammad Marri.

Guerrilla groups in Baluchistan have been operating almost continually since 1947. The history of the conflict between the central government and the Baluchis has been examined elsewhere.[32] Intermittent conflict throughout the sixties ended with a ceasefire in 1969, as the Yahya Government dissolved the one-unit scheme whereby Baluchistan had been forced into the artificial province of West Pakistan. However, some of the groups involved had developed a coherent Marxist-Leninist strategy of guerrilla warfare. Events in 1971, leading to the successful movement by the Bengalis to break away from Pakistan, had encouraged some guerrilla factions in Baluchistan. The principal group was the Pararis, led by Sher Mohammad Marri.[33] They sought military support from the Iraqi Government,[34] and appeared to be preparing for an armed struggle against the central government.

It is important, however, to reiterate that the NAP governments in Baluchistan and NWFP were not involved with the arming of guerrilla groups. They had, for the first time in Pakistan's history, formed an administration in their own provinces. As beneficiary of these constitutional arrangements, the NAP was eager to operate within the established institutional framework. However, instead of encouraging NAP's commitment to representative structures, the PPP ostracised the moderate Baluch and Pathan leadership by dismissing the provincial government. Ironically, the leading exponents of an accommodatory stance towards the new representative framework, Bizenjo and Wali Khan, were arrested and accused of plotting secession. Thus, precisely those groups who could have been relied upon to strengthen regional representative institutions were marginalised by the PPP. The democratic experiment had failed within a year of its inception.

In an atmosphere charged with accusations of treason, Bhutto insisted that behind the façade of a parliamentary framework, the NAP was operating as an underground group, "serving as the front line organisation for Afghan territorial designs on Pakistan".[35] The tactic of attacking parts of the civilian opposition as secessionists was sustained, even after the NAP was banned. The PPP's malicious policy towards the National Democratic Party (NDP) was outlined in a mischievous memo approved by Bhutto: "The following line of action is suggested . . . preventing the NDP from coming in the fold of the opposition alliance. This can be achieved by attacking their *secessionist* manifesto. An immediate attack can be launched on the similarity of their programme with Mujib's six-point demand and their plan to re-open the fundamentals of the constitution in proposing redefining of the boundaries of the provinces and encouraging local cultures and languages".[36] The dynamics of such a strategy generate outcomes which are a product of a self-fulfilling logic. Political parties are accused of treason and, on the basis of such libel, are excluded from the political structure. Expulsion and marginalisation provoke a violent reaction, as occurred in Baluchistan. This reaction is then presented as evidence of treacherous intent. This provides an ostensible legitimisation for the initial repression.

Bhutto's dismissal of the NAP Government was conditioned primarily by his deep mistrust of groups demanding greater provincial autonomy.[37] He viewed such platforms as superstructures for secessionist tendencies. This attitude had determined his tough stance towards Mujib's Awami League. Similarly, his government's approach towards the Baluchis and the Pathans was influenced less with the desire to accommodate them within a democratic structure. Bhutto, in collusion with the army, was more concerned with a military strategy to prevent perceived threats of a further dismemberment of Pakistan. A nervous élite feared a repetition of Bangladesh, and was quick to exploit the arms cache discovery in order to impose direct central rule over the provinces. Not surprisingly, there was strong support from the army high command for such a course of action. The second factor responsible for central intervention was the influence of the Shah of Iran. The Shah feared a regional Baluch-Pathan uprising fuelled by military assistance from Iraq and Afghanistan. Consequently there was Irani pressure, and financial support, for military intervention in Baluchistan. Finally, the removal of NAP governments in the two provinces imposed a strong, centralised power structure under the hegemony of a single party. Bhutto was favourably disposed towards such a framework; hence the removal of the two opposition-controlled provincial administrations eliminated the major impediments to a PPP-dominated political structure. As Bhutto was to concede later: "the Shah wanted us to take strong action of course. It was a convenient way to please him, but we knew what we were doing. We knew what we wanted".[38]

The adverse repercussions of the PPP's actions in Baluchistan cannot be over emphasised. Central intervention had three implications which collectively undermined the basis of a democratic structure, and therefore facilitated the return of military rule in 1977. First, the army was effectively back in power in one province, just over a year after it had allowed civilian leaders to form a government. Bhutto had allied himself with the army against a representative provincial government. Also, the fact that civilian leaders were being accused of treason by the PPP sustained a vocabulary in Pakistani politics which favours military intervention. The army élite sees itself as a national force, which must intervene to cement and preserve a nation threatened by treacherous politicians. Bhutto, by operating within this matrix, provided further evidence to the army that these dangers existed. Such perceptions strengthen the resolve of militaries to intervene. The second implication of the action in Baluchistan was its divisive impact on political leaders. By arbitrarily dismissing civilian governments, Bhutto had alienated his natural allies for the establishment of a democratic order. Indeed, civilian leaders pleaded with military commanders to disobey the orders of the PPP Government.[39] Opposition leaders, wary and suspicious of Bhutto, gradually gravitated into a position where they sought help of the military to remove the PPP Government. There is considerable evidence to suggest that some leaders of the PNA Movement[40] of 1977 saw a military *coup* as the only way of ousting Bhutto.[41] Indeed, one of the principal figures, Asghar Khan, had written to the military leaders requesting them to step in.[42] Finally, the dismissal of provincial governments, and the failure to hold fresh elections, effectively subverted the constitutional structure outlined in the '73 document. Of course, intervention by the centre is not uncommon elsewhere. Several instances have occurred in India, for example, particularly under Mrs Gandhi. However, great care is taken to ensure a return to an elected government, at the state level, as quickly as possible. Under the PPP, no such effort was made in Baluchistan and NWFP, since fresh elections would have produced an identical result. The dismissal of these governments entailed an effective suspension of the '73 Constitution. Thus, the legal framework, which Bhutto so desperately needed in his relationship with the army, ceased to operate in critical spheres.

The 1973 Constitution gave the civilian structure authority only to the extent that the principal parties involved accepted the legitimacy of the framework outlined therein. The three main constituents were the military, the PPP as the party in power and the opposition parties. The army's approval was involuntary. It had been forced to transfer power after the '71 surrender. Its interaction with the subsequent civilian structure was dependent on what form the democratic organism took. The tectonics of institution building required mass support. A national consensus had to be based on an effective *modus vivendi* between the PPP and the opposition parties. In terms of electoral support the opposition collectively represented a larger proportion of the people than those who had voted for the PPP. In addition, some opposition parties had a regional support base which had to be incorporated within a national, representative, institutional mechanism. The opposition's support for such a structure was dependent on the degree to which they were allowed to function within it. The systematic repression of the opposition, and the rigging of the electoral mechanism through which governments could be replaced, provoked a hostile extra-parliamentary movement which toppled the PPP regime.

The dismissal of the NAP-JUI governments was perhaps the most significant act in the process of alienating the opposition. It was, however, supplemented by a series of repressive measures. The constitution was changed arbitrarily to incorporate increasingly authoritarian policies. In April 1974, the government passed a constitutional amendment which limited the freedom of association as laid down in Article 17 of the constitution.[43] Further, it empowered the government to ban parties or organisations whose object was deemed to be against the 'sovereignty and integrity of Pakistan'. In 1975, personal liberties were curtailed by a constitutional amendment permitting indefinite detention, without trial, for persons deemed to be acting or "*attempting to act* in a way prejudicial to the security of the state".[44] Later the same year, the high courts were deprived of their right to grant bail to any person detained under preventive detention laws.[45]

The restrictions on civil liberties necessitated repression of the press. It is difficult to be repressive in certain key sectors and allow freedom in others. It was inevitable that the press would be prevented from freely reporting the withdrawal of rights. Asked why the liberal English language weekly *Outlook* was banned, Bhutto had a simple, chilling response. "It went too far".[46] Others, of course, had also transgressed these 'limits'. In 1972, for example, the *Sun* daily newspaper had operations suspended until its coverage conformed to government requirements. There is an exhaustive list of similar cases.[47] The National Press Trust (NPT), a government body used to control and censor the press, was retained in spite of firm pledges by the PPP to abolish it.[48] Another instrument of repression was the Federal Security Force (FSF). Its principal target, as noted above, were members of the civilian opposition. The methods used by the FSF, against both opposition members and individuals within the PPP who opposed Bhutto, were particularly brutal and nasty.[49]

In the sixties, the PPP had been the leader and symbol of a movement for extending civil liberties, for undertaking economic reforms to ensure a better distribution of income, and for the introduction of representative government. In power, the PPP failed to achieve any of these goals. The shortcoming lay not in poor implementation, but in a lack of serious commitment to any of these objectives. When it began to suppress those groups who genuinely believed in the rhetoric of the party, they became the most hostile enemies of Bhutto's PPP. These articulate, urban liberal groups were joined by a variety of groups, who had widely differing reasons for opposing the PPP. In particular, urban middle classes and traders, adversely affected by the economic and social policies of the PPP, played a crucial role in mobilising and sustaining the mass movement against Bhutto. The movement was launched by the nine-party electoral alliance, PNA, which had been formed to combat the PPP in the 1977 elections.[50] It was triggered by the rigging of these elections by the PPP. Bhutto had squandered a unique opportunity to build a democratic structure. Authoritarian populism represented the worst of both worlds. It was neither efficient in its economic management nor liberal in its political orientation. Bhutto's substantial achievements were in foreign policy. The 1972 Simla Accord with India, for example, brought back 90,000 prisoners of war through skilful negotiations under extremely difficult circumstances.

Footnotes:

1. See Johnson, J (ed):*The Role of the Military in Underdeveloped Countries;* Finer, S. E.: *The Man on Horseback*; Janowitz, M.: *The Military in the Political Development of New Nations.*
2. Even after such a crushing defeat, the military tried, initially, not to transfer power to the civilians. However, junior officers were not willing to accept a leadership which had surrendered in East Pakistan. Only when the generals felt that they would not be accepted by lower ranking officers did they agree to hand over. See, for example, Choudhry, G. W.: *Last Days of United Pakistan.*
3. For details see Lodhi, M.:*The Pakistan People's Party.* (Ph.D. thesis, L.S.E.)
4. The general concerned was Gul Hasan, who was later removed. The incident occurred in Lahore.
5. By way of contrast, India drafted its constitution by 1950. The Congress leadership did not face a challenge to their authority from any majority ethnic group.
6. White Paper on the Performance of the Bhutto Regime, volume 3: P. A. 68. Annex 24. (Government of Pakistan, Islamabad).
7. This was reminiscent of the army's reaction to Nkrumah's proposals in Ghana.
8. Bhutto had asked the army to attach FSF recruits to army units. The army refused to do this. See Lt. General M. Iqbal's interview in Lodhi, op cit, p. 679.
9. This was also related to a resource constraint. The army was not willing to take a cut in its allocation to accommodate FSF purchases. By the time Bhutto fell, FSF armoury included 60mm mortars, grenades, machine guns and tear gas equipment.
10. References to various incidents are contained in National Assembly of Pakistan (Legislature) Debates, 31.5.73. pp. 390-5.
11. For details, see Sayeed, K. B.: *The Nature and Direction of Political Change in Pakistan,* pp. 328-30.
12. Bhutto's comments on the FSF are illuminating: "I set up the FSF with the object of making it the most formidable calibred force in

the country . . . apparently my conception of the force was not understood by the organisers . . . chiefly on this account riff-raffs and leftovers have been picked up from here, there and everywhere to make the force . . . instead of controlling discipline and insubordination, if this force becomes a vehicle for promoting chaos it would indeed be a very sad commentary on our efforts and on our aims". Quoted in White Paper, op cit, Annex 25.

13 Even newsreel showing Pakistani surrender in East Pakistan was withdrawn.
14 Bhutto took a strident position against the Awami League. For details see Choudhry, G. W., op cit. Also Jahan, R.: *Pakistan, Failure in National Integration.*
15 The post of Commander-in-Chief was replaced by that of Chief of Staff. The functions of the latter were more limited. Some of the functions of former C-in-C came under the control of the Prime Minister, through his defence adviser and secretary. This reorganisation was aimed at the dispersion of power which would serve to limit the authority of any single general.
16 Interspaced were Bhutto's personal vendettas emanating from past rivalries while he was a minister, specially the enemies he made when he left the Ayub cabinet.
17 For details see Alavi, H.: "The Army and the Bureaucracy in Pakistan", *International Socialist Journal,* 1966.
18 In practice the CSP officers were recruited from a tiny quasi-caste group of families. See Habib, H; *Babus, Brahmins and Bureaucrats.*
19 For details see Ziring, L.: "The Pakistan Bureaucracy: Administrative Reforms", *Asian Survey,* December 1974. pp. 1086-94.
20 *Dawn,* 21.8.73.
21 For example; i) Vaqar Ahmed (Audit and Account service) was Cabinet and Establishment Secretary. ii) Afzal Saeed, Head of Prime Minister's Secretariat. iii) Rao Abdur Rashid, Special Secretary, Cabinet Division. iv) Saeed Ahmed Khan, Chief Security Adviser.
22 The Cornelius Commission, headed by Justice A. R. Cornelius in 1962, recommended the abolition of the CSP and the creation of a single, 7-tiered Civil Service structure. The government had sanctioned three other reports suggesting reform of the Civil Service. These were i) Pakistan Pay and Services Commission Report, 1948. ii) A study by R. Egger, a consultant in public administration, 1953. iii) A study by B. L. Galieux, 1955.
23 Entry to the Civil Service was increasingly regulated by the Establishment Division of the central government rather than the

Federal Service Commission. For details of recruitment see Burki, S. J.:*Pakistan under Bhutto.*
24 *Zindagi.* Lahore, July 1974.
25 For details see Harrison, S: *In Afghanistan's Shadow*; Hussain, A.: *Elite Politics in an Ideological State.* pp. 150-60.
26 Even those parties who had certain reservations, such as NAP, agreed to co-operate in view of the urgent need to establish a constitutional structure. The constitution contained a clause whereby the extent of provincial autonomy was to be reviewed within a decade. This was a concession made by the PPP to get support from regionally based parties.
27 Pakistan Economic Survey, 1982. p. 43.
28 Harrison, S.: op cit, p. 168.
29 For further details see ibid, pp. 160-80. This point was repeatedly emphasised during author's interviews with Baluch politicians.
30 Bizenjo had sought help from the federal government but insists that he had asked for federally-controlled civil armed forces, not army units.
31 Among those aware of the flow of arms to Baluch guerrillas was a leader of the Bugti tribe, Akbar Bugti. He informed the central government and was rewarded by being appointed Governor of the province after NAP's dismissal.
32 See Harrison, S.: op cit, for a more detailed account of Baluch politics.
33 The Pararis (the Baluchi word refers to irreconcilable conflicts) were to later evolve into the Baluch People's Liberation Front. Their founder, S. M. Marri, was a close ally of the Sardar of the powerful Marri tribe, Khair Buksh Marri.
34 See Harrison, S.: op cit, pp. 32-40, for account of Iraqi involvement.
35 *Pakistan Times,* 12.3.73.
36 The National Democratic Party (NDP) was formed in 1976 as a successor to the outlawed NAP. The memo in the text was written by Rao Abdur Rashid Khan, Special Secretary, Cabinet Division. See White Paper on Performance of Bhutto regime, volume 3, p. 25.
37 Bhutto's initial conciliatory gestures towards NAP were dismissed by one of the former NAP leaders as "necessitated by a desire to show a united front at Simla (venue for the Bhutto-Indira summit) so that he could negotiate as a democratic leader for the return of prisoners of war held by India". Interview with author.
38 Quoted in Harrison, S.: op cit, p. 156.
39 For details see Lodhi's thesis, op cit, pp. 345-50.

40 An electoral alliance of 9 parties formed to fight the PPP in the '77 elections.
41 Various instances are quoted in Lodhi, op cit.
42 The letter is reproduced in his book, *Generals and Politics.*
43 The constitution (first amendment) bill, 23.4.74.
44 The constitution (third amendment) bill, 12.2.75.
45 The constitution (fourth amendment) bill, 14.11.75.
46 *Outlook* was banned in July 1974. Bhutto's response in *Dawn*, 10.7.74.
47 *Punjab Punch, Zindagi* and *Urdu Digest* were banned. Editors of the latter two were jailed. The editor of *Dawn* was also arrested. For details see White Paper on Misuse of the Media under the PPP.
48 The NPT had acquired public notoriety in the sixties. Bhutto himself was a victim during the formative phase of the PPP.
49 J. A. Rahim, an old man and a founding member of the PPP, was physically assaulted after he had fallen foul of Bhutto. Details of what was done to him and his son, and similar gory stories, can be found in White Paper on the Misuse of Instruments of State Power. For an account of FSF activities against civilian politicians, see Asghar Khan: *Generals and Politics*, pp. 70-100.
50 Bhutto had called an early election in March 1977, feeling secure that the splits in the opposition would ensure a PPP victory.

Chapter Two

Economic Developments and Their Consequences

The political convulsions of the late sixties had inevitable adverse consequences for the economy; since 1969, the growth of *per capita* output had been negative. The PPP had, therefore, not only to revive the economy but also, due to the nature of its evolution, concern itself with distributional issues. Public intervention in the economy was linked to such concerns. However, it is worth noting that Pakistan's economic evolution had reached a stage where policy makers had committed themselves to greater state intervention even prior to the PPP's ascension to power. Until the late sixties, import-substituting industrialisation had led to the growth of consumer goods industries. In the last days of the Ayub Government, however, substantial progress had been made in negotiations with foreign powers regarding collaboration, in setting up large capital goods producing units, such as a steel mill. The intention was to expand the public sector into capital goods production, with the private sector being encouraged to establish downstream industries. When the PPP came to power there was an added dimension to the envisaged expansion of the public sector; existing private sector enterprises were nationalised and brought into the fold of public ownership.

Bhutto's mass appeal had revolved around his ability to articulate effectively, and capitalise on, the wave of sentiment for economic and social reform which swept through Pakistan in the late sixties. The economic strategy under Ayub, described by Bhutto as "a monstrous economic system of loot and plunder which the regime lauded as a free enterprise",[1] had successfully achieved its objective of creating a substantial class of large industrialists. Strong sentiment against this nascent bourgeoisie was shared, however, by *conservative* as well as radical groups in society. Support for a programme of economic and political reform came from a wide constituency —

the urban lower middle class, the peasantry, the proletariat and landlords from Bhutto's province, Sind. The antagonism of the latter was due to the preponderance of traders, who had migrated from India, amongst the new industrial élite. These non-Sindhis were the principal beneficiaries of industrialisation in Sind. The resultant friction with the Sindhi rural élite was reflected in the support given by this class to the PPP's nationalisation programme, which was aimed at clipping the wings of the industrialists. Sindhi landlords were well represented in the PPP, even in the initial phase of party formation.[2] This aspect of the PPP is worth emphasising, since it had considerable influence on the party's performance in government. Thus the radical rhetoric of the PPP, mass support for which had propelled the party into prominence in Punjab and Sind, should not be taken too seriously as an indicator of policy implementation. Landlords comprised a substantial component of the founding members of the PPP. They tolerated and even encouraged a radical programme as a basis for mass mobilisation. In power, they were not entirely indifferent to reform, but were careful in controlling its pace and minimising its magnitude. We shall analyse various aspects of the reform programme, such as land redistribution, later in the chapter. We begin with an evaluation of the nationalisation measures and the subsequent growth of the public sector.

It is important to distinguish between the two phases of nationalisation. The first phase, which began soon after the PPP came to power, was motivated mainly by distributional concerns. A concentration of physical and financial assets had accumulated in the hands of a tiny corporate élite. State intervention was the mechanism through which these excessive densities of economic power were to be curbed. By 1974, however, the left wing within the PPP had been marginalised or purged. None the less, a number of small and medium sized industrial units were taken over by the state. The motives and effects of the secondary nationalisations differed fundamentally from the initial phase of public ownership. Whereas the first set of measures was part of a coherent strategy, the subsequent phase was the outcome of *ad hoc* responses to various situations. By 1976, access to the state had become a primary avenue of accumulating a private fortune. Thus, groups and individuals in command of state institutions used public intervention in the economy as a means of extending their power and wealth. Corruption was a mechanism through which resources were being transferred, from public enterprises to private individuals. Unfettered by socialist concerns, the state intervened to redistribute resources arbitrarily in favour of those who had access to its patronage. The utility of public enterprises was gauged by the efficacy with which they could extend economic benefits and political patronage to those whom the regime favoured.

The first phase of nationalisation began in January 1972, when the government took over thirty-one industrial units, which fell under ten categories of basic industries. The nationalisation was not as extensive as it may appear. The take-over was confined to capital and intermediate goods sectors, which meant that only 20% of value added of the large-scale manufacturing sector came under public ownership. Most of the privately owned industrial units were in the consumer goods sector and were, therefore, unaffected by the nationalisation. The take-over of basic industries was followed by a restructuring of credit policies. In May 1972, the State Bank announced a new credit policy, the main beneficiaries of which were small landlords, rich peasants and the smaller industrial capitalists.[3] The credit policy mitigated the post-nationalisation fears of the private sector. As a consequence, both the stock market and industrial confidence — measured in terms of the number of loan applications made to financial institutions — recovered sharply.[4] At this stage, the nationalisation programme was being perceived as an attempt to curb the growth of large, monopoly capital. It did not threaten the structure of private enterprise *per se*. Indeed, government policies were encouraging smaller entrepreneurs, and appeared to be rectifying the imbalances of the Ayub era. State intervention under PPP was not part of a process culminating in socialist ownership of all the means of production. Public ownership was aimed at creating a mixed economy, with the state concentrating on heavy industry and curbing the growth of excessive inequalities. The success of such a strategy is contingent upon a clear demarcation regarding the role to be played by the private sector. In the absence of such a clarification, caution and confusion hampers the development process.

Private sector 'confidence' depends in large measure on the extent to which the capitalist class has faith in the promises and policy intentions of the government. When the PPP Administration undertook the initial nationalisations, it gave emphatic reassurances to private capital that it would not embark on further nationalisation of industrial units. It was, made clear, however, that financial institutions were under review, hence the 1974 take-over of banks and insurance companies[5] was anticipated. Private capital was willing to adjust to, and accommodate, a degree of state intervention which it saw as politically inevitable. The credit policy mentioned above added to a climate of accommodation. Other sympathetic official concessions, such as generous compensation for nationalised assets, had created an environment which promised the evolution of a stable equilibrium between private capital and the government. Indeed, the first year of PPP rule had witnessed a healthy economic recovery after the traumas of 1971. Particularly impressive had been the growth in exports facilitated by a massive devaluation of the rupee in May 1972.

The relatively harmonious interaction between the public and the private sectors was destroyed by a series of nationalisations of industrial units which began in 1973 and culminated in the take-over of rice husking units in 1976. These nationalisations reflected an *ad hoc* political response to various situations. In August 1973, floods swept across Pakistan, the first natural

Economic Developments and their Consequences

calamity of this nature to have struck Western Pakistan for two decades. An immediate consequence was a severe shortage of consumption goods in the flood-affected areas. For example, the price of cooking oil trebled, partly because of hoarding.[6] On 16 August, the government nationalised the cooking oil (ghee) industry. This renegation on the promise not to take over more industrial units caused a panic in the private sector. Rumours of further nationalisations were given sustenance by somewhat ambiguous statements by members of the PPP.[7] Consequently, private investment fell to less than a quarter of the projected figure.[8]

The January '72 nationalisation had mainly affected the 'top twenty-two families' mentioned in the Ayub chapter; a sizeable section of the cooking oil industry was, in contrast, owned by small and medium sized capitalists.[9] Further, owing to shortages anticipated from flood damage, the cotton market 'went wild'. Consequently, the export of raw cotton was banned on 27 August, to be resumed in October, but only through the state, for which purpose a Cotton Export Corporation was established. However, the fatal blow to private sector confidence was struck in July 1976. The government, arbitrarily and unexpectedly,[10] nationalised the flour milling, cotton ginning and rice husking mills.[11] These units processed and distributed agricultural produce to the market. Through the public seizure, the government eliminated these intermediaries and directly undertook the marketing of agricultural output. The action served the function of merely transferring resources from small entrepreneurs to groups who took over control of the appropriated enterprises. This annexation provided incontrovertible proof to private capital that the PPP regime could not be relied upon to adhere to its promise of no further nationalisation. Moreover, very serious political costs were attached to the 1976 nationalisations. The *petite bourgoisie*, comprising small industrialists, traders and shopkeepers, were outraged by measures which threatened their livelihood. The antagonisms, and power, of this class were evident in the opposition movement which toppled the PPP Government in 1977. It played a critical role in paralysing economic activity during national strikes, thus ensuring the efficacy of the protest.

Before we examine the adverse macro-economic and political consequences of arbitrary nationalisations, we should acknowledge that the government did achieve its objective of clipping the wings of the large industrial families. This is reflected in Table 1 below. The efficacy of the government's measures is indicated by the effect they had on the two dominant families, Saigol and Habib. Perhaps more damaging than the loss of assets was a diminution in official respect for the leading industrial families.[12] None the less, some caveats need to be noted. Political patronage is reflected in the fact that some of the large families to have done relatively well out of nationalisation, such as Hyesons (see Table 1), gave generous financial support to the PPP.[13] Further, a substantial number of the large families were unaffected, in terms of asset ownership, by the nationalisations. One must also bear in mind that terms of compensation, for acquired units, were generous.[14] Although the reforms cannot be accused of excessive severity, they did curb the growth of industrial-financial monopolies.

Table 1: *Position of Major Industrial Families: Impact of Nationalisation. (Rupees in millions).*

Family	Pre Nationalisation		Post Nationalisation	
	Position	Net Assets*	Net Assets	Position
Saigol	1	529.8	165.3	3
Habib	2	228.0	68.8	11
Dawood	3	210.8	767.5†	1
Crescent	4	201.7	201.7	2
Adamjee	5	201.3	146.3	5
Colony (N.)	6	189.7	95.8	6
Valika	7	183.5	62.2	12
Hoti	8	148.6	148.6	4
Amins	9	137.9	137.9	–
Wazir Ali	10	102.6	87.6	–
Fancy	11	102.4	–	–
Beco	12	101.4	–	–
Hussain	13	81.7	81.7	9
Colony (F.)	14	89.9	19.8	–
Ghandara	15	79.9	25.8	–
Hyesons	16	79.4	83.5‡	8
Zafar-ul-Ahsan	17	77.2	22.1	–
Bawany	18	69.3	69.3	10
Premier	19	56.1	56.1	13
Nishat	20	54.3	54.3	14
Gul Ahmed	21	52.3	52.3	15
Arag	22	50.1	50.1	16
Rahimtoola	23	49.9	49.9	17
Noon	24	48.8	48.8	18
Shahnawaz	25	46.0	46.0	19
Monnoo	26	45.0	45.0	20

Notes: *Includes Non-Manufacturing, Banking and Insurance.
 †Includes Dawood-Hercules (1971).
 ‡Includes Hyesons Sugar Mills (1974).
Source: Rashid Amjad, 'Industrial Concentration and Economic Power', *Pakistan Economic and Social Review*, Vol. XIV, Nos. 1-4 (1976), p. 254.

Economic Developments and their Consequences

There are three broad categories into which one can classify public intervention programmes[15] in developing countries. First, public ownership of economic assets is the central component of a Marxian, socialist society. In such a context, the private sector is either non-existent or plays a marginal role. A second category of state intervention may be referred to as corporatist. The state operates as an adjunct to private capital. Indeed, in many cases the state helps to create entrepreneurs by starting industries and then handing them over to private ownership. Successful corporatist strategies have been followed in South East Asian countries such as Taiwan and Korea. A model of such intervention is provided by Japan. In between these conceptually clear rationales for public intervention is a third category. This refers to public intervention in the context of mixed economies[16] where the role assigned to the private sector is ambiguous. This also implies a lack of coherence regarding the role of the public sector. Quite often public intervention is arbitrary and subject to random political pressures. This apparent lack of a strategy creates uncertainty and confusion. State-owned enterprises become a device for political patronage and are used to pay political debts, or to accumulate power. The managers of these state enterprises are recruited on the basis of loyalty rather than ability. The inevitable consequence is the creation of an inefficient, corrupt public sector.[17] Not only does this eventually lead to unnecessarily high budget deficits, but it also entails monetary financing of this deficit, which has adverse inflationary consequences. An escalation in inflation often harms, most severely, those classes which the government was trying to help through public intervention.

The nationalisation programme under the PPP, particularly in the latter stages, was neither efficient in the corporatist sense nor was it a part of a serious commitment to socialism. The managers of state enterprises saw public intervention, not in terms of a step towards socialism, but as an instrument through which power and income could be redistributed in their favour. It is worth emphasising that the PPP continued to nationalise industrial units well after the left wing within the party had been purged. Each nationalisation was accompanied by socialist rhetoric but its appeal to the conservative PPP élite lay in its promise of personal enrichment, wealth and power. It is difficult to attribute the persistent use of nationalisation to any other source.

The expansion of public enterprises became a symbol of the PPP's potency, as successive interventions were increasingly determined by political pressures, irrespective of economic logic. Nevertheless, the Administration was not entirely indifferent to the economic performance of public enterprises. In any case, there was considerable pressure from Pakistan's external creditors to increase the efficiency of public enterprises.[18] However, in assessing the efficiency of public sector enterprises under the PPP, it is worth bearing in mind that the nationalised units brought with them accumulated losses of Rs. 254 million.[19] Subsequent constraints worsened the financial situation of these enterprises. Nationalised units were expected to limit price increases despite high and accelerating inflation. They also had to employ surplus workers due to political pressure. This resulted in over-manning and a fall in productivity. Initially, however, the performance of public sector enterprises was not altogether disheartening,[20] as indicated in Table 2. Some of the public sector industries performed well. The cement industry, for example, showed impressive profits, as did the automotive, petroleum and fertiliser industries.[21] The aggregate performance of the public sector was, however, adversely affected by some chronic cases. Public enterprises were quite often established with a view to meeting some social or political objective. Units were frequently set up in remote, backward areas. Such measures are welcome and the economic costs may be, within reason, worth bearing. Yet the merits of such a policy were distorted by the method in which the remote areas were selected for favourable treatment. Projects mushroomed around places such as Larkana, Bhutto's home town. In these cases, the government appeared to be less concerned with promoting balanced regional development and more with token measures to please politically powerful groups. An example of inefficient location is provided by Bannu Sugar Mills. The absence of a sufficiently well-developed local infrastructure made the plant uncompetitive. On average, 90% of the plant's capacity was not utilised.[22] Insufficient attention to economic criteria for investment also led to huge losses at Sind Engineering and Anti-Biotics Ltd. This is evident in Table 2, especially in the 1976-77 and 1978-79 columns for the overall average rate of return. The figures in brackets exclude Bannu Sugar Mills, Anti-Biotics Ltd. and Sind Engineering.

Unfortunately, jobs in the public sector were also used as a reward mechanism to extend political patronage. Jobs ranging from managerial appointments to clerical posts were distributed accordingly. Not surprisingly, the consequent over-manning and inefficient management appointees affected financial performance. In 1972-73, for example, enterprises under the Board of Industrial Management employed 40,817 people. The number rose by 58% in 1976-77, whereas production did not increase correspondingly.[23] Indeed, in many cases it declined. A similar, but even more dramatic, fall in productivity due to excessive employment was experienced by the Cotton Trading Corporation.[24] In general, employment pressures took two forms. First was the pressure to keep uneconomic units functioning. For example, the old Valika Chemical Plant was kept in operation despite its extremely poor economic and technical position, largely to avoid laying off workers. The second form of pressure was directly on employment — pressure not to dismiss surplus workers. For example, the Lahore Engineering and Foundry Unit was carrying 1,500 extra workers which it could not release for political reasons. These measures to protect employment directly were self-defeating. Particular jobs were protected by

Table 2: *Rate of Return on Investment in Public Enterprises (1974-75 to 1979-80). (Percent).*

Industrial Groups	1974-75	1975-76	1976-77	1977-78	1978-79	1979-80
Chemicals and Ceramics	37.3	26.3	0.6	−5.3	−100.9 (−7.8)[2]	−2.7
Fertilisers	14.4	8.8	5.1	15.2	19.3	17.8
Automobiles	69.1	74.3	105.6	52.7	−1715.0 (35.6)[3]	52.9
PIDC	4.0	28.5	−680.1 (−7.4)[1]	19.6	1.3	4.9
Cement	25.4	21.7	12.0	12.9	10.1	13.2
Engineering	32.2	37.1	40.9	33.6	−3.5	7.1
Overall Average Rate of Return	41.9	21.9	3.3 (56.8)[1]	29.7	−693.9 (14.6)[2,3]	27.7

Source: Naqvi and Sarmad: *Pakistan's Economy through the Seventies.*
Note: 1, 2 and 3 indicate rates of return when 'Bannu Sugar Mills', 'Anti-Biotics Limited' and 'Sind Engineering' respectively are excluded.
The rates of return have been calculated from the following formula and weighted by current assets:

$$\text{Return on Investment (\%)} = \frac{\text{Net Profit before Interest and Taxes}}{\text{Net Equity} + \text{Long-Term Debt}} \times 100$$

increased inefficiency which indirectly led to jobs being lost elsewhere in the economy.

The poor performance of public sector enterprises hampered their ability to raise investment resources internally. The failure to generate investment funds was due partly to pricing policies. Nationalised units pricing seemed to allow only the recovery of operating cost, with an allowance for inventory and fixed capital, calculated on the basis of historical costs and not current market replacement costs.[25] Consequently, internally generated funds for financing investment only contributed 7% of the amount required. As a result, nationalised industries had to borrow from the government. This borrowing added to the budget deficits financed largely through monetary expansion, which accelerated the rate of inflation. This rise in prices hurt those groups whom the government was trying to help.

The burdens imposed by public enterprises were not, of course, the only source of expanding budget deficits. The growth in non-development expenditure, especially defence, was substantial. This was accompanied by the inability of the government, largely due to political factors, to raise more revenues from direct taxation. Indirect taxes accounted for 82% of tax revenues. Thus, not only did the tax system have a regressive effect on income distribution, but it also imposed fiscal strains due to poor coverage of direct taxation.[26] The government attempted to curb the budget deficit by reducing subsidies on consumption goods. The reduction of subsidies hit urban groups. At the same time, nominal earnings failed to keep up with inflation. This not only reduced living standards for those on low incomes, but also encouraged corruption in the public sector among employees who had to 'supplement' their diminishing official incomes.[27]

Nationalisation was not the only factor responsible for the growth of the public sector under the PPP. As we have mentioned above, the PPP came to power at a time when policy makers had committed themselves to involving the state directly in the production of capital goods. The most significant inheritance in this context was the decision to build a steel mill. In 1968, the government had set up the Pakistan Steel Mill Corporation. This was for negotiating financial and technical assistance with the USSR for a project with an annual steel capacity of one million tons. On 22 January 1971 the Soviet Government signed an agreement to render such assistance. When the PPP came to power they recommended a change in location,[28] after which the final go-ahead was given in May 1973. The cost of the steel mill was substantial. The mill absorbed the bulk of investment funds. In 1977-78, for example, 63% of public sector investment was confined to the steel mill.

The government's objective, relating to the above, was to rectify the imbalance in Pakistan's industrial sector. During the sixties, Pakistan had developed an industrial structure capable only of producing consumer goods. By investing resources into the capital goods sector, the PPP Government helped to establish a more diversified production base. These projects also entailed an implicit investment in human capital since they required the development of Pakistani scientists and engineers to run these enterprises. Nevertheless, although the objective was laudable, the choice of projects was questionable. Since there is surplus capacity in the world steel market and the cost of producing steel in Pakistan is excessively high, the prospect of exporting any steel was remote. Consequently, all of the steel output had to be absorbed domestically. This implied a substantial steel subsidy, if downstream engineering firms were to be competitive, imposing considerable fiscal constraints on the government. In view of these inefficiencies, it may well have made more sense to import cheaper steel for the development of a competitive capital goods sector in Pakistan. In other words, the government could have used its resources more productively and still met the objective of creating a more balanced industrial structure.

In addition to the steel mill, the state sector tended to concentrate on other large capital-intensive projects. One of these, the nuclear reprocessing plant, was conditioned primarily by security perceptions. In 1971, Pakistan had been dismembered through Indian military intervention. To prevent the recurrence of such an event, Pakistan sought to develop a military deterrent. Thus, Bhutto launched a programme of complex subterfuge through which technology to develop a nuclear bomb was imported in bits and pieces, and then developed by Pakistani scientists.[29]

The PPP's electoral platform had raised expectations regarding the creation of employment opportunities. This objective could not be reconciled with the government's emphasis on capital-intensive projects. Public sector investment in these long-gestating projects accentuated the capital bias in the economy, which had initially been encouraged by the over-valued exchange rate in the sixties. The capital-labour ratio rose, further aggravating poor employment generation by the industrial sector. In 1976, for example, the total employment of the ten sector corporations, set up by the government to manage the nationalised industries under the aegis of the Board of Industrial Management (BIM), amounted to 61,731.[30] The figure is insignificant when gauged in relation to the annual increase in the country's labour force of approximately 600,000.

In terms of factor use, Pakistan's experience was not too different from that predicted by Hollis Chenery in his comparative statistical survey of developing countries.[31] Accordingly, there had been a shift of labour from the agricultural sector to the industrial and service sectors, although this shift lagged behind the structural change in production. This means that the growth in output of the industrial sector was greater than the growth of employment in that sector. The industrial sector was a poor absorber of labour.[32] As a consequence, the agricultural sector had to play a critical role in generating employment if increases to the labour force were to be productively absorbed. On account of the Land Reform Programme and the associated political uncertainties, as well as adverse weather conditions in 1974 and 1975, the agricultural sector was not performing well under the PPP. Thus, employment generation became an acute problem. The government launched direct employment campaigns aimed at absorbing particular sectors of the labour market, e.g. the National Development Volunteer Programme (NDVP) aimed at professional and technical unemployed manpower. Another example was the People's Work Programme (PWP), launched in 1973, which was designed to encourage labour-intensive projects in rural areas. These programmes were inadequate, in terms of financial resources and coverage, and their impact can at best be described as marginal. The major avenue through which the government sought to resolve the explosive employment tensions of a stagnating economy whose population was growing at 3%, was migration to the oil booming Gulf. The government was quick to exploit geographical proximity and combined it with appropriate appeals of Muslim brotherhood to promote migration to the Gulf. The economic benefits of the migratory process have been substantial, as we document in part 3. It is ironic, however, that the primary political beneficiary of the process was the Zia regime, under whom the full impact of the remittances began to hit home.

The expansion of the public sector, and the effects of arbitrary nationalisation, are reflected in Figure 1. The graph illustrates annual investment undertaken by the private and public sectors. In direct contrast to the sixties, most of the investment under the PPP was undertaken by the public sector. Private investment dried up, out of fear of nationalisation. The dramatic fall is illustrated in Figure 1. In 1974, private investment in large-scale manufacturing was reduced to a third of what it was in 1970. It increased gradually in subsequent years but even by 1978 it was still less than half of the 1970 value. Private capital, paralysed by erratic nationalisations, 'flew' out of the country. This occurred at a time when Far Eastern economies were emerging as major exporters of competitively produced goods. Substantial sections of private industry in Pakistan, which was already inefficient, fell further behind in the seventies due to lack of investment. Aggregate industrial investment, however, increased under the PPP. The fall in private investment was compensated for by a substantial increase in public sector investment (see Figure 1). The share of the public sector in total investment grew from 5% in 1970-71 to 74% in 1976-77. The sharp contrast from the Ayub period can be seen in Figure 2 (p. 86), which shows the shift in relative contributions to investment made by the public and private sectors.

The aggregate growth of the economy under the PPP, as measured by the annual rise in the GNP, was 4.6% per year. This was an impressive average growth rate, especially in view of the uncertainties produced by institutional reform. Most of the growth, however, was accounted for by the service sector, as can be seen in Table 3 (p. 87). The fastest growing sector in the economy was defence and public administration. The rapid 11% annual

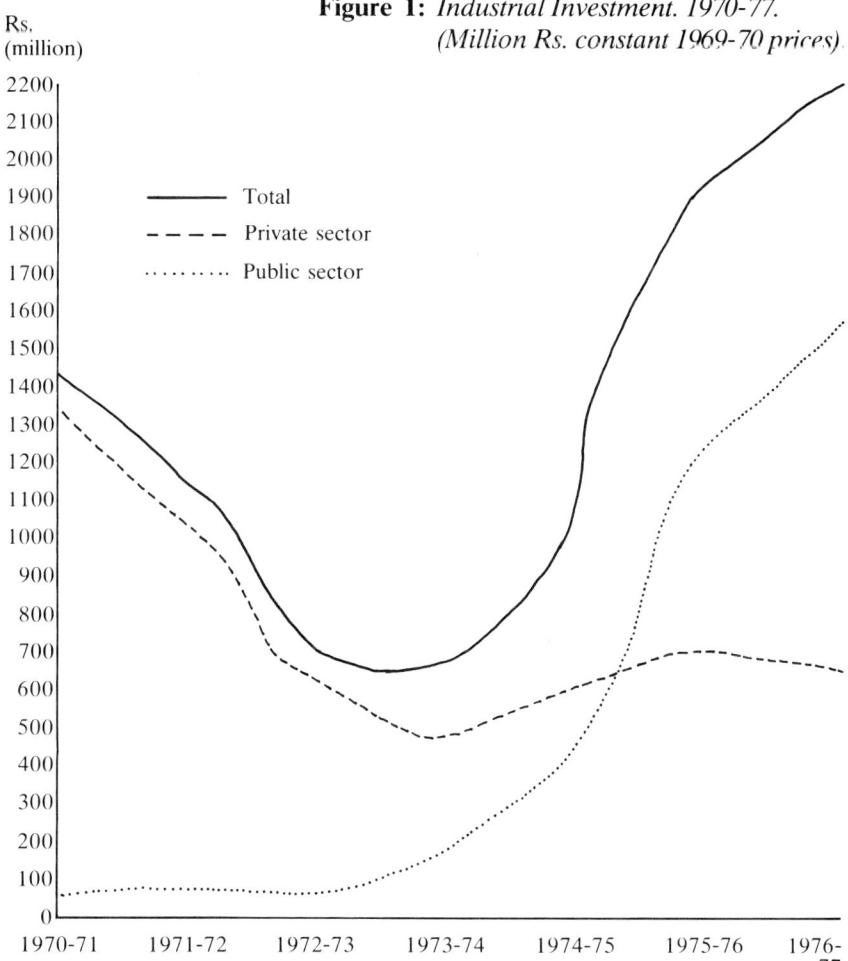

Figure 1: *Industrial Investment. 1970-77. (Million Rs. constant 1969-70 prices)*

Source: Pakistan Economic Survey, 1979 — Government of Pakistan, Islamabad.

growth of this sector was caused by measures to increase the scale of the armed forces as well as reflecting the rising administrative costs of an expanding public sector. This fast growth in the service sector was offset by relative stagnation in the commodity-producing sectors. Agriculture grew at a rate less than the growth of population, leading to a decline in *per capita* agricultural production (see Table 3). The poor performance was accounted for partly by exogenous factors — there were droughts and floods in two years out of the five of PPP rule. There were also short-term production losses due to the erratic implementation of land reforms. Similarly, the growth of manufacturing output, especially large scale, was affected by insti-

Figure 2: *Relative shares of public and private sectors in total investment. (%).*

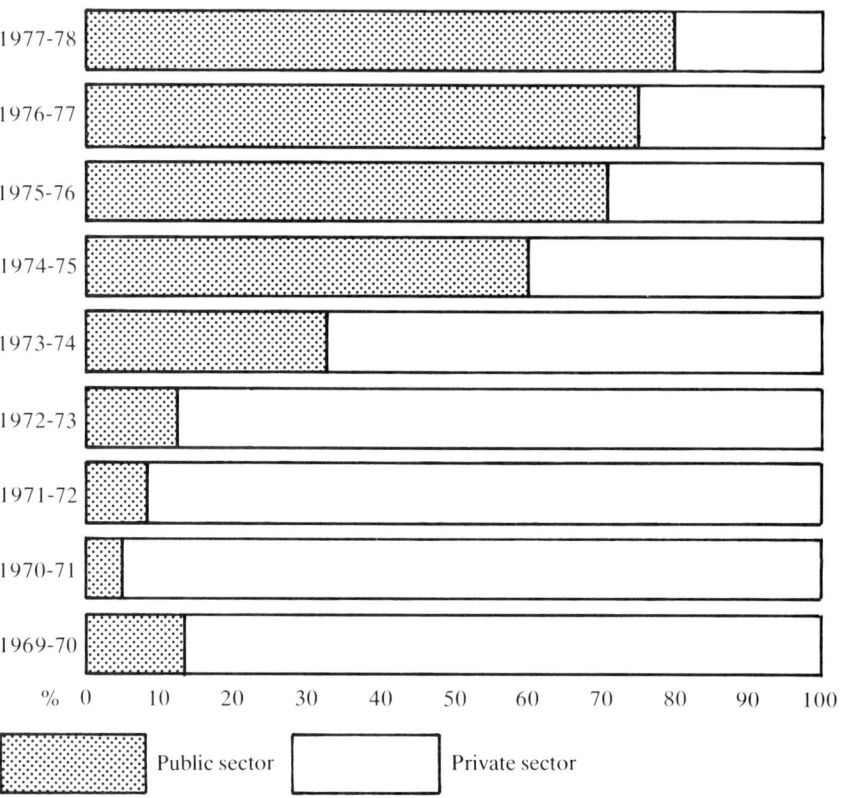

tutional reforms. Large-scale manufacturing grew at a rate of 1.91%. This represented a substantial decline from the sixties, when growth rates exceeded 10%.[33]

In view of Pakistan's abysmal record in the provision of social services, and the PPP's electoral pledges to alleviate poverty, one would have expected the growth in the service sector to have been based on increased allocations for social services. In practice, however, priority was assigned to the defence services. Consequently, the plan for expansion of social services was squeezed by the diversion of resources to defence and public administration. Not only was there a moral imperative for the PPP to increase the paltry allocations for health and education, but such a course would also have strengthened the mass base of the party. The failure to provide adequate funding for social services meant that schemes launched by the PPP, such as free primary education,[34] were doomed to failure. Another potentially popular plan was the People's Health Scheme, which incorporated the

Table 3: *Growth Rates of Different Production Sectors, GDP and GNP. (At Constant Prices) (Percent per year).*

Sectors	1969-70 to 1976-77	
COMMODITY — PRODUCING		2.21
Agriculture	1.75	
Mining and Quarrying	3.54	
Manufacturing	3.23	
Large-scale	1.91	
Small-scale	7.04	
SERVICE		6.40
Construction	7.57	
Public Administration and Defence	11.40	
Other Services	5.11	
GDP	4.22	
GNP	4.60	

Source: Pakistan Economic Survey, 1981-2, Islamabad.

Chinese idea of 'barefoot doctors' being sent to rural areas. Again, poor funding effectively subverted the programme.

A policy of diverting resources to defence and administration, while launching schemes to expand social services, could not be accused of prudence. Such follies helped to develop and sustain a perception that official schemes were incompetent and inadequate. For example, nationalisation of private schools led to a marked deterioration in standards, as increased enrolment was not matched by resource allocations. Indeed, it may have been more sensible, in view of the resource constraints, to expand educational facilities in rural areas rather than nationalise urban middle-class schools.[35] In an interview with the author, a former PPP education minister described the education strategy "as a way of fooling the people, since the money to finance schemes was never made available".[36] Thus, precisely those policies which could have cultivated support for the PPP across a wide social spectrum were responsible for earning it a reputation of administrative incompetence. Indeed, the disintegration of whatever little there was by way of urban health and education facilities, had a serious political consequence. The urban middle classes supported the opposition movement against Bhutto, partly because of their anger at the PPP for having recklessly destroyed the prevailing structure of social services, of which they were the primary beneficiaries.

Another economic phenomenon to have affected the response of the middle class was inflation. Indeed, a poll commissioned by the PPP in 1977 revealed that inflation and corruption were listed as the two major criticisms of the government.[37] The acceleration in inflation is illustrated in Figure 3. The peak was reached in 1973-74, when the inflation rate rose to 30%. This rise in prices was due, to a considerable extent, to factors beyond the government's control, particularly the rise in the price of oil. However, domestic economic policies also contributed towards the rising inflation rate.[38] Two factors in particular were responsible for inflationary pressures: the rapid expansion of the money supply and the slow growth of the commodity-producing sectors. The excessive expansion in the money supply was due largely to financing of the government's budget deficit, by creating money. One of the primary reasons for the growth in the budget deficit was the increase in non-development public expenditures, such as defence. At the same time, the government was not able to mobilise domestic resources to finance this expenditure. Indirect taxes grew slowly, because of the relative stagnation in economic activity. Growth in direct taxation was limited by political pressure and the leakages implicit in corrupt administration. Public savings were negligible due to the poor performance of public sector enterprises. Finally, a fall in private savings deprived the government of an alternative source of resource mobilisation. The fall in savings can be explained by the financial penalties imposed on savers, as well as political uncertainties, which made the private sector take savings out of the country. Savings were effectively discouraged by negative real rates of interest. The poor return on deposits is illustrated in Figure 3. During the period 1972-75, with inflation well in excess of deposit interest rates, savings placed in banks lost as much as 20% of their real value. This led to a decline in private savings. Thus the poor mobilisation of domestic resources implied monetary financing of budget deficits, and consequent inflationary pressures. The second domestic cause of inflation was the inadequate performance of the commodity-producing sectors, documented earlier in the chapter. This led to supply shortages of goods, resulting in upward pressure on their price level.[39]

The rate of inflation was brought down, however, by a series of measures aimed at reducing the budget deficit. Expenditures were curtailed by reducing subsidies, including those on food.[40] The government reacted to resulting urban protests by cushioning the blow to the poorer segments of the population. This was done through wage increases for low-income government employees and industrial labour. The middle class bore the brunt of the subsidy reduction, which is justifiable on distributional grounds, but served to further antagonise the middle classes — already angry at the government's education policies. Other measures to control inflation included a tighter monetary policy, in the form of credit controls. Consequently, inflation came down from 30% in 1974 to less than 10% by 1977.

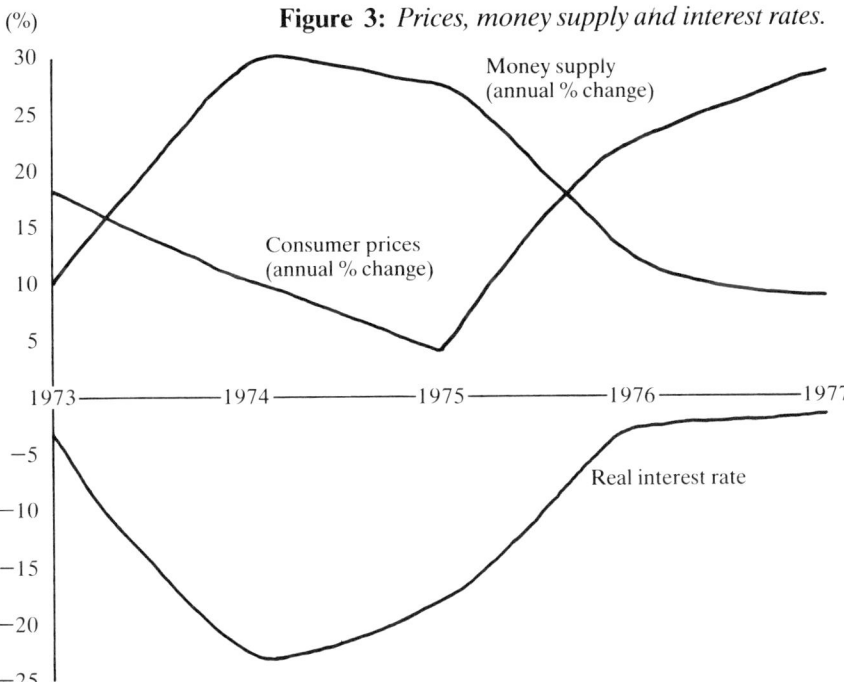

Figure 3: *Prices, money supply and interest rates.*

Source: IMF, International Financial Statistics, 1979.

As far as aid inflows are concerned, the PPP era witnessed a consistent rise in reliance on foreign capital. Despite strenuous efforts, the government failed to prevent an overall decline in aggregate investment.[41] The public sector had partially compensated for the sharp decline in private investment by a substantial increase in public investment. The domestic resources to finance this investment were inadequate. An indication of the shortage of resources is provided by Table 4 (p. 90). As the table shows, investment requirements exceeded domestic savings by a wide margin. For example, domestic savings could finance only 36% of investment in 1974-5. Another indicator of the inadequacy of domestic resources is provided by Table 5 (p. 91), which shows how most of the domestic resources went into financing non-development expenditure. As a consequence, nearly 65% of development expenditure was financed by foreign capital in some years. The secular rise in foreign loans is illustrated in Table 6 (p. 91).

The accumulation of debt was reflected in an increase in Pakistan's debt service ratio, *viz*: debt service payments as a percentage of foreign exchange earnings. By 1976-77, Pakistan had a debt service ratio of 20%. This ratio far exceeds the average, of 10%, for low-income countries. There is, of course, nothing wrong in borrowing from external sources, provided that these resources are invested towards enhancing domestic productive capa-

Table 4: *The Magnitude of the Resource Gap (1969-70 to 1977-78).*

Years	Savings as Percentage of Investment	Resource Gap (Investment-Saving) (Million rupees)	Resource Gap as Percentage of GNP
(1)	(2)	(3)	(4)
1969-70	56.8	3,257	6.8
1970-71	54.5	3,568	7.1
1971-72	66.5	2,566	4.7
1972-73	83.5	1,428	2.1
1973-74	53.2	5,431	6.2
1974-75	36.5	11,560	10.2
1975-76	58.8	9,386	7.0
1976-77	62.0	10,408	6.7
1977-78	80.1	5,968	3.2

Source: Pakistan Economic Survey, 1980-81.

city. The growth in Pakistan's debt obligations suggests that its ability to service this debt did not grow at a satisfactory pace. Although the terms on which Pakistan borrowed were far more favourable than middle-income Latin American countries, who relied on private capital, it is none the less true that the terms of external assistance have become a lot harsher when compared with the early stages of Pakistan's development. As Table 7 (p. 92) indicates, the proportion of grants in total external assistance fell from 64% immediately after Partition to 15% in 1977-78. Similarly, the proportion of loans repayable in foreign exchange went up from 30% to 85%. The inability of export revenues to rise sufficiently to service debt repayments meant that a substantial proportion of foreign loans was used to pay back past debts. For example, almost 60% of aid disbursement between 1974 and 1980 was returned to donors in the form of debt servicing.[42]

The PPP government's relationship with Western financial institutions, such as the World Bank, differed substantially from the harmonious interaction enjoyed by the Ayub regime. Critical of the government's macroeconomic strategy, the World Bank stipulated a set of reforms, particularly in the area of domestic resource mobilisation, as a precondition for further Bank lending. The refusal of the PPP Government to accept these conditions led to deadlock in 1974-75. Because of the tension over conditionality issues, the World Bank refused to provide much-needed support for the expansion of social services. PPP's health, education and welfare programmes remained inadequately funded, in spite of their compatibility with the 'basic needs' approach favoured by the Bank in those days.

The PPP regime's policies, which led to a deadlock with the World Bank,

Table 5: *Government revenues and expenditures.*

	1972-73	1973-74	1974-75	1975-76	1976-77	1977-78
1) External resources as a percentage of development expenditure	68.97	50.87	69.34	62.43	41.11	38.56
2) Non-development expenditure as a percentage of domestic resources	92.85	82.31	92.12	86.82	71.22	72.47

Sources: Pakistan Basic Facts, 1979-80.
Annual Report 1979-80, State Bank of Pakistan.

Table 6: *Foreign aid commitments.*

	1952	1956	1960	1964	1968	1973	1977
Foreign Aid (Rs. million)	5	472	1,068	3,105	3,577	3,557	13,902
Proportion of GNP (%)	0.02	2.1	3.4	7.5	5.8	5.9	10.5

Sources: Annual Report of the State Bank, 1979-80.
Pakistan Basic Facts, 1979-80.

Table 7: *Commitments of External Assistance (U.S.$ Million).*

Period	Total assistance	Grants		Loans repayable in foreign exchange	
		Amount	% share	Amount	% share
Pre-1st Plan	337	216	64	101	30
First Plan	1,073	578	54	221	21
Second Plan	2,757	1,105	40	1,559	57
Third Plan	2,746	704	26	2,042	74
Five Years (1970-75)	3,944	375	9	3,569	91
1975-76	958	102	11	856	89
1976-77	1,115	187	17	928	83
1977-78	979	151	15	828	85

Source: Pakistan Economic Survey, 1981-82.

were elaborated in the government spokesman's address to the Pakistan Aid Consortium:[43] "During the last four years we have been beset by a succession of events. . . . The impact of worsening terms of trade has been in the order of $600 million per annum, i.e. about a third of our imports and half the gross capital inflow. . . . In this situation our response could have been to cut consumption or to reduce our development targets and investment level . . . [a third option] was to attempt to increase the overall inflow of resources from abroad while increasing our development efforts and maintaining consumption levels, particularly for the poorer sections of the population. . . . It was the third alternative we chose". The choice did not please the Bank. In view of Pakistan's poor record of domestic resource mobilisation and the oil price hike of 1974, the Bank felt that the expansionist policies of the PPP would lead to an acceleration in inflation and an excessively high debt burden. The PPP regime refused to accept the Bank's demands for curtailment of government expenditure and suggested measures to raise taxes and domestic savings. One of the casualties of the Bank's hostility to the PPP's macro-economic strategy was the government's programme to expand social services. The PPP regime gave greater priority to the development of a capital goods sector, whereas the Bank's conditionality deadlock prevented it from providing finance for projects designed to meet basic needs.

An essential component of the PPP's initial reform programme was a commitment to reduce the size of land holdings. On 1 March 1972 Bhutto announced a Land Reform Programme: "We are as much against the ignorant and tyrannical landlord as we are against the robber barons of industry. We are as much for the creative and humane landowner as we are for a productive and conscientious owner of industry.[44] . . . I can't nationalise the land. It's not possible. At the same time, I can't allow bigger estates to remain. I must cut them down so that production increases".[45] Accordingly, the 1972 land reforms restricted ownership to 150 acres of irrigated, or 300 acres of unirrigated, land. PPP institutional reforms were accompanied by policy changes which removed the previous bias towards the industrial sector. In 1973-74, the terms of trade were more favourable to agriculture than they were in any previous year in Pakistan's history.[46] The '72 devaluation had removed the effective subsidy and protection received by the industrialists due to an overvalued exchange rate. In addition, the government encouraged agricultural production by substantially increasing the procurement prices for major crops,[47] as well as subsidising inputs, such as fertilisers and seeds. In accordance with the objective of promoting entrepreneurial farmers, the ceilings on holdings were subject to certain incentive-related exemptions. These included allowances of fifty acres per holding above the stipulated ceiling for purchase of a tractor or tube well.[48] Similarly, the restructuring of the agricultural tax system contained measures for the promotion of modern technology. Generous tax deductions were allowed for the purchase of agricultural machinery, as well as for the costs incurred for land development, in order to increase productivity. Agricultural credit was also channelled into financing mechanisation.[49]

The broad framework of the PPP's policy was clear. Mild land reforms were to be accompanied by measures to promote agricultural productivity. There were, however, three factors which distorted the effective implementation of this strategy. The administrative machinery was controlled and manipulated by the large landlords. A corollary to this was the lack of an honest administration capable of implementing the legislated measures. Finally, the Land Reform Programme was marred by arbitrary political interference punishing recalcitrant landlords and rewarding loyal supporters of the PPP.[50] It is not surprising, therefore, that the redistributive impact was negligible. Indeed, land tenure reforms ended up as little more than a cosmetic exercise. Since the holding on ceilings was defined in terms of the individual, and not the family, large landowners had little difficulty in retaining most holdings through division within the family.[51] The total resumed area was less than 1% of the total area of 36.4 million acres in Punjab, and less than 3% of the total area of 11.4 million acres in Sind. Indeed, the area resumed in these provinces was much smaller than land resumed under the 1959 land reforms. Barely 1% of the landless tenants and small owners benefited from the 1972 land reforms.[52] A recent study indicates that income distribution in rural areas may have *worsened* under the PPP.[53] A similar trend was evident in urban areas.[54]

In the political sphere, the Land Reform Programme served two functions for the PPP. First, it is no coincidence that land reforms were most effective in NWFP. The number of peasants receiving land in the NWFP amounted approximately to 33% of the total number of landless tenants in the province.[55] Almost 12% of the total farm area in NWFP was redistributed. This was a creditable achievement, and the positive distributional effects go a long way towards explaining the growth of PPP support in the frontier. Nevertheless, it is tempting, as an analysis of the '72 land reform suggested, to "interpret implementation of land reforms in the province as tactical politics in the struggle of the Bhutto regime against the National Awami Party (NAP)."[56] To use land reform to gain political support is perfectly legitimate, but to use it crudely to punish political opponents, such as Baluchi NAP leaders Bizenjo, Mengal and Marri,[57] distorted the fundamental purpose of land tenure reform. The second political function of land reforms was to reward loyalty to the PPP among landowners. Within three years of assuming office, Bhutto had purged the party of its left wing leaders and had begun to cultivate the traditional rural élite of the Punjab. The landlords flocked to the PPP, partly because they were wooed, but partly because they were threatened. Joining the PPP became a route through which they could subvert resumption of their land holdings.[58] Thus, land reforms became a source of political patronage, with the dominant classes recognising the need to cultivate access to the PPP, since a formal commitment to the party in power could mitigate the scale of land resumed.

It is, however, worth stressing that the PPP never lost its core support among the working classes in Punjab and Sind. Although there was a large gap between what the PPP promised and what it delivered, the attempt at reform represented a perceived improvement from the days of Ayub Khan and his predecessors. Regimes prior to the PPP had refused to even *acknowledge* claims of distributive justice, propounding publicly a view that even greater inequalities were necessary to promote economic growth. Thus, even relatively mild reforms under the PPP symbolised, for the poor, a favourable shift in the government's attitude. Indeed, the divergence between objectives and performance did little damage to Bhutto's personal popularity among the poorer segments of rural society. This was partly due to popular perceptions that Bhutto was personally keen on reforms but was subverted by 'vested interests' and 'corrupt party colleagues'. This is not to suggest that the PPP's reforms did not have a positive impact on specific disadvantaged classes. In the urban areas, for example, the government introduced changes in the structure of industrial relations. The 1972 labour laws[59] improved pension rights, provided educational allowances for the children of workers, as well as greater provision for medical and welfare funds for workers. The new labour legislation, which covered over 50% of workers in the manufacturing sector,[60] also provided protection from arbitrary dismissal and the right to appeal to a labour court. Industrialists complained bitterly that these labour laws led to lower productivity and eroded profit margins due to 'labour indiscipline'.[61] The government was also more sensitive to protecting the real wages of low-income urban groups than the relatively affluent middle classes. While the real incomes of shopkeepers fell,[62] four pay increases were granted to workers in public sector enterprises in the first three years of PPP rule. Similarly, when food subsidies were reduced, low-income government employees and workers were partially compensated by wage increases. The real wages of organised factory workers rose under the PPP. According to one study, the real wages of this group rose by approximately 6% per annum.[63] The growth of real wages is documented in Table 8 below.

Finally, it is worth stressing the psychological boost to the poor of a regime which constantly engaged in rhetoric emphasising the need to redistribute incomes to create a more just social order. The acknowledgement, by the government, of the economic *rights* of the poor represented a distinct progress in rhetoric, if not in substance. The attempt at economic reforms, irrespective of degree of success in implementation, was sufficient to sustain popular support for the PPP. It partly explains why Bhutto remained, till his death in 1979, the most popular politician in Pakistan.

Table 8: *Real wages of organised labour, 1970-75.*

	Rupees	:	Real wages Index (1959-60 = 100)
1970-71	1384	:	127
1971-72	1504	:	138
1972-73	1679	:	143
1973-74	1775	:	163
1974-75	1730	:	159

Source: Guisinger, Hicks and Pilvin: 'Wages and relative factor prices in Pakistan'. Mimeo — September 1977.

Summary

The PPP's popularity was based on a programme of social and economic reform. The implementation of economic reforms fell far short of expectations. Initially, state intervention in the economy was predicated by distributional concerns. Gradually members of the left within the party were either purged or marginalised. The state continued, none the less, to intervene in the economy. Public ownership was based on criteria which were erratic and arbitrary. Public intervention became a mechanism through which political and economic patronage was distributed. Successive nationalisations, despite assurance that the government would not take over more industrial units, created deep insecurities within the private sector. This led to a flight of private capital abroad as industrialists, not surprisingly, stopped investing in units which faced the prospect of being nationalised.

In agriculture, a combination of uncertainty over institutional reforms and bad weather led to a decline in *per capita* output. Other exogenous shocks which the PPP administration had to contend with included the oil price hike of 1973.

The concentration of the public sector on large capital-intensive projects, such as the steel mill, absorbed the major share of investment resources. The situation was exacerbated by the inability of nationalised industries to internally generate sufficient funds for investment. Consequently there were not enough resources available for investment in the provision of basic needs, such as health and education.

The underfunding of the ambitious social sector programmes deprived the government of an important component in its strategy to extend its mass base. At the same time, the mismanagement of these programmes antagonised the middle classes, who were the beneficiaries of the existing educational structure.

It would appear to be the case, however, that inadequate implementation of economic reforms did not substantially reduce mass support for Bhutto. The very introduction of economic reforms, based ostensibly on concerns for distributional justice, represented an improvement from military regimes who had openly advocated greater inequality.

There is much substance to the argument that it is unfair to compare the economic policy performance of the PPP with the Ayub or Zia regime. The PPP had a relatively brief tenure in office, which started under conditions of extreme adversity — the country had just been dismembered through a debilitating civil war. In addition, the PPP had to contend with the devastating impact of the '73 oil price hike. While one accepts that such exogenous shocks need to be taken into account, one finds it hard to escape the conclusion that the situation was made worse by erratic and inconsistent policies.

Footnotes:

1. Quoted in H. A. Rizvi: *PPP-The first Phase, 1967-71*, p. 7.
2. ibid, pp. 30-35, has details.
3. For a brief review, see S. J. Burki: *Pakistan under Bhutto*, pp. 110-120.
4. ibid, pp. 116-20.
5. See J. Rashid: 'Economic Causes of Political Crises in Pakistan' *Developing Economies*, Tokyo, June 1978.
6. *Dawn*, 14.8.73.
7. See H. Feldman: "Pakistan — 1973", *Asian Survey*, February 1974 and issues of *Dawn*, 19.8.73 to 30.8.73.
8. *Pakistan Economic Survey*, 1974, p. 20.
9. Feldman, op cit. Also see Burki, op cit.
10. The Minister of Finance had previously issued a public statement saying that the January 1974 nationalisations completed the fulfilment of the PPP's election manifesto pledges. See *Dawn*, 31.1.74.
11. For a background to the '76 nationalisations see Amjad and Ahmed: *The Management of Pakistan's Economy*, chapter 4, and Burki, op cit, pp. 116-130.
12. Some leading industrialists, such as Dawood, were arrested and humiliated publicly.

13 The Hyesons backed Bhutto financially, even during his 1970 election campaign.
14 On 7 March 1974, private sector hopes were revived by amendment of an earlier ordinance to provide compensation to owners of nationalised firms listed on the stock exchange. This was done on the basis of market values, not on the generally lower book values. The compensation was to be paid either in cash or in 15-year bonds convertible to cash.
15 These three categories are not exhaustive. None the less, they cover most cases of public intervention in developing countries.
16 By mixed economies, we refer to the co-existence of private capital and public enterprises. Neither sector performs a marginal economic role.
17 These issues are explored in greater detail by Y. Aharoni: *Markets, Planning and Development.*
18 Prominent among these were the Aid to Pakistan Consortium, IMF and the World Bank.
19 Some of the nationalised units in the red at the time of the take-over were Valika Chemicals, Ravi Rayon and Pakistan PVC. By taking over units based on outmoded technology, the public sector was burdened from the start. See A. T. Chaudhry's article in *Dawn*, 9.1.78 which explores similar issues.
20 This point is forcefully argued by Naqvi and Sarmad: *Pakistan's Economy through the Seventies.* The authors do not argue that public sector enterprises were particularly efficient, especially when evaluated at world prices, but that their inefficiency was no greater than that of private sector units.
21 For a review see World Bank: *Pakistan; Development Issues and Policies*, volume 1, 1978, p. 115. The profit performance of the automobile industry declined in 1975-76.
22 Sarmad and Naqvi, op cit, p. 48.
23 White Paper on the Economy under the PPP, p. 41.
24 ibid, p. 32.
25 See the World Bank report on *Public Sector Resource Mobilisation*, April 1978, for further discussion.
26 Agricultural incomes are not taxed. There is also large scale 'tax avoidance'. Of course, not all indirect taxes are regressive. If selectively imposed, as a number of them were, the burden is borne by the richer segments of society.
27 Thus corruption has a circular flow. High-level corruption leads to public sector inefficiency, this contributes towards budget deficits, the monetary financing of which leads to higher inflation. Wages fail to keep up, leading to corruption among lower level employees to maintain their real income levels.

28 From Buligi (West Karachi) to Pipri, which is 40km east of Karachi, in close proximity to Port Qasim.
29 Financial support for the bomb came from Libya. The process was the subject of a BBC television documentary. See Panorama: The Islamic Bomb? March, 1981.
30 *Pakistan Economic Survey*, 1978, pp. 20-21.
31 H. Chenery: *Structural Change and Development Policy.*
32 For details see A. Nôman (B. Phil. thesis, Oxford University), where the author compares Pakistan's performance with other Asian countries.
33 In some years, poor industrial performance was aggravated by exogenous factors. For example, in 1974-75, textile output was affected by the damage done to cotton output by floods.
34 On 1 October 1972, education for all children up to the age of 13 was made free, although not compulsory. The second phase, which was to have started in 1974, was designed to achieve the goal of free, compulsory education.
35 Nationalisation of urban private schools was completed in October 1974.
36 Author's interview with A. H. Peerzada.
37 Poll conducted by research cell of the Prime Minister's Secretariat in preparation for 1977 elections.
38 See H. A. Pasha: "Measurement of the contribution of different factors to inflation in Pakistan". *P.I.D.E. Discussion paper* — 21.
39 For discussion, see ibid, pp. 12-15.
40 In April 1974, food subsidies were reduced on wheat, sugar and ghee. Another measure to reduce the budget deficit was an increase in export duties to enhance revenues.
41 See Sarmad and Naqvi, op cit, pp. 60-70.
42 Amjad and Ahmed, op cit, p. 293. Higher inflation in Pakistan, relative to other Asian countries (average increase in consumer price index in Asian countries was 11.6%, while in Pakistan it was 17.3%) had an adverse impact on export competitiveness, which had been given a substantial boost by the '72 devaluation. As a consequence, Pakistan's share in world exports declined from .16% to .12% in 1976.
43 Statement of Shahid Hussain to the Pakistan Aid Consortium, 28 April 1976.
44 Z. A. Bhutto's television address to the nation, 1 March 1972.
45 Interview to West German magazine, *Stern*, 15 June 1972.
46 Brown and Gotsch: "Pakistan agricultural prices". World Bank, mimeo, 1977. Terms of trade moved against agriculture in later years.

47 Procurement prices for wheat, cotton, rice and sugarcane more than doubled during 1972-76.
48 For a discussion, see Chaudhry and Herring: "The 1972 Land Reforms in Pakistan and their Economic Implications", *Pakistan Development Review*, Autumn, 1974.
49 *Pakistan Economic Survey*, 1975-76, has a table illustrating these allocative priorities, p. 42.
50 For instances see White Paper on Performance of the Bhutto Regime: The Economy, pp, 14-15. Cases are also documented by M. Lodhi in her thesis on the PPP (Ph.D., London School of Economics), pp. 455-60.
51 For details of how landlords could avoid land reforms see M. H. Khan: *Underdevelopment and Agrarian Structure in Pakistan*, pp. 180-200.
52 ibid, p. 110.
53 Z. Mahmood: *Income Inequality in Pakistan: An Analysis of Existing Evidence*, Paper presented at the conference of the Pakistan Society of Development Economists, Islamabad, March 1984.
54 According to Mahmood, ibid, the share of the highest quintile of rural households increased from 24.1 to 27.3% between 1971 and 1979. In urban households it rose from 30.6 to 36.1%. The Gini co-efficient climbed from 0.295 to 0.324 for rural households and from 0.36 to 0.41 for the urban group.
55 R. J. Herring: "Z. A. Bhutto and the "eradication of feudalism in Pakistan" *Economic and Political Weekly*, 22.3.1980.
56 ibid, p. 606.
57 Punitive action under land reform legislation was taken against almost all the leaders of the NAP, the main opposition party.
58 For observations on this point see A. Malik: "Elections 1977: what will be the Bhutto strategy?". *Viewpoint*, 4.2.77.
59 It is, of course, true that the labour laws fell short of expectations held by a number of radical trade union leaders. This led to continuation of labour unrest throughout 1972, especially in Karachi, which was suppressed by police firing on workers.
60 One must, however, bear in mind that workers in the organised sector represent a very small proportion of the workforce.
61 See Meekal Ahmed: *Factors Which Hinder or Help Productivity*, mimeo. Asian Productivity Organisation, Tokyo. 1978.
62 See survey of Rawalpindi shopkeepers done by the Pakistan Institute of Development Economics (P.I.D.E.), Islamabad, 1975.
63 Guisinger, Hicks and Pilvin: *Wages and Relative Factor Prices in Pakistan*. mimeo. September, 1977. World Bank.

Chapter Three

Populism and Ideology

In the late sixties, the growth of the PPP had been spontaneous. Much of the vitality, energy and enthusiasm of the early years was infused by young left wing cadres. They were galvanised into organising effective mass protests by a dynamic and vibrant landlord from Sind, who possessed the explosive ability to translate widespread grievances into an agitation which debilitated a military regime. A critical component in Bhutto's meteoric success in mass politics, was a realisation that it was not sufficient to confine himself to a critique of Ayub Khan's rule. The PPP symbolised and articulated an alternative — a vision of a democratic, socialist society. On this basis Bhutto courted mass appeal, and it was on this basis that virtually the whole of the left in Punjab and Sind swarmed to the PPP. Also well represented in the PPP, however, were Sindhi landlords, even at the initial stage of party formation. Some of them supported reforms of the existing political and economic structure, although they naturally differed with members of the urban left on the scale of necessary reforms. Other landlords in the party fold were more conservative but politically astute. They saw the PPP as a party which would promote greater representation for Sindhis at the national level. The PPP's strategy in the 1970 election campaign was thus based on the support of traditional feudal forces in Sind combined with an appeal to the disadvantaged social groups in urban Punjab and Sind. A third aspect of the PPP's evolution was the support given to Bhutto by factions within the army. Unlike Mujib, Bhutto's relationship with the army was not entirely adversarial. Not only had Bhutto been a leading member of a military government, but he also had substantial support *within* the army, when he launched his campaign against Ayub Khan. These factions were dissatisfied with Ayub, particularly with his handling of the 1965 war. In harmony with their frustrations were Bhutto's accusations that Ayub lost on the negotiating table in Tashkent what the Pakistan army had won in the '65 war. This encouraged the dangerous belief that Pakistan was capable of defeating India militarily, if only its leaders showed greater resolve.

These three variables — a radical reform programme, feudal support in Sind and Bhutto's ambivalent relationship with the army — constituted a diaphanous equilibrium which was preserved by the frenzied cement of a mass movement. In power, the manner in which these contradictions were resolved was to dictate the course of politics under the PPP.

Within three years of forming a government, the PPP leadership had been purged of its left wing elements. The left within the party had never represented a united bloc. It constituted more of an amorphous ideological matrix, elements of which had joined the PPP independently of each other. Each group had been useful in mobilising support among different sections of workers and peasants. In spite of their splintered nature, left wing groups could none the less be divided into two broad categories, the 'hard' and the 'soft' left. The radical left was removed from the party within months of the PPP coming to power. The second stage of the internal power struggle witnessed the removal of the reformist left. The radical left advocated a swift transformation to a socialist economic and political structure. They argued that 1972 offered a unique opportunity for the PPP to undertake fundamental reforms. The ruling class was not in a position to resist a shift in power towards workers and peasants, due to its debilitating defeat in 1971. In line with this argument, these radical groups organised worker's occupation of a number of factories, as well as encouraging establishment of people's courts, which sentenced individuals for being pro-capitalist or anti-labour.[1] Similarly, clashes between landlords and tenants in rural areas were organised in Punjab, Sind and NWFP.[2]

The PPP Government reacted swiftly to these disturbances. The police were ordered to fire on workers attempting to seize or burn factories.[3] At the same time, Bhutto moved against those elements within his party who were seen to be encouraging a state of industrial anarchy. Accordingly, the Mukhtar Rana group, who had a support base among radical trade union groups in Punjab,[4] was eased out when its leader was expelled from the party. He was sentenced to five years' rigorous imprisonment for making a speech in which he advocated a public trial of Bhutto for having 'betrayed the toiling masses'. Similarly, Mairaj Mohammed Khan, a member of Bhutto's cabinet, who had substantial support among radical student and labour unions in Sind, was forced to resign in October 1972. He had little choice after police fired on industrial labour in his constituency, as well as Bhutto's tacit approval of a voluble campaign, launched by the right within the PPP, to rid itself of 'troublesome communists'. Public abuse, directed at Mairaj *et al*, was orchestrated by an ex-member of the fundamentalist Jamaat-e-Islami party, Maulana Kauser Niazi, who had become a prominent figure in the PPP. Like Rana, Mairaj was later imprisoned for a speech in which he accused Bhutto of class betrayal.

The formal and emphatic repudiation of the radical left occurred at the December 1972 convention of the party held at Rawalpindi — the first since the PPP had formed a government.⁵ Bhutto's address to the convention stressed that the PPP did not intend to establish complete state control over private enterprise. To 'smash feudalism and capitalism' was an objective of the radical left within the party. The mainstream of the PPP, Bhutto reminded the convention, was concerned with reforms of the system, not its overthrow. Irritated by complaints from the radical left, that the PPP reforms did not go far enough, Bhutto warned militant groups within the party that they would face his wrath, if they persisted in their agitprop activities among workers and peasants. Bhutto's strong public denunciation of militant groups within the party ("most of our troubles come from the left") effectively signalled a formal purge of the radical left.

The reformist left, however, was well represented in Bhutto's first cabinet. It had four members who were committed to the creation of a more egalitarian social structure: J. A. Rahim (Minister for Industrial Production), Mubashir Hasan (Finance Minister), Sheikh Rashid (Health) and Khurshid Hasan Meer (Establishment). The initial implementation of land reforms and the nationalisation of industrial units was carried out under their command. By 1974, however, even the reformist left was marginalised, as its representatives were ousted from the cabinet. The departure of J. A. Rahim was significant not only in its ideological implications but also as a symbol of the form of brutality which became the hallmark of the FSF's dealings with those who opposed Bhutto. Rahim, a founding member and an old man, was beaten up as security forces raided his house after he had fallen out of favour.⁶

The ousting of the reformist left was more significant than the purge of the radical elements. The distancing of the PPP leadership from militant groups came as no great surprise. The departure of the reformist left, on the other hand, marked a crucial turning point in the direction towards which the PPP was headed. The removal of left wing members from the cabinet could not be attributed to Bhutto's response to the failures of policies initiated by the left.⁷ A year or so is hardly long enough to assess the impact of substantial institutional reforms. Indeed, the left was marginalised within months of the 1974 nationalisation of financial institutions — a period of time barely long enough to oversee the enactment of measures, let alone evaluate the success of the reform package. The left's confinement to the periphery was linked with Bhutto's cultivation of the Punjabi landed élite. At the time of its inception, Punjabi landlords had remained aloof from the PPP. In power, Bhutto assiduously wooed the Punjabi landed aristocracy. But the shift in PPP class alignments in the Punjab required absolute control over the party's reform programme. This necessitated the removal of senior left wing members, after which Bhutto had complete command over implementation and formulation of policy. The removal of the left signalled to the rural élite that the power struggle within the party, such as there was, had been won decisively by the right. For Punjabi landlords it was an opportune moment to join the PPP and establish access to the state's patronage over financial and political resources. This was particularly important in the context of land reforms, since joining the PPP could minimise the resumption of land. The scale and rapid pace of the process is reflected in the astonishing fact that twenty-eight out of the thirty-three leading aristocratic families of the Punjab had representatives in the PPP by 1976.[8] Virtually all of the feudal families were given party nominations for the 1977 elections.[9] Another indication of the dominant position acquired by landlords is given in Table 1. As the table indicates, 66% of the PPP's top leadership were members of the landed élite.

Table 1: *Social Background of the top 50 PPP leaders — 1975-76.*

Social Background	Number
Landlord	27
Tribal Chief	6
Businessman	5
Middle-class Professional (Lawyer, Engineer, Teacher, etc.)	7
Former Ruler of Princely State	2
Retired Civil Servant/Armed Force Personnel	2
Trade Union Leader	1

Source: M. Lodhi: *The Pakistan People's Party*, p. 413.

This shift towards landlord-based support can be contrasted with the 1970 election, in which the PPP's support in Punjab had been based on overcoming traditional landlord-manipulated mobilisation of votes. Accordingly, the PPP's popularity had been concentrated in the relatively modernised areas of Lahore, Faisalabad, Eastern Multan district and along the industrial belt of the grand trunk road. In areas of Punjab where landlords had continued to exert authority over vote mobilisation, the PPP had not performed well in 1970.[10] By 1976, these landlords had joined the party, partially reversing the modern methods of voter mobilisation adopted by the PPP in 1970.

The removal of the left, and the entry of landlords on a large scale, should not be seen as representing a transformation of a radical left wing party into a conservative force. The People's Party was the outcome of a factional struggle within the West Pakistani ruling élite. Dissatisfaction with Ayub's handling of the '65 war, as well as fears regarding the growing inequalities, had led to the formation of an informal caucus of dissidents within the junta. This clique included Foreign Minister Bhutto, as well as military officers such as Gul Hasan, Tikka Khan and Rahim. In 1966, Bhutto resigned from the government. In addition to some members of the junta, Bhutto had the support of Sindhi landlords, who had reasons to feel antagonistic towards the Ayub government, since the primary beneficiaries of economic development in Sind had been non-Sindhi industrialists. To unsettle the military government, Bhutto sought to mobilise mass support in those provinces that mattered to the military: Punjab and Sind. He was the principal architect of a strategy which accentuated consciousness of class antagonisms in society as a basis for cultivating mass support. The harnessing of popular opinion required a platform for the redistribution of economic and political power in favour of the dominated classes. For this purpose, radical left wing groups were cultivated in Punjab and Sind. The élite faction was not entirely in control of the process of mobilisation. It had to rely on radical elements to harness support. These groups utilised this opportunity to promise radical reforms, in the hope that a public commitment from vulnerable leadership would be binding if and when a government were formed by them. The mobilising vigour of these left wing groups, and their prominence in organising mass rallies, gave the PPP the appearance of a radical party. This public profile tended to cover the more conservative forces, which were far more powerful and were to determine the direction that the PPP took when it assumed office.[11]

Two broad characterisations of Bhutto are common. The first sees him as an ideological schizophrenic.[12] One dimension consists of a secular, modern socialist; the other of a conservative, repressive 'wadera'[13]. The latter tendency dominated, hence the conservative flavour of PPP rule. The second characterisation dismisses this theory of personality conflict. It sees Bhutto primarily as a 'power craftsman'[14] and a practitioner of *realpolitik*, interested in power, and moving according to the conception of what was most advantageous in the gaining and maintaining of it. While the former view is somewhat superficial, attributing excessive importance to Bhutto's supposed split personality, the latter perception can be supplemented by specifying the structural choices facing Bhutto. They determined the matrix within which Bhutto could operate. One of the critical determinants was Bhutto's relationship with the existing power structure. The disenchantment of factions, within the power bloc, with the policies of the Ayub regime, and their consequent support for the breakaway member of cabinet, has been documented elsewhere.[15] Support from army factions was symbolised by Major-General Peerzada's assurance to Bhutto that the army would not back Ayub's efforts to suppress his demonstrations.[16] Thus, at one level, the PPP represented a movement in which a section of the élite had cultivated mass support, by accentuating existing antagonisms towards the ruling class. Class consciousness was also heightened by a form of mobilisation, which encouraged revolt against a government representing the dominant classes. However, once the party had come to power, Bhutto had to contain and neutralise the class polarisation evoked by the PPP's radical rhetoric.[17] Such containment required absolute control over the reform programme; a command swiftly acquired by Bhutto under pressure from powerful social forces. The removal of the left was as much a sign of Bhutto's weakness as his strength. It was a crude incision and seriously damaged the party's credibility. The left wing ministers, however, represented the most threatening ideological group in the party. To retain them in critical positions would have continued to alienate and threaten the traditional rural élite. It would also have entailed incessant pressure to seriously implement the social and economic reforms enacted by the PPP. This would have involved committing the PPP towards effecting a fundamental alteration in the distribution of economic and political resources. Bhutto himself was representative of the powerful social forces which would have been marginalised by such a strategy.

With the removal of the left, the PPP leadership had to perform the complex task of retaining mass support by sustaining the illusion of reforms, while ensuring that the implementation lacked substance. Bhutto became central to this political sleight of hand. The imperatives of the situation necessitated the personalisation of the reform programme. Bhutto acquired the role of benefactor, personally dispensing the state's resources to correct social inequalities. This was done through token gestures, such as open kutcheries, in which selected peasants could take their grievances directly to Bhutto. This form of political articulation increased the party's reliance on Bhutto, since he was the only figure capable of sustaining the vision that the PPP was seriously concerned with social transformation.

The resolution of the PPP's internal contradictions in favour of powerful conservative forces led to the revival of faction-ridden feudal politics. For example, intense rivalry between G. Mustafa Jatoi and Mumtaz Bhutto was the source of bitter conflict within the party in Sind.[18] Similarly, party squabbles in the Punjab between G. M. Khar, K. H. Meer and S. Rashid involved patronisation of shady underworld figures.[19] Khar's 'advisers' included men of considerable notoriety, such as Mian Tari. Bhutto's concern at the growth of 'gangsterism' was evident in his memo to Governor Khar (16 August 1973): "Pistols to the right of us, pistols to the left of us, pistols all around us. This seems to be the motto of the party. For the most trivial of things pistols are drawn and flashed ... gangsters who do this sort of thing must feel they have protection, because this was not their brave habit before we assumed office. How are we going to end if this becomes the order of the day?" Concerned though he may have been, Bhutto was too reliant on these feudal factions to take strong action against 'goondaism' — 'goonda' being the Urdu word for thug — and prevent the PPP from taking on the appearance of a revamped Muslim League.

In addition to the above, Bhutto's deep mistrust of groups demanding greater regional autonomy had serious implications for political development. Pressure from the army high command, and the Shah of Iran, to take strong action against the Baluchis, met little resistance from the PPP leadership. This unfortunate identity of attitude led to the dismissal of NAP provincial governments and an armed insurrection in Baluchistan. The action effectively aborted the incipient democratic structure, involving the army in provincial administration. In a country with weak civilian institutions, the PPP's conduct aided the return of military rule.

By 1974, the direction towards which the PPP was guiding Pakistan's political structure was increasingly evident. Early in his career Bhutto had advocated the need for a controlled democracy. The practical manifestation of this vision was a centralised, one-party dominated political structure. Leaders of the main opposition party, NAP, were in jail. The press had been gagged. At the same time the PPP extended its control over all sectors of society, with political and economic resources increasingly concentrated in the hands of the central government. The PPP exerted command over these resources, with Bhutto himself at the apex of this structure. Access to these resources was used as a magnet to attract the allegiance of a wide spectrum of groups in Punjab, Sind and NWFP. The move towards a centralised, single-party dominated structure was evident in Bhutto's plan to convert the parliamentary system into a presidential one.[20] The design was not too different from that of Sheikh Mujib, in Bangladesh.[21] Although not quite as extreme as Mujib's scheme, the PPP's desire for a single-party dominated structure was motivated by similar dictatorial tendencies. Bhutto did not, however, have the required majority in the legislature to implement the change to a presidential system. The conversion required a two-thirds majority in the house. It may be unkind to suggest that the rigging of the '77 election was connected with the above.

The PPP's objective of establishing its hegemony over a single-party dominated civilian structure, rather than developing a democratic participatory framework, had unfortunate implications for the opposition. Had the PPP taken its responsibility for creating a democratic structure seriously, it would have ensured that the mechanism for a transfer of power to an alternative civilian government would not be distorted. The rigging of the 1977 elections provided distasteful evidence that the PPP had abandoned its commitment to a free, democratic structure. It had degenerated into a party of patronage, dominated by the traditional rural élite, and reliant on Bhutto's populist appeal to retain mass support.

Ideology

During the phase of mass mobilisation, the PPP had adopted the concept of

'Islamic Socialism', as articulated by a number of liberal scholars.[22] The framework outlined therein was based on an eclectic interpretation of Islam. Instead of deriving a theory of the state from the Quran, as fundamentalists do, the liberal interpretation of a modern Muslim state approached theological sources in a diametrically opposed manner. First, desirable economic and social objectives were stated. This normative articulation of aims was then given theological sanction by a somewhat random reference to the Quran. Passages from the Quran which have a progressive, egalitarian connotation were used in support of a reforming, socialist platform. Needless to say, those injunctions of the Quran which did not conform to stated policy objectives were discarded on grounds that these were specific to that era of Arabian history. Such a formulation emphasised that all religions were revolutionary, in the sense that they inherently represented a doctrine of change. This empathy with the idea of progressive change provided the intertemporal link. Since socialism represented change in the modern era, it follows that it is in conformity with the spirit of Islam: "Islam and the principles of socialism are not mutually repugnant. Islam preaches equality, and socialism is the modern technique of attaining it."[23]

The adoption of this ingenious formulation[24] enabled the PPP to achieve several objectives simultaneously. First, it clarified the distinction between socialist reforms and communism; the latter charge could have seriously hindered the growth of the PPP in Pakistan.[25] Second, it appealed to a wide cross section of social groups who favoured a more egalitarian society and adhered to the view that change was central to the spirit of their religion. Third, it prevented the conservative religious parties from monopolising religion as a source of mass appeal. Bhutto sensed that, given Pakistan's history, it would be unwise to abdicate from taking a public stance on religion. If religion were to be used, and this he considered necessary, it had to be integrated into the progressive, reformist discourse which characterised the PPP's election platform. Accordingly, emphasis was placed on the concept of musawaat (equality) as "preached by the prophet Mohammad".

Invoking theological sanction did, however, shift the parameters of ideological debate. Under Ayub the orientation of government, if not of society, was secular. The reintroduction of religion as the ultimate source of authority entailed dangers of manipulation, damaging consequences of which became evident during the course of PPP rule. Indeed, the shift of power within the PPP was mirrored in the manner in which religion was used. The marginalisation of the left and the consolidation of the right, were reflected in a shift in the party's discourse. The road to ideological transition was led by Maulana Kauser Niazi, a leading member of Bhutto's cabinet and a former leader of the fundamentalist Jamaat-e-Islami. Collectively, the conservative and religious parties had polled a higher number of votes than the PPP in the 1970 election. The PPP began to cultivate this constituency through a series of concessions which culminated in the ignominious surrender to fundamentalism in 1977, when the PPP government imposed a set of measures designed to placate conservative forces. It was ironic that the PPP, erstwhile promoters of Islamic socialism, were responsible for initiating legislation which introduced the Muslim equivalent of Calvinist puritanism.

Perhaps the most significant concession to religious parties was granted in 1974. In that year seventy people died in anti-Qadiani riots in Punjab, provoked by an incident at the sect's headquarters in Rabwah.[26] The religious parties revived the demand to declare the sect beyond the pale of Islam, due to the belief that its founder, Mirza Ghulam Ahmed, claimed to be a prophet. This claim, which militated against the finality of Mohammad's prophet-hood, incensed religious parties, particularly the Jamaat-e-Islami. As we documented in part one, similar demands for ostracising the Qadianis were made in the fifties. At that time, the government had resisted demands to declare the Qadianis as non-Muslims. The PPP Government, on the other hand, gave in to pressure from the religious parties and Saudi Arabia.[27] The Qadianis were declared a non-Muslim sect, an unfortunate concession to fundamentalist pressures.

The PPP's drift towards conservative Islam was also influenced by international factors. The '73 oil price hike led to the growth in the economic and political power of Arabs, in particular Saudi Arabia. Subsequently, Pakistan's links with the wider ecumenical community of Islam received greater attention, for the first time since the late forties.[28] The Arab world began to figure prominently in Bhutto's foreign policy. The Pakistani military was the most advanced in the Muslim world; hence increasing Arab demands for military personnel and training were met by Pakistan. In addition, the PPP Government hoped to exploit Pakistan's geographical and religious proximity to seek preferential access to the expanding labour market of rapidly growing Gulf economies. The export of manpower to the Arab world was important not only because it eased the problem of poor labour absorption within Pakistan, but also because it provided an opportunity to raise the standard of living of a substantial section of Pakistan's population. Links with the Arab world offered other benefits as well. Bhutto sought financial support for the development of nuclear power. Bhutto's primary interest in a nuclear bomb lay in its deterrent effect on India.[29] During the sixties, Bhutto had displayed strong militaristic chauvinism against India, encouraging Pakistan's entanglement in Kashmir in 1965. Later, his public utterances regarding a 'thousand-year war' with India symbolised his persistent hostility. When he came to power, India's military supremacy had been firmly established. 90,000 prisoners of war were captured by India after the surrender of Pakistani troops in Bangladesh. Under these circumstances, Bhutto was keen to prevent a repetition of Indian intervention to dismember Pakistan, as it had done in 1971. A nuclear bomb would serve as an effective deterrent.[30]

Pakistan's closer association with the Arab world was symbolised by the holding of the summit of Islamic heads of state in Lahore. The summit, held in 1974, was a diplomatic *coup* for Bhutto.[31] The collection of heads of state from all the major Muslim countries for such a conference, emphasised the importance Pakistan sought, and to some extent gained, within the Muslim world. This revival in international prestige was particularly important for Bhutto, after the '71 debacle in East Pakistan. However, the price of gaining acceptance into the Muslim world was an increase in influence over domestic issues by powerful governments such as Saudi Arabia. The Saudi Government often made it clear to aid recipients that secularism should be discouraged in Muslim countries.[32] Thus, international factors reinforced the conservative shift within the PPP. The PPP's concessions to theocratic demands also set in motion tendencies which facilitated the subsequent drift into fundamentalism under General Zia. In 1970, when the religious parties accused the PPP's socialism of being un-Islamic, Bhutto retorted by stressing that the compatibility between Islam and socialism was not 'properly understood'. In 1977, by way of contrast, Bhutto attempted to diffuse the opposition movement by giving in to puritanical theocratic demands, which were by no means central to the opposition's campaign against the PPP.[33] The PPP banned alcohol, gambling and night clubs, as well as replacing Sunday with Friday, the Muslim sabbath, as the weekly holiday. The effect of the concessions was opposite to what was intended. The measures further weakened the PPP Administration, since they were seen to be a somewhat pathetic response of a cynical regime desperately clinging to power.

Bhutto had called early elections in March 1977, confident of extending the PPP's hegemony over the political structure. From the outset, there were fears that the electoral process would be tampered with, to ensure a substantial majority for the ruling party. Distortions were evident even before votes were cast. Fifteen candidates of the PPP, including Bhutto and the four provincial chief ministers, were elected unopposed to the National Assembly. PPP nominees, elected without contest to the four provincial assemblies, totalled 55, giving the party a majority in the legislatures of Baluchistan and Sind even before a vote was cast!

The rigging of the elections gave the PPP's rival civilian parties an opportunity to mobilise a mass movement against the distortion of constitutional procedures. Based primarily in urban areas, the revolt was sustained by a wide coalition of groups who had suffered politically, or economically, under the PPP. Traders and shopkeepers had been incensed by the 1976 nationalisation of small industrial units, as well as by a decline in their real incomes during the seventies.[34] The urban professional middle-class groups supported the PNA Movement as an expression of their anger at bearing the brunt of tax increases, while suffering a deterioration in the provision of services, such as education. Those who suffered under the PPP were joined by those who had never supported it — such as the religious sections of the *petite bourgeoisie.* In contrast to the anti-Ayub movement, the PNA's mobilisation drew most of its inspiration and sustenance from middle-class groups. This was evident in the surprisingly large number of women's demonstrations in Punjab and Sind.[35] The PNA Movement spread across a wide network of mandi (market) towns whose economic life was controlled by traders. The organisation and cohesion of these merchants was particularly important in the effective implementation of national strikes.

It was ironic that the *civilian* opposition, in the form of the nine-party Pakistan National Alliance (PNA), had mobilised a mass movement to topple a civilian government. Indeed, opposition leaders urged the military to take over, in the naive expectation that it would be willing to act as an intermediary in the transfer of power from one civilian government to another.[36] The army, eager to seize any opportunity to regain power, ensured the demise of the five-year civilian interlude. Bhutto's downfall through a military *coup* seemed, ironically, to indicate how institutional features can dominate personalities.

Although Bhutto's reforms were not radical, they did alter the élite equilibrium established in the sixties. None of the groups which dominated Pakistan in that era felt secure under the PPP. First, the bourgeoisie and the landed élite were rattled by uncertain nationalisations and land reforms. A volatile policy environment was not conducive to long-term investment plans. Consequently, the bourgeoisie had little to gain by the PPP remaining in power and, by and large, supported opposition parties or the military. The second dominant élite group of the sixties — the bureaucracy — had felt undermined by the administrative reforms under the PPP. Deprived of their previous prestige and authority they, too, had little reason to support the PPP. Finally, the army. Bhutto did not, of course, envisage a weak army; he wanted a militarily strong army subservient to domestic civilian authority. For a short period the army accepted this role. But as the insecurities generated by the PPP accumulated, the army intervened to re-establish the élite equilibrium evolved in the sixties. The élite reconstituted itself, but the dilemmas it confronted were different from the sixties and its responses were, as we shall see in the following chapters, conditioned by the changed environment.

Footnotes:

1. For details see M. Lodhi: *Pakistan People's Party* (Ph.D. thesis. pp. 300-50).
2. See issues of *Dawn*, between 1.1.72 and 1.4.72.
3. The worst incident, in terms of casualties, occurred on 8 June 1972, when 11 workers were killed in Karachi.
4. The support base of this group was particularly strong in Faisalabad.
5. The December 1972 convention in Rawalpindi was the third since the party was formed.
6. Rahim's son was also subjected to physical and sexual assault. For details of similar treatment handed out to opponents, see White Paper on the Performance of the Bhutto Regime: Misuse of the Instruments of State Power, pp. 44-65. For examples of FSF intimidation of the opposition, see Aghar Khan, *Generals and Politics*. pp. 75-100.
7. A number of commentators seem to be suggesting this. See works on the Bhutto era by Taseer, Burki and Sayeed cited in the bibliography.
8. M. Lodhi: op cit, pp. 413-19.
9. See P. J. Jones: *Pakistan People's Party* (Ph.D. thesis).
10. See Baxter and Burki: "Socio-economic Indicators of the People's Party Vote in the Punjab", *Journal of Asian Studies*, August 1975. Also see C. Baxter: "People's Party vs. Punjab Feudalists" in J. Korson(ed): *Contemporary Problems of Pakistan*.
11. For excellent, detailed documentation of this process see M. Lodhi: op cit.
12. Studies which appear to take this view include Moody, Taseer and Burki. See bibliography.
13. Term used to describe large landlords in Sind.
14. Forcefully argued by M. Lodhi in her thesis, op cit.
15. See S. Taseer: *Bhutto a political biography*, and H. Alavi: "The Army and the Bureaucracy in Pakistan", *International Socialist Journal*, March-April 1966.
16. See Denzil Peiris article in *Far Eastern Economic Review*, 15 July 1977, p. 12.
17. For a theoretical discussion of this issue see E. Laclau: *Politics and Ideology in Marxist Theory*.
18. For details of factional politics under the PPP see A. H. Syed: "The PPP — phases one and two" in Ziring et al: *Pakistan — the long view*. For specific factional struggles the reader may find it

useful to refer to issues of the weekly *Outlook* between 2.6.1973 and 6.6.74.
19 See A. H. Syed: op cit. Also, M. Lodhi: op cit.
20 L. Wolf-Phillips, constitutional expert at the L.S.E., was consulted in this regard. Confirmed by Wolf-Phillips in a meeting with the author.
21 For details of Mujib's one-party system see R. Jahan: *Bangladesh Politics.*
22 For details see A. Ahmed: *Islamic Modernism in India and Pakistan*, chapter 11. Also see I. Ahmed: *The Islamic State Controversy in Pakistan* (Ph.D. thesis) and M. Usman: *Islamic Socialism.*
23 *PPP Political Series,* — 1, "Political Situation in Pakistan" by Z. A. Bhutto, 1968, Lahore.
24 The term Islamic socialism did not appear in the foundation documents of the PPP or its manifesto. It was used extensively, however, in Bhutto's speeches during his election campaign.
25 In 1969, Maulvis had issued a fatwa (religious decree) stating that socialism was un-Islamic and that Bhutto was a non-believer (Kafir) for espousing it.
26 For details see A. Syed: *Islam, Politics and National Solidarity.* The Qadiani sect is also referred to as Ahmedis, in memory of the founder of the group, Mirza Ghulam Ahmed. Qadiani refers to the geographical base of the sect in Qadian, about 30 miles from Amritsar.
27 Qadianis are not allowed into the holy places and cities of Saudi Arabia.
28 In the immediate aftermath of its formation, Pakistan's leaders, buoyed by the accomplishment of creating the largest Muslim state in the world, sought a dominant role in the wider Muslim world. They were strongly rebuffed by men such as Nasser and Mossadeq, who were extremely critical of Pakistan's alliance with the U.S.
29 Bhutto's fears of India are evident in *The Myth of Independence*, published in 1969. His fears of an Indian nuclear bomb, and its consequences for Pakistan, are expressed therein. See pp. 175-78.
30 For the Arabs, particularly Libya, Pakistan's acquisition of nuclear technology facilitated their access to technology denied to them by Western prohibition.
31 Bhutto also used the occasion to recognise Bangladesh by extending an invitation to Mujib.
32 The Bangladesh government faced similar pressures from Saudi Arabia, See A. Mascaranhas *Bangladesh: Legacy of Blood.*

33 Indeed, one analysis of PNA's public pronouncements during the campaign revealed that 70% of major addresses were concerned with Bhutto, civil rights and socio-economic issues. The Islamic state theme received a weight of approximately 12%. By responding to this issue, Bhutto appears to have increased its significance. See S. Mujahid's review article in *Pakistan Horizon*, Karachi, Volume 37, 4. 1984. Pakistan Institute of International Affairs.
34 See, for example, the evidence of survey of Rawalpindi shopkeepers done by the Pakistan Institute of Development Economics, Islamabad, 1975.
35 Details of demonstrations are contained in A. K. Brohi's statement in the Supreme Court of Pakistan, p. 65. Islamabad, 1977.
36 The leader of the Tehrik-e-Istaqlal, Asghar Khan, wrote a letter to the army chief suggesting military intervention. The letter is reproduced in his book, *Generals and Politics*. The Punjab chief of the Jamaat-e-Islami had asked the military to step in as early as 1973. He was arrested for making such a suggestion.

Part Three
MILITARY RULE UNDER ZIA, 1977 — 1985

"When he seizes a state the new ruler must determine all the injuries that he will need to inflict. He must inflict them once for all, and not have to renew them every day, and in that way he will be able to set men's minds at rest and win them over to him when he confers benefits . . . violence must be inflicted once for all; people will then forget what it tastes like and so be less resentful. Benefits must be conferred gradually; in that way they will taste better."

Machiavelli, The Prince.

Chapter One

Strategies for Self-Preservation

In 1977 the military seized power under circumstances which differed fundamentally from those prevailing in 1958. Unlike Ayub, Zia had deposed an elected civilian government, an act of treason under the '73 Constitution. In addition, the military no longer commanded the public prestige that it enjoyed when Ayub had stepped in to oust a weak, incompetent and unrepresentative government. Pakistan had experienced thirteen years of military rule which had culminated in a civil war. The military bore the stigma of responsibility for the shame and humiliation of 1971. Both these factors accentuated the need for the army to redefine its role in society in order to acquire the legitimacy to govern. The ideological imperatives for justifying the usurpation of power led the army to seek a remedy in the conversion of Pakistan into a theocratic state. The structural changes necessary for such a mutation will be examined later. The context is provided by the following summary of political events between 1977 and 1985.

Until 1986, the Zia period can be divided into three phases. During the first section, 1977-79, the regime deceived and outmanoeuvred the civilian opposition parties by publicly reiterating its commitment to hold elections while it undertook measures to entrench itself and consolidate its position. In 1979, Zia dropped the pretence of being the leader of an interim regime. Between 1979 and 1983 the army tightened its grip. The military wrapped itself into the role of an ideological vanguard for a theocratic state. Political opposition was smothered by the uninterrupted use of martial law. The third phase began in 1983 with the junta desperately seeking to break its isolation. It had successfully withstood the risks involved in eliminating Bhutto. Similarly, the military had little difficulty in containing public protests for the restoration of democratic rule. Powerless the people may have been to prevent these events, but endeared they were not. Consequently, Zia's junta was more isolated than any other government in Pakistan's history. To overcome this ostracism, the outlines of a political order were announced in 1983. Under this scheme civilians were to be assimilated into the administration as adjuncts to military supremacy.

The First Phase: 1977-79

The army *coup* of 5 July occurred two days after the outlines of an accord to settle the political crisis had been accepted by both protaganists, *viz*, the opposition alliance (PNA) and the ruling PPP. Bhutto, fearing military intervention,[1] had conceded the demand for holding fresh elections in place of the rigged March '77 polls. Indeed, virtually all of the opposition demands had been accepted.[2] A few relatively minor issues were still to be resolved. However, two leaders of the nine-party opposition alliance favoured a takeover by the military to a deal with the PPP.[3] One of them, Asghar Khan, had earlier written to the chiefs of the armed forces pleading for a *coup*.[4] The plea for military intervention was based on the naive expectation that the military would take over, hold elections, transfer power and return to the barracks. In the abstract, such optimism could kindly be described as frivolous. Given Pakistan's history, and what the military did after holding elections in '70, such invitations were suicidal.

The army justified its intervention by making the somewhat incredible claim that Pakistan was on the verge of a civil war.[5] Such a grave polarisation was not, however, going to prevent the military from holding elections and "transferring power within ninety days".[6] Yet the policy measures undertaken were hardly those of an avowedly interim regime. Instead of announcing an annual plan, long-term economic policy changes were incorporated in a five-year plan. The fifth plan (1978-83) was announced in early '78 but work on it had started within two months of the *coup*.[7] The plan emphasised the shift in strategy whereby the private sector was to regain the prominence it had lost under the PPP.[8] Other structural changes were made, such as the denationalisation of rice husking and flour milling units. Long-term measures were not confined to the economy. Just six weeks after the *coup*, Zia announced the formation of the Islamic Ideology Council.[9] The council was entrusted with the task of preparing an outline of an Islamic theocratic state. It had two panels, one on Islamic Law and social reforms, while the other dealt with matters relating to economics and finance. Zia also announced plans to establish separate women's universities.[10] These measures conformed to the intentions expressed by Zia in his first speech: "I consider the introduction of an Islamic system as an essential *prerequisite* for the country".[11] Later, President Zia recalled that, after taking over, he had clearly defined priorities before his government of which the "introduction of an

Islamic order was on the top",[12] implying that the transfer of power to civilians was a secondary consideration.

Indeed, not only was it a secondary issue, it was an alternative which had to be prevented. However, it was awkward and difficult to deny the right of democratic government, especially in view of the fact that Pakistan had been embroiled in a mass movement, since March '77, for free democratic elections. Accordingly, the military devised a strategy whereby the political leaders were to be held responsible for the postponement of elections. *They were not fit to hold high office, while the army was seen to be willing, even anxious, to uphold democracy.*[13] This public subterfuge camouflaged more sinister concerns. The military were acutely aware that the most significant threat to its retention of power came from Bhutto. Not only had he played a critical role in mobilising mass protests to topple the military government of Ayub in '68, he had also, in the process, become the first political leader to have created a popular mass base in the Punjab. Worse still, there seemed to have been a revival in his popularity after his downfall. His rallies in Karachi and Lahore attracted awesome audiences. These were reasons enough for the junta to collectively support a strategy to eliminate Bhutto physically. Any further convincing they may have required was provided by Zia, for whom this grave issue had personal implications. It was most unlikely that Bhutto would have spared Zia's life were he to return to power. After all, he simply needed to invoke the '73 Constitution, which prescribed the death penalty for a *coup.*

Accordingly, a special investigation cell was established, by the martial law authorities, to probe into malpractices committed by the PPP leaders.[14] Within a month of the take-over, the Federal Investigation Agency (FIA) completed inquiries into the murder of an ex-member of the National Assembly, Dr Nazir Ahmed, and claimed that Bhutto and Punjab Governor Khar were responsible for it.[15] The FIA filed a further seven cases against Bhutto.[16] Five cases were registered in a special court.[17] Within two months of the take-over, the special public prosecutor claimed that the "state has got conclusive evidence of Mr. Bhutto's complicity in the murder of Kasuri's father".[18] It appears that Zia may have also considered the possibility of trying Bhutto for the murder of Ataullah Mengal's son.[19] Initially Zia announced that Bhutto would be tried for murder by a military court.[20] Later, the junta thought better of involving the military directly, considering it to be politically prudent to have the sentence announced through the judiciary.

The tirade against Bhutto produced a response, among some of the political leaders, which the army had hoped to elicit. While a number of them insisted that Bhutto's trial should be left to a civilian government,[21] others demanded that 'accountability' should precede the polls.[22] Former Civil Servants joined a government-orchestrated campaign to postpone elections until the process of purging the political structure of 'undesirable' elements was completed.²³ Ironically, the diatribe against Bhutto increased, rather than diminished, his popular support.The public response was one of sympathy for a deposed leader who was, seemingly, being persecuted by a regime whose motives were suspect. Senior opposition leaders admitted that they had little chance of electorally defeating Bhutto's PPP.²⁴ General Zia postponed the October polls ostensibly because 'public opinion so demanded'.²⁵

On 4 April 1979 Bhutto was hanged. The seven-member bench of the Supreme Court had upheld the verdict of the Punjab High Court. The split judgement was divided along ethnic lines.The four Punjabi judges, two of whom were permanent judges of the Punjab High Court, and had been made *ad hoc* judges of the Supreme Court, found Bhutto guilty of ordering the murder. The three non-Punjabi judges acquitted him. It was no coincidence that Zia's last promise of an election date was made a few days before the execution.²⁶ Throughout Bhutto's trial, the election bait had outwitted not only the parties opposed to Bhutto but also the leadership of the PPP. As long as Zia publicly adhered to the promise of elections, they were careful not to antagonise him into cancelling them. This ensured that they would not attempt jointly to mobilise a mass movement to demand elections and clemency for Bhutto. Shortly after the hanging, elections were cancelled and political parties banned.²⁷

The Second Phase: 1979-83

In contrast to the first period, the second phase was characterised by the explicit public disclosure of the army's intentions. "There is no possibility of an early end to the third and longest martial law . . . we have come to stay", declared Zia.²⁸ Elsewhere he warned "I will neither leave the scene nor allow anyone else to rise".²⁹ The overt affirmations of intent coincided with a fortuitous exogenous development. For the Zia regime, several beneficial consequences followed from the Soviet invasion of Afghanistan in December 1979. The significance of the gains was accentuated by the precarious position of the military dictatorship, as it entered the second stage of its rule. It faced both domestic and international revulsion and isolation in the wake of Bhutto's hanging and the introduction of savage punitive measures such as public flogging and amputation. Relations with the U.S. were severely strained. The U.S. had suspended all military supplies to Pakistan, in response to the latter's pursuit of a nuclear capability. The deterioration in relations was symbolised by the burning down of the American embassy in Islamabad, more or less with official approval. The economy was also under severe strain. The Aid to Pakistan Consortium had refused to reschedule debt servicing. In addition, private sector investment was being hindered by continuing political uncertainty.

Thus, the alteration in Pakistan's geopolitical significance for the West could not have come at a better time for Zia. Aware of his temporarily strong bargaining position, he was keen to extract a reasonable price for allegiance, rejecting Carter's initial aid offer as 'peanuts'. In the event, the regime derived numerous advantages. First, in exchange for providing a base for sustained guerrilla activity against the Soviet-Afghan Administration, Pakistan negotiated a $3.2 billion package of American military and economic loans. As part of the deal, the military regained access to sophisticated military hardware. Second, the U.S. subsequently ignored Pakistan's nuclear programme, enabling her to proceed without excessive hindrance or the adverse publicity and pressure exerted by the Carter regime. Third, the increased flow of foreign capital contributed towards a macro-economic revival. During the second phase, the average GNP growth rate rose to 6.2%. Increased international accommodation, due to American influence, also led to the rescheduling of Pakistan's debt. Fourth, central government support for Pathan Afghan groups has had a corrosive effect on parochial forces in the Frontier Province of Pakistan. The movement for provincial autonomy has been overwhelmed by events across the international border and the influx of three million refugees. These events have eroded support for Pushtunistan, a separate Pathan state merging Pakistan's frontier province with Afghanistan.[30] The Russian invasion had initially contributed towards a marked diminution in provincial hostility towards the Pakistani central government. Pathan integration within Pakistan has been aided by economic developments such as migration of Pathan workers to Karachi and the Gulf, as well as by the cementing power of an external threat. The Soviet Union, prior to the invasion, was considered to be a potential ally among those sections of the Pathans disenchanted with the centralisation of the Pakistani political structure. However, once Russian troops invaded a Pathan country, the desirability of such an allegiance was supplanted by open hostility and suspicion. We are referring here to the immediate impact of the Afghan crisis on the NWFP. After the initial shock, Pakistani Pathan attitudes towards Afghanistan and the refugees have changed. The 'costs' of the Afghan crisis are analysed in another section. Finally, the support of the U.S. and the Middle Eastern Muslim countries for Zia gave international legitimacy to military rule in Pakistan, on the ground of regional necessity. Thus, at a critical juncture, Zia was able to distract domestic attention to the threat posed by Afghanistan. Sudden international prestige also increased Zia's stature within the military.

Internally, Pakistan was being gradually transformed into a theocratic state with totalitarian connotations.[31] Theopneustic measures are discussed in the section on religion (see the following chapter, 'A Military Theocracy'). Here we shall concentrate on the relentless coercion of the second phase, designed to suffocate independent institutions and bludgeon public resistance.

The latter objective was achieved by empowering military courts with indiscriminate and comprehensive powers. Unmitigated by judicial checks, the arbitrary martial law that these courts dispensed was used as a conscious instrument of a policy to instil fear. These military courts operated in a framework of absolute power, defined by a decree empowering the government to detain any person speaking or acting against the regime.[32] Political activity itself was made liable to be punished by seven years' rigorous imprisonment and twenty lashes.[33] President Zia publicly expressed the necessity for such coercion: "Martial law *should* be based on fear".[34] Brigadier Malik was a more articulate exponent of the general philosophy: "Terror struck into the hearts of enemies is not only a means, it is the end in itself. Once a condition of terror into the opponent's heart is obtained, hardly anything is left to be achieved ... Terror is not a means of imposing decisions upon the enemy, it is *the decision* we wish to impose upon him".[35] In a similar vein the Federal Minister for Labour and Manpower, Lt. General Faiz Ali Chisti, advocated that the "enemies of Islam must be hunted down and killed like snakes even when they were offering prayers".[36] In this context it is significant that measures to inject terror, such as hand amputation and public lashings, were announced initially as martial law regulations *prior* to the Islamisation process.[37] Only later were they incorporated into the religious arena.

The conscious use of terror as an instrument of domestic policy was implemented through the uninterrupted use of martial law between 1977 and 1985. Unlike Ayub's military Government, President Zia's regime felt the necessity for retaining martial law for nearly a decade. The prolonged rule through decree was a sympton of the regime's isolation and insecurity. This ostracism was the result of the infinitely more complex task that Zia tackled than Ayub had faced, of justifying his *coup* and finding acceptance for military rule. The frequency with which the junta had to resort to arrests and lashings to quell resistance is indicated by the table below.

The drift towards a military-theocratic society required, in addition to the obedience imposed by fear, the elimination of independent sources of authority. Up to 1979, the judicial structure had been, to a limited extent, protecting citizens against arbitrary coercion by the state. For example, the Supreme Court judgement on Mrs N. Bhutto's petition[38] stressed the right of the court to review the legality of martial law instruments, and to issue writs of *habeas corpus*. Invoking these provisions, the high courts frequently quashed detention orders issued by the military and stayed flogging sentences meted out to political prisoners.[39] The Baluchistan High Court stayed the execution of death sentences passed by a special military court.[40] The same court declared that Zia's measures for curbing the judiciary were illegal.[41] Indeed, the Supreme Court judgement accepting the legitimacy of the '77 *coup* on the grounds of the 'doctrine of necessity'[42] stressed the con-

Table 1: *Punishments for political activity*

	Arrests
1978	1,327
1979	1,831
1980	612
1981	1,197
1982	4,212
1983	6,012
1984	2,100
1985	2,513

	Flogging sentences
Total	4,214

Sources: Newspaper reports and official statements in *Dawn, Jang* and *Morning News*. Reports of Amnesty International on Pakistan. Due to strict press censorship, the figures in the above table are likely to be gross underestimates.

ditional nature of the judicial vindication:[43] "The new regime represents not a new legal order but only a phase of constitutional deviation dictated by necessity ... the court would like to state in clear terms that it has found it possible to validate the extra-constitutional action of the chief martial law administrator not only for the reason that he stepped in to save the country at a time of a grave national crisis ... but also because of the solemn pledge given by him that the period of constitutional deviation shall be of as short a duration as possible and that during this period all his energies shall be directed towards creating conditions conducive to the holding of free and fair elections leading to the restoration of democratic rule in accordance to the dictates of the constitution".[44]

Measures taken against the judiciary were directed at removing two critical powers. First, the power of judicial review of the legality and constitutionality of executive decisions was removed. Second, the judiciary was deprived of the authority to protect civil rights. These were taken away through successive annual measures between 1979 and 1981. The Constitution (second amendment) order of '79 established a system of military courts, parallel to the civilian courts, to try offences under martial law. In the following year, the regime extended the jurisdiction of military tribunals, at the expense of the judiciary. The same order[45] barred the higher courts from reviewing the actions of the military courts. However, by far the most severe measures to curtail the jurisdiction of the law courts were contained in the Provisional Constitutional Order (PCO) of March 1980.[46]

The PCO terminated judicial scrutiny of any politically important executive action. It declared void all court decisions on the legality of martial law, thus rendering the 'doctrine of necessity' irrelevant. Judicial protection against arbitrary arrest was eliminated by the removal of the right of a prisoner to *habeas corpus*,[47] the first time this right had been annulled in Pakistan. Another notorious precedent was set by the military's removal of a judge.[48] This was made possible by a clause in the PCO whereby the executive was granted the power to remove judges directly, thus overriding the prevailing arrangement in which tenurial changes were made through the Supreme Judicial Council.[49] The PCO effectively extinguished the important constitutional role of the judiciary, forcing it to confine its attention to purely criminal and civil cases not involving issues of political substance.[50]

Control over the judiciary was inherent in the logic of extending military hegemony over all sectors of society. This process also entailed prohibiting access to information. That such restraints were part of the structure of military rule, was publicly acknowledged by President Zia: "Democracy means freedom of the press ... martial law its very negation".[51] Previous regimes have been content with curtailing the independence of the media, hence ensuring allegiance to the government. The Zia regime has in addition, sought a more vigorous role for the media as a catalyst in the transformation of Pakistan into a theocratic state. One indication of this role is the substantial increase in time devoted to religious issues on television. During the sixties, daily average television time devoted to religion was ten minutes.[52] Under Bhutto, fifteen minutes were taken up by religious commentaries.[53] Since the proclivity to Islamise society began in earnest, average daily exposure has risen to one hour and five minutes.[54] The increase in quantity incorporates a qualitative change. Previously, religious programmes were concerned mainly with commentaries and recitation of the Quran. Since 1977, television has become a zealous advocate of the practical application of a theocratic social and political order. For example, programmes on state-owned television have recommended, inter alia, the confinement of women within the house, more extensive use of the burqa and the acceptance, on religious grounds, of a dictator whose piety is sufficient to command obedience.[55]

The incorporation of the privately owned press into a supportive discourse for a theocratic order was preceded by brazen threats issued by President Zia: "I could close down all newspapers for five years and nobody would be in a position to raise a voice against it".[56] Thus, measures to muzzle the press came as no surprise. Pre-censorship of papers was introduced in 1978. Later, this was replaced by 'responsible journalism', a euphemism for self-censorship under strictly defined limits, with heavy penalties for violation. The press which refused to behave was confronted with the familiar paraphernalia of repression. Weeklies were banned and newspapers closed.[57] Arrested journalists[58] were given flogging sentences by military courts.⁵⁹ Trade unions were banned in radio and television.⁶⁰ Totalitarian control was extended by the government's decision to constitute committees, at the district level, to ensure that no newspaper published articles 'repugnant to the ideology of Pakistan'.⁶¹ Perhaps the most insidious aspect of military rule is that actions which are considered to be disgraceful for a civilian government are presented and justified as a necessary part of the genetic construction of martial law.

By 1983, President Zia had contained rival sources of authority, both outside and within the military. Political parties were banned and made impotent by the continuous incarceration of political leaders. The judiciary and the press had been marginalised. Zia had also withstood attempts from within the army to stage coups. These were led by officers who were cynical about Zia's use of Islam to retain power, and the consequent loss of the army's prestige in the country. On 17 March 1980 Zia confirmed that a *coup* had been attempted against him.⁶² In early 1983, forty middle-ranking officers were arrested for planning a conspiracy to oust and assassinate Zia.⁶³

Contrary to popular expectations, the Zia regime had survived both internal and external threats. However, survival had not enabled the regime to overcome its isolation. A wider social and institutional base was still proving to be elusive. Zia had hoped to create a mass base by eliciting support for the theocratic order being implemented by the government. Popular enthusiasm for this venture was not forthcoming. The inability to create a social base was of obvious concern to the junta. Zia's sensitivity to this failure was underlined by the lessons the military had learnt from Ayub's downfall. Zia stressed that lack of popular participation was a key factor in the sudden capitulation of the military regime in 1969.⁶⁴ To break the regime's isolation, and to overcome the insecurity it bred, Zia initiated a programme designed to widen participation while retaining the supremacy of the military. Thus, the third phase of Zia's rule began in 1983, with the announcement of a schedule for the induction of civilians into the administration through a restricted electoral process.

The Third Phase: 1983-?

Unless forced to do so by a debilitating setback, such as defeat in war and/or a grave economic crisis, military regimes in the Third World have not been prone to surrendering power. None the less, the military has to contend with popular demands for democratic rule. An inability to respond to such claims involves constant recourse to coercion, which aggravates the military's isolation and breeds fragility. Consequently, military governments endeavour to implement a political structure which seeks to absorb and channel popular participation. Two basic alternatives exist for the military to retain effective power, while it institutes the appearance of representative government. First, the military can transfer the administration to a civilian government, but maintain a mechanism through which its policy preferences are implemented. An example of a mechanism ensuring civilian compliance is a constitutional role for the military, whereby it accords to itself the right to intervene if the political framework deviates beyond prescribed limits.[65] The second alternative is for the junta leaders to resign their military rank and/or assimilate civilians into the government. The Zia regime finally chose the second course, although it had earlier contemplated the first option.[66]

On 12 August 1983, Zia announced details of a framework whereby civilians were to be inducted into the administration. Elections to the national and provincial assemblies were to be held by March '85. Although the mode of elections was not specified, President Zia had earlier indicated that political parties would be excluded from the electoral contest.[67] These elections were to be preceded by local elections, on a non-party basis, and followed by the lifting of martial law.

The plan evoked an immediate response from the political parties. Conscious that its success would ensure the prolongation of military rule behind the buffer of civilian personnel, the parties launched a national protest movement. Organised by the Movement for the Restoration of Democracy (MRD), an alliance of the major political parties, the agitation hoped to force Zia into transferring power through free, democratic elections. The movement, details of which are analysed later, proved to be an important landmark in the politics of Sind; but its failure lay in its inability to provoke a response in Punjab.

Having successfully withstood the MRD assault, the junta began to implement the proposed structure. Accordingly, local (municipal) elections were held, in 1984, on a non-party basis. More significant were the preparations for the National Assembly polls. The government began negotiations with the classes who could be expected to accommodate themselves to, and be easily incorporated within, the proposed structure. These elections provided an opportunity for the major landowning families and the large industrialists to gain direct access to the government and thus reap the benefits that success in such a contest would provide. The large landlords of the Punjab and NWFP assured the government of their support and participation. Even in Sind, substantial sections of the landowning class made their peace with the government. On the basis of the talks between Zia and the representatives of the dominant classes, the government was confident that the PPP would be split in Punjab and Sind. A government spokesman, commenting on Zia's negotiations, correctly predicted that "twenty-three out of thirty-two members of the national assembly elected in '77 from Sind on the PPP ticket will stand irrespective of the MRD boycott".[68]

Zia made it clear that the induction of civilians would not hinder the process of imposing a theocracy. "Elections will be held but they will be for the purpose of strengthening the ideological foundations of the nation ... Islam has no room for political parties or Western democracy. We will not imitate the Western system and the army will hand over power to an elected government by March '85 *on condition that the Islamisation process be continued*".[69] Indeed, the elections were preceded by a referendum on the Islamisation process. The result of the referendum, in which people were asked whether they supported the measures undertaken by the regime to Islamise Pakistan, was an embarrassment for the government. The turnout was approximately 10%.[70]

The referendum was followed by a muted campaign for elections to the National and Provincial Assemblies. Political parties were banned. Processions and demonstrations were illegal. Under these constraints, the campaigns by individual candidates resembled those of a municipal, rather than a national, election. Issues of economic, political and social substance, normally contained in manifestos, were not part of the electoral discourse. Indeed, a legislature was being elected through a campaign which did not permit political debate.

In the absence of policy prescriptions, the candidates mobilised support from traditional sources of authority and power. First, as local influences, landlords retained their ability to deliver votes to any aspirant for power. Most of the large landowning families of the Punjab either stood themselves or put up candidates of their choice.[71] The pattern was repeated in NWFP. There was a more limited participation by the tribal leaders and landlords of Baluchistan[72] and Sind.[73] The dominance of the propertied classes is reflected in the composition of the National Assembly, shown in Table 2 below.

Table 2: *Background of National Assembly Members. 1985.*

Landlords and tribal leaders	157
Businessmen	54
Urban professionals	18
Religious leaders	6
Other	3

Sources: *Dawn, Jang* and *Herald.*

The second determinant of voter mobilisation in the electoral campaign was clan or 'biradari' allegiance.[74] The evocation of personal, traditional and local ties replaced conventional mobilisation along party lines: "Tribe, clan, sect and ethnicity are factors that appear to be serving as frames of reference for the voters in today's electoral contest. Electioneering has, for the most part, focused on local issues which are more normally the concern of representatives of municipal bodies, rather than the legislature, who is expected to make laws for the entire country".[75]

The sheer magnitude of the turnout, 52%, was a surprise to all groups — the military, the candidates and the opposition. The critical factor responsible for such an impressive turnout, after a bland and timid campaign, appeared to be a perception among voters that the elections represented, however imperfectly, a decisive phase in the transfer of power to the civilians, i.e., success of this process would lead initially to the sharing of power among civilians and the military, and eventually to the withdrawal of the army to the barracks. Zia helped to create and sustain this impression, promising a withdrawal of martial law soon after the elections, as part of a phased departure of the military from politics.[76] Another factor responsible for the large turnout was the split within the political parties. Two of them, the Muslim League (Pagaro group) and the Jamaat-e-Islami, officially backed the elections. Since parties were banned they put up candidates as individuals, but made their party allegiance obvious. Indeed, workers of the component parties of the MRD, which officially boycotted the elections, openly defied directives and participated in the electoral process. The MRD's decision was based on the conviction that real power would not lie in the Assembly. Thus, it hoped that its boycott would lead to a poor turnout and deprive the Assembly of any claim to representation. The decision led to substantial defections. The most serious impact was on the PPP. The party expelled thirty-one members in Sind for standing in the elections.[77] In Punjab, sixty members were expelled.[78] Most of these were from landowning families, who had stood for the PPP in the '77 elections. Another important component of the MRD, Tehrik-e-Istaqlal, expelled nine members, who included an ex-MNA and a district chairman.[79]

The government did receive a few minor setbacks — five of the nine cabinet ministers were defeated, sixty-three members of the advisory council lost and the party most closely associated with the government, the Jamaat, suffered serious losses.[80] However, these reversals were sufficiently offset by the overall success of the exercise. First, the other major party to have supported and fought the election, the Muslim League, emerged as the major organised force. Pagaro-supported candidates won forty-two of the 237 National Assembly seats. PPP defectors won thirty-eight seats. Second, and most significant, the extent of the turnout had lent legitimacy to the exercise. The government had scored a decisive victory over the MRD, who had predicted a 10-15% turnout.

The perception that had resulted in the large turnout, namely that the civilianisation process marked a decisive stage towards democratic rule, was shattered almost immediately after the elections. Less than a week after the polls, President Zia announced his new constitution[81] without consultation with, or requiring ratification by, the legislature. The constitutional changes

Table 3: *Comparison of Electoral Turnout.*

	1970		1985
Average	57.96%	:	52.93%
Punjab	66.48	:	59.59
Sind	58.44	:	44.05
Baluchistan	39.04	:	35.13
NWFP	46.83	:	38.81

formalised the concentration of power in the hands of President Zia. Indeed, the constitution prescribed procedures for the arbitrary use of power by the President. Zia appropriated the authority to decide his powers and indemnity clauses ensured that he could not be challenged. For example, Article 48 gave the President the discretion to extend his powers without any effective constitutional safeguards limiting his capacity to accumulate personal authority. The arbiter of these powers is the President, whose decision on the matter "shall be final and the validity of anything done by the President shall not be called into question". In addition, the President's orders are deemed valid even if they violate fundamental rights.[82] The military's actions since 1977 were also declared to be 'constitutional'. A provision was introduced, whereby the assembly could not repeal or amend any of Zia's martial law orders since the *coup* without his approval.[83]

Whereas the above powers constrained the actions of the Assembly, safeguards were introduced in case it transgressed these limits. President Zia has the power to dissolve the National Assembly without the Prime Minister's consent.[84] In addition, he has been empowered to go above the National Assembly and call a referendum on any important national issue. His extensive powers of appointment include the posts of Prime Minister, ministers of state, provincial governors and the three armed forces chiefs. In brief, all critical functionaries of the state, including officials of the judiciary, are to be appointed by the President.

Constitutional sanction has also been given to the measures undertaken for the creation of a theocratic order.[85] Thus, the political and ideological parameters have been defined. Given this matrix, a degree of constrained choice has been given to the Assembly to formulate public policy. This role — of an assembly operating within broad policy outlines defined exogenously — is more akin to the functioning of assemblies in Eastern Europe rather than the task they perform in democratic systems.[86]

For the voters, the '85 elections provided an opportunity to exert pressure on the army to end martial law. As we have stressed above, the electorate and a number of candidates saw these elections as a concession towards an ultimate transfer of power to the civilians. For the military, on the other hand, the objectives of the exercise were different. The generals needed civilian participation to end their isolation. The legislature, elected on a non-party basis, was to provide the institutional buffer to absorb a degree of political activity. To concede a degree of power to civilians was the necessary price to pay for the army to retain long-term control over the state. Doubts about the permanent supremacy of the military within this structure were removed by the constitutional changes announced immediately after the elections. Thus a contradiction is inherent in this institutional structure. The powers that the military are willing to grant to the legislature make its position untenable. The large turnout is seen as a mandate to end military rule, albeit in stages. The phased nature of the process imposes constant pressure on the legislature to be seen to be acting with a degree of independence from the military and to take steps towards the gradual transfer of power to the civilians. The military has to curb this stridency, but if President Zia continues to be as brazen as suggested by his constitutional amendments, then the whole purpose of the exercise is nullified. Ironically, irritation at the impotence of the Assembly was expressed by one of the most ardent supporters of the military, the leader of the Muslim League, Pir Pagaro: "The National Assembly belongs to the President and is sub-sovereign while the President himself is super-sovereign".[87] If Parliament is seen to be a rubber stamp the popular legitimacy, which the military so urgently sought through the creation of this structure, will crumble.

Zia's institutional scheme for incorporating civilians has similar objectives to Ayub's 'basic democracies' (see part 1). First, such a framework creates a loyal network of beneficiaries who lend and canvass support for the regime. The civilians who are inducted into such a framework develop access to the state's resources. Such linkages can usually provide an effective mechanism for the accumulation of private fortunes. The second objective that the military hopes to achieve through such reforms is to contain the demand for democratic rule. The introduction of representative elements in government, in however limited a form, represents an important symbolic change. Although the military will retain effective power, Zia would be able to initiate changes which are cosmetic, yet have symbolic significance. One such measure would be the removal of martial law, which is inevitable. This would not alter the political power of the military, nor would it lead to the emergence of a strong judiciary. Stringent checks are likely to be imposed on the courts. However, the military will withdraw from a number of relatively petty judicial matters. These measures were partly necessitated by the widespread resentment against the brutality and corruption of summary military courts.

It is, however, critical to realise that institutional mechanisms, such as Zia's non-party legislature and Ayub's basic democracies, do *not* represent institutionalisation of a political community. By definition, institutionalisation refers to the creation of public bodies which are independent of

Strategies for Self-Preservation

Table 4:

Group:	Impact of developments on group between 1977-86	Relationship with Zia regime
A Vertical cleavages		
1. Traditional landed élite	1977 land reform rescinded. Members of this class prominent in local bodies elections of 1979 and 1983. The dominant class in the national party-less elections of 1985. Successfully aborted the recommendations for the introduction of an agricultural income tax in 1986.	Strong supporters of Zia regime.
2. Industrialists	A number of industries denationalised. Government economic policy aimed at reviving private sector 'confidence' and investment. Muted investment response from private sector, partly due to political uncertainty.	Strong support for current regime, based partly on fear that the alternative is the PPP.
3. Urban shopkeepers/traders	Beneficiaries of booming economy, particularly the multiplier effects of Gulf remittances.	By and large content with developments under present regime. Section of this class are strong supporters of Islamisation.
4. Urban working class	Substantial working-class migration to the Middle East. Rise in real wages of workers in organised sector of industry. Union activity banned.	Migration has led to working-class indifference to opposition movements to topple government.
5. Peasants	Government rhetoric or reforms no longer concerned with distributional issues. Reassertion of the dominance of the traditional élite.	Opposition to government is largely ineffective since it is isolated and difficult to mobilise. In Sind, however, substantial peasant involvement in nationalist movement.

131

Table 4: — *continued.*

Group:	Impact of developments on group between 1977-86	Relationship with Zia regime
6. Urban professionals (lawyers, journalists etc.)	Judiciary marginalised and controlled. Military courts have exercised supreme authority. Islamic legal practices introduced. Journalists under several constraints. Some flogged.	Sections of this group have been vocal opponents of the regime.
B Horizontal cleavages		
1. Sunni clerics	Greater power, authority and influence acquired by religious functionaries. Clerics involved with policy making for the first time, as members of Shariat courts and Islamic Ideology Council.	Strong allies of Islamisation programme, particularly the Jamaat-e-Islami.
2. Ahmedis	Increased persecution of Ahmedi sect, formalised in Ordinance XX (26.4.1986) which prescribes prison sentences for Ahmedi individuals who refer to themselves as Muslims, or who antagonise other Muslims by their behaviour. (Ahmedis were declared to be a non-Muslim sect by the PPP government in 1976.) There are nearly 3.5 million Ahmedis in Pakistan.	Facing increased persecution, Ahmedis have retained a low profile, fearing violent reaction.
3. Shias	Approximately 20% of Pakistan's population are Shia Muslims. Due to doctrinal differences with the Sunni sect, Shias have strongly opposed Zia's Islamisation programme. Increase in Shia-Sunni clashes.	Vehement protests against Islamisation, which they see as imposition of Sunni interpretation of Islamic state. Opposition has been negative, i.e., restricted to removing Shias from fold of Islamisation, rather than against the regime *per se*.

Table 4: — *continued.*

Group:	Impact of developments on group between 1977-86	Relationship with Zia regime
4. Students	Important political category in previous mass mobilisation, students have been cowed by a series of repressive measures. Tight government control over campuses, exercised through Jamiat-e-Tulaba — the student wing of the right wing religious cadre party, Jamaat-e-Islami. 1981 university ordinance increased government control over appointments. MLR 51 used to dismiss teachers. Student unions banned in 1984.	Subdued by tight, coercive control by right wing groups. Not able to mobilise collectively. Sporadic opposition, controlled by swift and tough government action.
5. Women	Constitutional changes detrimental to women include Law of Evidence which stipulates that the testimony of two women is equal to one man's on certain cases.	Formation of urban women's groups such as WAF. Sustained, organised vocal opposition to regime by these urban-based pressure groups.

particular individuals. The structures mentioned above do not outlive the incumbent. They are personalised and their tenure tends to expire with the removal of the leader. However complex the institutional-'democratic' façade, the structure is firmly based on personal rule. What is almost certain is that Zia's departure will be accompanied by a renewal of the elusive quest for a stable political structure.

The three phases of the Zia regime, which we have briefly outlined above, have witnessed a marked departure of state policy from previous patterns. In particular, the change relates to the implementation, by the state, of a theocracy. We now turn to a more detailed analysis of the process. This is followed by examinations of economic policy and the government's measures relating to the troubled intra-provincial relations. An overview of the regime's relationship with various sectors of society, is provided in Table 4 on page 131-3.

Footnotes:

1. Bhutto's fears of a *coup* are documented in letters contained in the White Paper on '77 elections. (Publication details of all articles and books quoted in the text are given in the bibliography.)
2. Indeed, Zia acknowledged that Bhutto had done "everything he could" to accommodate the opposition. See his statement in *Dawn*, 10.7.77.
3. This was subsequently confirmed by one of the senior members of the PNA's negotiating team. See Professor Ghafoor's statement in *Dawn*, 25.11.81.
4. A copy of this letter is reproduced in Asghar Khan: *Generals in Politics*, p. 89. Zia referred to this letter in an interview with *South* in January 1985.
5. See Zia's statement in *Dawn*, 7.7.77.
6. ibid.
7. Work on the fifth five-year plan (1978-83) began a few months after the *coup*. Confirmed by Civil Servants in interviews with the author.
8. Zia also stressed this change in strategy. See his statement in *Jang*, 2.9.77.
9. Strictly speaking, this was a reconstitution of the moribund council.
10. *Dawn*, 2.9.77.
11. *Morning News*, 6.7.77.

12 *Dawn*, 11.2.78. Press interviews also reflected concern over the army's real intentions. The interviewer of *Keyan*, an Iranian journal, suggested to Zia that measures taken by him indicate that the regime is preparing for a long stay. See *Keyan*, 10.4.78. Similarly, Zia's assurance that he will transfer power and go back to soldiering were met with cynicism by *Newsweek*: "That's what Ayub said and he held on to power for 11 years". See *Newsweek*, 14.7.77.
13 See, for example, Zia's speech in *Dawn*, 16.8.77.
14 See reports in *Dawn*, 23.7.77 and 4.8.77.
15 For a report of the investigation see *Dawn*, 16.8.77.
16 On charges which included corruption, malpractices and misuse of state instruments.
17 On 3.2.78.
18 Barrister M. Anwar's statement in the *Pakistan Times*, 11.9.77. Evidence was based on the confession of Mahmud Masud, director of the para-military FSF. Masud was arrested the day after the *coup* and subsequently turned state approver.
19 In Zia's first meeting with Mengal he indicated that "persons responsible" would be tried. However, once the Kasuri case started, Zia made no further reference to the Mengal murder. Interview of author with A. Mengal, London 1985.
20 *Jang*, 18.9.77.
21 These included PDP chief Nasrullah Khan, JUI leader Mufti Mahmud and PNP's Bizenjo. See *Pakistan Times*, 1.9.77.
22 Prominent among them were Tehrik chief Asghar Khan, NAP leaders Wali Khan and Mazari, as well as Muslim League leader Pir Pagaro. See *Jang*, 31.8.77.
23 Four ex-judges "publicly demanded Zia to try Bhutto before the poll", *Pakistan Times*, 31.8.77. Retired General Gul Hasan also demanded action against Bhutto, *Jang*, 28.8.77.
24 See, for example, Asghar Khan's admission in *Morning News*, 5.1.78.
25 Zia had noted that "public opinion seemed to be against October polls" in his press conference on 1.9.77.
26 For a chronology of broken promises on the election issue see Kamal, K. L.: *Pakistan, the Garrison State*. pp. 86-7; Wolf-Phillips, L: *Constitutional Legitimacy*. pp. 30-5.
27 Zia banned political activity on the day he took over, for a "cooling off" period. This ensured that the momentum of the '77 mass movement was broken.
28 Interview with *Ittefaq* (Bangladesh), April 1982.
29 Quoted in the Quarterly Report on Pakistan, Economist Intelligence Unit, second quarter, 1982, p. 4.

30 For details see chapter on provincial relations.
31 For a definition of totalitarianism see chapter on ideology.
32 Martial Law Regulation issued on 22.7.77.
33 Martial Law Regulation issued on 1.3.78.
34 Interview with BBC television, 4 April 1978.
35 Zia wrote a foreword to the book from which this quotation is taken. Brigadier S. K. Malik: *The Quranic Concept of War.* p. 30.
36 *Morning News,* Karachi. 20.1.80. Chisti, like Zia, is ideologically close to the religious cadre party, Jamaat-e-Islami.
37 On 10 July 1977, just five days after the *coup*, military courts were set up. Simultaneously, a martial law regulation instituted punishments of hand amputation, public lashing and death by hanging.
38 Pakistan Legal Decisions, 10.11.77. Supreme Court judgement on Mrs Bhutto's petition.
39 For an account of judicial resistance to martial law orders see Amnesty's report on Pakistan, 1982.
40 In the farcical trial of A. H. Baluch, the name of the victim was changed twice, because it was discovered that the alleged murder victim was still alive.
41 *Dawn*, 3.3.80.
42 The doctrine of necessity is derived from Bracton's maxim that necessity confers legality on what would otherwise be illegal, because the security of the state and the safety of the people is the supreme purpose of law.
43 Supreme Court judgement, 10.11.77.
44 For further discussion of how Kelsen's doctrine relating to constitutional breakdown has been (mis) used, see L. Wolf-Phillips: *Constitutional Legitimacy* — a study of the doctrine of necessity.
45 Shortly after the issuance of this order, over a hundred military courts started functioning.
46 Presidential Order 1 (1980).
47 Writ requiring a person to be brought before a judge or into court, especially to investigate the legality of his restraint.
48 Amnesty International Report, op cit.
49 In March '80, the military replaced the Chief Justice of the Lahore High Court, prior to the court's judgement of the illegality of military rule.
50 Those who wish to pursue the constitutional significance of these changes are referred to J. D. Casper. "The Supreme Court and National Policy Making" *APSR*, March, 1976. For a view on the Soviet system see H. J. Berman: *Justice in the USSR.* New York, 1963.

51 *Dawn*, 12.7.77.
52 Calculated from a sample of television transmissions. Sample of 300 listings.
53 Calculated from a random sample of 300 listings between 1972 and 1977.
54 Random sample of 300 daily transmission listings between 1978 and 1984.
55 The government was forced to discontinue a series by Dr Israr, which recommended that women should leave their jobs and return to the house.
56 Zia's threat issued to the press on 21 March 1982.
57 Five dailies were banned in 1979. These included the PPP's *Musawat* and two dailies from Quetta and Sadaqat. Declaration of the Daily *Hayat*, Lahore was annulled in March '78. *Daily Sun* closed down after its editor and leading journalists were all arrested.
58 Approximately 150 journalists were arrested in May 1978.
59 In 1978, a summary military court sentenced the editor and a journalist of the *Sun* to ten lashes and a year's rigorous imprisonment for printing an article critical of the military. In May '79, six newsmen were awarded flogging sentences.
60 Trade unions were banned on television and radio in April 1978.
61 *Dawn*, 15.4.84.
62 *Asian Recorder*, 21.4.80.
63 EIU report on Pakistan, 2, 1984. For another account see S. Cohen: *The Pakistan Army*, p. 255, where it is alleged that senior generals informed Zia of the plot.
64 Zia has referred to this shortcoming several times. See, for example, *Pakistan Times* 3.5.85.
65 Turkey is, of course, one such example.
66 In 1980-81, Zia made several references to the need for guaranteeing a constitutional role for the army to intervene in moments such as a grave national crisis. What constituted a crisis permitting subsequent intervention was to be decided by the military.
67 In 1982, Zia had indicated that future polls would be held on a non-party basis. See *Pakistan Times*, 6.5.82.
68 FEER, 29.11.84.
69 FEER. YB, 1985.
70 According to reports by both the BBC and the *Daily Muslim*, Rawalpindi. The first edition of the *Muslim* after the referendum reported a 10% turnout. The issue was withdrawn from public circulation by the government.

71 For details see constituency reports in Pakistani newspapers between December '84 and March '85. Large landlords standing in the Punjab included PPP defectors such as Sadiq Hussain Qureshi (Punjab Governor under PPP), ex-MNA Taj Ahmed Noon and ex-MPA Ashiq Gardezi.
72 In Baluchistan, candidates were put up mainly by the Bugti, Ahmedzai and Jamali tribes as well as the Jogezai in Pushto-speaking areas. Notable candidates included Ahmed Nawaz Bugti, Finance Minister in NAP-JUI Government; Salim Bugti, son of ex-Governor Akbar Bugti; S. K. Marri, nephew of Baluch leader K. B. Marri.
72 In Sind, the landlords were split among those who conformed to the MRD boycott and others who chose to accommodate themselves to the proposed structure.
74 Thus, for example, Kashmiri, Shaikh and Moghal biradaris formed a coalition in Gujranwala. In Tando Allahyar, the Qaimkhani biradari supported a retired major against Federal Minister Ali Ahmed Talpur. The latter lost.
75 Editorial in *Dawn*, 25.2.85.
76 In his final television broadcast before the elections, Zia laid considerable emphasis on the gradual withdrawal of military rule.
77 Sixteen were expelled on 30.1.85; fifteen on 13.2.85.
78 *Morning News*, 3.2.85.
79 District Chairman of Sialkot. See *Pakistan Times*, 31.1.85. These expulsions could well lead to a radicalisation of opinion within political parties along regional and class lines. Large land-owning groups in Punjab have left the political parties and joined the National Assembly. This could well lead to the emergence of a leadership with a different class background. Sindhi landlords are split. Those who have remained with the parties are becoming strident regionalists. Within Baluchistan, the major political figures abstained from the electoral process.
80 Only nine of its fifty candidates won.
81 'Revival of the Constitution of 1973 Order, 1985'. These constitutional changes were introduced as amendments to the '73 Constitution, which was not abrogated. In practice, the '85 amendments defined a new constitution in which a non-elective presidential system was introduced.
82 Amendment to Article 8 of the '73 Constitution.
83 Amendment to Article 270a of the '73 Constitution.
84 Although the President does not have the power to veto bills emanating in the National Assembly, he can delay the bill for 45 days — time enough to exercise the kind of gentle executive

persuasion which was so effective in changing the minds of legislators in the fifties.
85 The Objectives Resolution of 1949 (see part 1, chapter 1) has been moved from the preamble of the '73 Constitution into the main part of the '85 Constitution. More significant is a shift in practical application. Previous regimes have paid lip service to the Objectives Resolution. Only since Zia's commitment to a theocracy has there been a will to implement its provisions.
86 See, for example, G. Ionescu: *The Politics of the European Communist States.* pp. 20-50.
87 *Dawn*, 15.4.85.

Chapter Two

A Military Theocracy

In many respects, the military's repressive control of society, between 1977 and 1985, resembles that of successive authoritarian governments which have ruled Pakistan. None the less, the Zia period has contained a qualitative change in the relationship between state and society. The critical difference related to the ideological sphere. In 1977, the government unilaterally initiated a process referred to as Islamisation. In effect, it represented an attempt to convert Pakistan into a theocratic society. Consequently, the period between 1977 and 1984 was traumatic, even by Pakistan's standards. During this phase Pakistan's political system began to exhibit characteristics commonly associated with totalitarian regimes. The fundamentalist Islamic social code, as defined by the military, consisted of elements central to a totalitarian state:[1]

(i) The articulation of a comprehensive ideology which provides the *raison d'être* for a particular social structure. The state is responsible for the practical implementation of this ideology. Opposition to the officially endorsed belief system is not permitted.

(ii) The state has a monopoly over communications. It has complete control over the flow of information to the public. All sources of information are censored.

(iii) Power is concentrated in the central government. The centre is usually dominated by a chief executive with dictatorial powers.

(iv) Extensive and arbitrary powers are used by the government to enforce obedience. The extent to which the use of fear is required may vary from period to period. But powerful mechanisms exist, such as martial law, as deterrents to active political opposition.

The *combined* effect of the above characteristics is to enable the state to exercise exhaustive control over all sectors of society. In the last chapter, we have noted the use of terror as an instrument of state policy to control dissent, the use of the media as an agency of religious indoctrination and the accumulation of supreme arbitrary power in the hands of President Zia. In this section we shall concentrate on the critical component of totalitarian rule — the articulation of a monolithic ideological framework. In Pakistan, an overall view of the social formation has been provided by a theocratic discourse. In the fundamentalist perspective, there is a binding unity between the idea of an Islamic state and the creation of an Islamic order. An Islamic state consists of institutions which implement a social code of life, i.e. an Islamic order.[2] These rules of human conduct extend to all spheres of social interaction. A comprehensive moral code permeates social, political and economic life.

Zia has invoked divine guidance for the implementation of an Islamic society: "I have a mission, given by God, to bring Islamic order to Pakistan".[3] The mission requires the creation of a social system "in which all sectors of life including administration, judiciary, banking, trade, education, agriculture, industry and foreign affairs are regulated in accordance with Islamic principles".[4] The penetration of religion into all sectors of society is justified by the notion that "sovereignty belongs to Allah".[5] The practical application of the sovereignty of God implies that the state shall implement a social order based on His injunctions. The divine law has been transmitted through two sources, the Quran and the Sunnah. The latter refers to the conduct of the prophet Mohammad which clarifies, explains and exemplifies the teachings of the Quran. It follows that a Muslim state cannot resort to totally independent legislation. Nor can it modify laws that God has explicitly laid down in the Quran. However, this does not imply that Islam totally excludes human legislation. It only limits its scope.[6] Where the Quran and Sunnah provide clear-cut injunctions, nothing can be changed it follows that independent legislation can only be resorted to in areas where the Sharia[7] is silent.

Zia's conception of an Islamic state is similar to that of the founder of the religious cadre party, the Jamaat-e-Islami, A. A. Maududi. Indeed, measures taken by the Zia regime are identical to those advocated by Maududi.[8] His orthodox conception of an Islamic state is that of an all-powerful, monolithic, public institution upholding a coherent religious ideology. The full weight of state power must ensure that all aspects of the social order reflect the character of an Islamic polity.[9]

Religious measures implemented by the Zia regime to "mould every aspect of life and activity in consonance with its moral norms"[10] can be divided into three spheres: social, political and economic.

In the social domain, individual and group behaviour has been controlled through the enforcement of barbaric measures derived from the seventh-century Arabic penal code. Primitive — but legal — punishments include the amputation of wrists and ankles for theft,[11] stoning to death for adultery[12] and eighty lashes for drinking alcohol.[13] However, the most retrogressive aspect of reverting to a seventh-century social code has been the legislation of an inferior status for women. In 1984, a law was passed whereby the evidence of two women was equivalent to that of one man in certain legal situations.[14] According to the law of Qisas and Diyat, the right to claim retribution (Qisas) or compensation (Diyat) is sanctioned by traditional Islamic practice. A woman's evidence in case of retribution is only half that of a Muslim man. In addition, a quantification of inferior status for women is contained in the provision that the amount of compensation payable for a murdered woman is half that payable for a murdered man.[15]

The '73 Constitution contained provisions against sexual discrimination.[16] Although the extent to which such legal sanctions achieved anything concrete is debatable, it is none the less true that the early seventies was a period which witnessed formal advances in the status of women. By contrast, the '84 legislation is, perhaps, the only instance in the contemporary world where the state has initiated reforms which have taken away women's constitutional rights. The sexually repressive spirit embodied in this law has been prominent in other aspects of Zia's rule. The President has publicly stated that a woman cannot be the Prime Minister.[17] This view echoed the recommendations of the government-appointed Ansari Commission, which declared that a woman cannot be a head of state. The Commission also recommended that a woman should have her husband's permission to participate in the legislature, and that a woman should be at least fifty years old before standing for the Assembly.[18]

The overt association of the state with institutionalised male domination has been justified by recourse to the Quran's religious authority: "Men are in charge of women because Allah has made one superior to the other . . . good women are the obedient" (4;34). A critical component of the fundamentalist conception of a theocratic society consists of enforcing this superiority. Thus a process of cultural retardation, generated by a strident assertion of male domination, has transformed the whole atmosphere. For example, in 1978, female dancing on television was prohibited on the grounds that such 'erotic practices' are part of Hindu, not Muslim, culture.[19] An unusual insight into the development process was provided by the Broadcasting Minister, Zafar-ul-Haq: "Pakistan will never be a truly independent and sovereign country so long as its people remain such ardent fans of music".[20] In 1981, a women's athletics team was not permitted to participate in Tokyo, because they would be performing before men.[21] In the following year, an official circular ordered female doctors to wear chaddars, since their long white coats were not 'sufficiently modest'.[22]

The totalitarian implications of a military theocracy were evident in a sinister proposal announced, ironically, in 1984. In his sermon to the nation on 14 August, President Zia launched a national campaign for the widespread adoption of the practice of five daily prayers. The critical aspect of the Nizam-e-salat campaign is the entailed direct physical intervention of the state to exhort compliance to a religious code of behaviour. This is being done through the appointment of 100,000 prayer wardens for village and urban localities.[23] The monitoring of religious activity by official appointees represents a further encroachment of the state into areas considered private by previous regimes.

Religious measures in the political domain have had the objective of defining an institutional structure compatible with the supremacy of the military. First, free democratic elections were attacked as components of a secular political order. Democracy is based on majority opinion which is translated, through the concept of popular sovereignty, into powers of legislation conferred on the elected representatives. The specific content of majority opinion is not defined. It was claimed that the democratic procedure was, therefore, in contradiction with a theocratic order where legislation and government are constrained by divine law. Elections do have a place in the political order defined by fundamentalist theoreticians such as Maududi.[24] But their role is similar to that of elections in Eastern Europe. People chose candidates considered to be, in theory at least, the most suitable available to implement an Islamic order.

Such a conception could accommodate the retention of power by the military, since piety, not representation, became the critical qualification. Thus, in a television address a few months after Bhutto's execution, Zia claimed that elections on the basis of adult franchise were un-Islamic.[25] The President announced that he wanted to "introduce Islam in Pakistan in the true sense. Our present political edifice is based on the secular democratic system of the West which has no place in Islam . . . In Islam there is no place for Western-type elections".[26] Illiteracy was a further impediment: "Elections are not the remedy for Pakistan today . . . 75% of the people of Pakistan are illiterate. How do you expect illiterates to decide for themselves what is good and what is bad for them?"[27]

A corollary to the prohibition on 'secular' democratic elections was the ban on political parties. Again, the exclusion of parties was justified through an interpretation of a theocracy which served the immediate interests of the army. The cynical use of religion as an apologia for the denial of civilian rule, was echoed in Zia's reiteration of Maududi's opposition to parties.[28] The formation of parties for the legislature in an Islamic state was prohibited on the grounds that they promote sectarian prejudices and weaken the Muslim community. Zia's modification of Maududi's doctrine lay in the replacement of religious leaders by a 'pious' military General as wielder of supreme authority.[29]

Not surprisingly, the third component of the theocratic framework defined by President Zia consisted of an extremely powerful president. As early as September 1977, Zia indicated that the presidential system was most suitable for Pakistan, since it was very close to the Islamic concept of Amir.[30] Subsequently, he put forward the somewhat linear argument that "Muslims believed in one God, one prophet and one book and their mentality is such that they should be ruled by one man".[31] The pervasive and expansive powers of a dictatorial head of government were formalised in the '85 Constitutional Amendments.[32]

Collectively, the above measures provide a framework for a centralised, monolithic state to implement a theocratic order under military supremacy. The conception of the state as a tool for realising the details of an overall conception of society has certain similarities, ironically, with communism.[33] Therein, the monopoly of the communist party is justified on grounds that political parties are a reflection of the class struggle and, since the state embodies the institutional framework of a classless communist society, there is no need for parties. Similarly, the Islamic state, in the fundamentalist conception, is seen as the sole agent for creating a comprehensive social order. As noted above, similarities also exist in electoral procedures; candidates can stand as individuals without representing an independent programme of legislation since the broad contours of an Islamic social order are already determined. It was under such a framework that non-party polls were held in March '85.

Islamisation of society has extended beyond the social and political domain to embrace the economic sphere. Measures to incorporate religious injunctions, which applied to the economic structure of seventh-century Arabia, have run into obvious contradictions in the context of a modern economy. This is nowhere more evident than in the attempt to abolish interest. The measures to introduce Islamic banking, discussed below, entail inventing innovative legal fictions whereby interest is avoided through technicalities or choice of terminology. Instead of charging interest the banks adopted the practice of making a 'service charge'. A brief digression into the historical origins of the controversy will provide an insight into why the irrational and dogmatic attempt to eliminate interest is so damaging for a modern private economy.

The idea of economic activity as administration of resources on behalf of God is a central feature of Muslim, Jewish and Christian thought.[34] The early chapters of the Bible embody this approach to economic life.[35] Similarly, within Islam economic resources belonged ultimately to God and economic activity was an aspect of the exercise of the stewardship of these resources extended to man. These religious conceptions of economic activity were conducted in a paradigm originating in Greek philosophy.[36] By and large Greek philosophers did not conceive of the economy as a group of relationships which could be considered apart from other forms of social interaction.[37] For both Aristotle and Plato economics was a branch of ethics, hence economic analysis was undertaken as part of the investigation of moral and political issues.[38] Their main concern was to formulate a framework of economic organisation which would sustain a stable social order. Political chaos could better be averted without the disruptive effects of excessively rapid economic growth.[39] The primary concern for a stable social order led Plato to express a general opposition to the practice of interest payment on loans. He belived that the existence of obligations to pay interest could be a major threat to the maintainance of peace and social solidarity in society. This belief was based on the occurrence of military conflict in the Greek city states, due to defaults on debt.[40] Aristotle opposed interest, since he saw money's role as that of facilitating exchange. To use it for another purpose was a distortion of its character as a social institution. Similar restrictions on interest were placed by religions. The Jews permitted interest on trade with foreigners but forbade interest charges to fellow countrymen.[41] St. Thomas's reformulation of the doctrine of usury provided the intellectual foundations with which the canonists and theologians supported the prohibition of interest. The Quran explicitly and emphatically prohibits *riba* (usury).[42]

In keeping with religious injunctions, the theocratisation of Pakistani society has extended into the credit markets, with a view to eliminating interest. A profit and loss sharing system (PLS) has been introduced for deposit accounts. A fixed interest is not paid on these deposits. The bank's profits and, in theory, losses are shared with the depositor. Not surprisingly, the nationalised banks have shown a 1% higher rate of return on PLS accounts compared with interest-bearing deposits.[43] Another set of Islamic banking measures relates to corporate financing. A syndicate of major banks, headed by the Investment Corporation of Pakistan, was set up to lend working capital without interest, instead of debentures, to meet corporate financing needs. This mode of lending is known as Musharaka (partnership) loans. Banks have approached the scheme with extreme caution, restricting Musharaka deals to a handful of well-established firms with healthy profit records.[44] A second type of partnership, introduced in 1982, is the Mudaraba. Private investors can participate in Mudaraba loans to corporations by buying shares, known as participation term certificates. Until 1985, the PLS and interest-bearing accounts were co-existing. By June of that year, however, interest was phased out.

The measures relating to interest are symptomatic of how fundamentalist dogma has determined public policy in recent years. The Quran's concern is with the social damage and exploitation through usury. The role of interest in a modern economy, however, differs fundamentally from that of usury. An economy based on private ownership has to undergo a complex intermediary process, through which funds are channelled into productive sectors. Scarcity of capital and its efficient allocation necessitate a price of capital, whatever this price is called. Interest is, of course, the price of capital. It is the rental value of using money. Obviously, in particular circumstances, such as consumption loans to peasants on exorbitant rates of interest, repayment burdens can have adverse social effects. There would be no harm in eliminating usury by reforms in those capital markets which make loans more easily available to peasants. Other complementary reforms to raise peasant incomes would, of course, be necessary. But to eliminate interest in a growing inflationary capitalist economy is simply not possible. We have already mentioned the necessity for pricing capital. There is also the contemporary problem of inflation, which did not exist as a sustained phenomenon in seventh-century Arabia. Any lender in an inflationary economy must be guaranteed a nominal rate of interest, just to preserve the value of the deposit. Thus, at the very least, the dogma-induced financial reforms produce complicated and inefficient subterfuges to call interest by another name. A confused financial system has been created, which undergoes complex distortions to charge interest to borrowers and to pay it to lenders through ideologically sound nomenclature.

There are more damaging effects on the economy than mere obfuscation. The most important has been the adverse effect on domestic savings. Pakistan saves 4.5% of its GDP. This compares with 20% for India and 17% for Sri Lanka. The uncertainty associated with returns under the Islamisation measures has encouraged the growth of the black economy. The lack of confidence in the financial system also restricted the ability of the government to raise domestic resources[45] which led, as we shall see in the chapter on the economy, to the virtual abandonment of both the five-year plans. In addition, there are no safety provisions in the Islamised financial system against panic withdrawals by depositors, if they have to share losses with a bank — perfectly plausible within the lending structure of profit and loss accounts.

Other measures to Islamise the economy are related to the fiscal sphere. Conceptually steps taken in this area are similar to welfare provisions.[46] From 1982, 2.5% is levied annually on all savings accounts. Zakat, as this tax is called, is then supposed to be used for welfare purposes. The imposition of this tax led to sectarian controversy. The substantial Shia minority, 20% of the population, refused to pay it, since it considers this tax to be voluntary. After mass demonstrations by the Shias in Islamabad, they were exempted from the tax. The amount collected from Zakat, on account of both the exemption to Shias and the low religious stipulation of 2.5%, is far too small to have any serious redistributive impact. In 1981-82, the total Zakat collection was equal to 0.2% of the GNP.[47] Zakat, which is levied on wealth including savings, also does not provide the right incentives to increase domestic resources. Apart from Zakat, the other Islamic tax to be introduced was Ushr, an agricultural tax levied from the '83 rabi crop.

We have outlined above the broad contours of how a fundamentalist religious ideology has provided the basis for state intervention in the economic, political and social spheres. We shall now examine why the military has embarked on this course and how it was possible that a hitherto secular élite participated in the religious transformation of society.

The contrast in ideological orientation of the military under Zia and Ayub could hardly have been more marked. The Ayub regime dropped the title of Islamic Republic from the '62 constitution, to emphasise the secular nature of the state. The military and the bureaucracy in command of the state apparatus saw their role as a modernising élite of a backward and traditional society. To them, religion and, in particular, religious leaders, represented symbols of the obstacles to development and modernisation. Less than a decade after Ayub's fall, the military élite wrapped itself in religion.

The religious discourse adopted was a response to two aspects of the political crisis engendered by the military intervention. Not only had Zia replaced an elected government, but he was also the leader of an army tarnished by the humiliations of 1971. At one level, therefore, the creation of a theocracy was an attempt to fill the political vacuum created by Zia's renegation on his promise to hold elections. Islamisation provided an objective for utilising state power, which the military had refused to transfer to civilians. At another level, the creation of a theocracy was a delayed response to 1971. Events in that year had eroded confidence in the validity of the original demand for Pakistan. It was evident that religion alone did not provide a sufficient basis for a nation-state, contrary to the claims of the two-nation theory.[48] Islamisation implicitly provided an explanation for the failure of national integration. The failure was ascribed to the abandonment of religion by Zia's military predecessors. Such a version avoided confrontation with unpleasant reminders of the real cause — the denial of democratic government and, consequently, majority rule to the Bengalis on account of Punjabi-dominated military supremacy.

The nature of the military élite's response to the political crisis was influenced by the post-'71 emergence of religiously-oriented leaders. Zia, backed by other East Punjabi generals with a religious background such as Chisti and Arif, turned to a paradigm with which he was familiar. He utilised his deeply religious upbringing to make the necessary alterations in the institutional structure. The military developed an interpretation of a theocratic order, within which their retention of power could be justified. Emphasis was placed on outlining the objectives of a religious state. Since the primary goal of the state became the creation of a theocracy, piety and commitment to religion acquired critical significance. Since Zia could legitimately claim such religious zeal, the metamorphosis of society could, simultaneously, serve the function of self-preservation. In addition, elections, in which manifestos did not necessarily conform to the idea of a theocracy, were not only unnecessary but harmful, since they would distract attention from the task for which Pakistan was created.

The possibility for implementation of a theocracy was inherent in the logic of Pakistan, even though its leaders had always refuted such implications. Zia invoked the origins of Pakistan as providers of historical legitimacy for the creation of a theocracy. Indeed, the separation of religion and politics had led, it was claimed, to the country's dismemberment. To prevent such a recurrence the army adopted the mantle of a vanguard for a theocracy. Religion was the panacea; "had the Islamic system been introduced at the appropriate time all basic necessities of every citizen would have been met easily", proclaimed Zia.[49] The role of a religious vanguard sought to provide the military with the sense of moral duty and purpose which it had lost after 1971. Simultaneously, it provided an explanation, to themselves, of the causes of past failures of military rule. In the early years of the junta, there were grave doubts within the military, especially among junior officers, about the wisdom of Bhutto's execution and the loss of credibility and respect for the army, as Zia broke successive promises to hold elections.[50] Indeed Zia's initial speeches had stressed the necessity for the military to abstain from politics as this would cause 'irreparable damage to the institution'.[51] Thus, the pervasive self-doubt within the military, as the generals retained power, was quelled by recourse to religion. Addressing graduates at the officers' training academy at Kakul, Zia emphasised their role as 'soldiers of Islam' who are — "guardians of *ideological* as well as geographical frontiers".[52] The idea of a military-theocratic state has a degree of support among those junior officers who were inducted in large numbers from lower middle-class households after the '65 war. These officers, a substantial proportion of whom come from the Lahore district, tend to be more religious than the officers recruited traditionally from the rural gentry.[53] Although there is no marked difference in the class background of the senior military officials, the fact that the powerful triumvirate of Zia, Chisti and Arif are all East Punjabi migrants is significant. The religious parties, in particular the fundamentalist Jamaat-e-Islami, have substantial support among the migrant community, which was consolidated by their relief work in the refugee camps in 1947. The Jamaat established forty-two medical dispensaries in Punjab and Karachi, which benefited an estimated one million refugees.[54] The support for a theocracy, within the army, tends to be concentrated in the East Punjabi migrant group.

Apart from motivational objectives internal to the military, an appeal to a wider constituency was sought through the religious discourse. The aim was to create popular legitimacy for the army, as an instrument for a radical religious transformation of society. However, the government was singularly unsuccessful in creating a mass base for a theocracy. Unlike Iran, the Islamisation process was launched unilaterally by the regime. The lack of a popular mandate was evident in the '85 referendum on Islamic policies, in which the abysmal turnout indicated lack of enthusiasm for a theocracy. Although there is popular respect for religion and widespread observance of religious practices, this has never been translated into a popular demand for a fundamentalist theocracy. Historical evidence is provided by electoral preference for secular parties, such as the PPP and NAP, over religious parties. Moreover, in Zia's case the cynical use of religion for self-preservation is so transparent that it has prevented even those groups who would be sympathetic towards a theocracy from lending support to Zia's Islamisation. A related reason for the lack of mass support is the association of the military with the Islamisation process. The army, as an institution, has not regained the prestige it lost in 1971. Although the PPP did not make public the results of the official inquiry into the East Pakistan debacle, most Pakistanis would agree with its principal conclusion. The Hamood-ur-Rahman Commission, which conducted the inquiry, concluded that the military was primarily responsible for the break-up of the country.[55] The political parties, the AL and the PPP, are admonished by the relatively minor rebuke of "political immaturity". Not surprisingly, the Zia government has not released the report.[56]

The attempt to create popular legitimacy for a theocratic state has had other ominous implications. The process has entailed a rewriting of history by government officials, which is reminiscent of Eastern Europe. Not only has there been a conscious distortion in the interpretation of historical events, but facts have also been altered to suit an ideological position.[57] An example of such distortion is Zia's claim that Jinnah was a devoutly religious man, wanting to create a theocratic state.[58] Such a vision of Jinnah is purely hallucinatory. Prayer and religious ritual were not a part of Jinnah's personal life.[59] In his public life he ardently opposed a theocracy, stating that "religion is merely a matter between man and God ... it should not be allowed to come into politics".[60] Similarly, his much quoted first address to the Constituent Assembly categorically rejected a theocracy: "you may belong to any religion or caste or creed — that has nothing to do with the business of the state ... in the course of time Hindus will cease to be Hindus and Muslims will cease to be Muslims, not in the religious sense because that is the personal faith of each individual, but in the political sense as citizens of the state". The current distortion of Jinnah as an advocate of theocracy is in such sharp contrast with reality that it could only have been attempted in a society where the state has complete control over information.

The reasons for the apparent ease with which a secular élite was transformed into a vanguard of a theocratic order are complex. First, institutional changes within the military-bureaucratic élite have eroded the ascendency of secular groups. Bhutto's administrative reforms (see part two) substantially reduced the power and influence of the Civil Servants. This led to a readjustment in the relationship between the generals and the bureaucrats in favour of the former. Whereas the bureaucratic reforms were far-reaching, the shuffling of senior military posts did not significantly reduce the power of the generals. Obviously they did not exercise supreme power under a civilian government, but their authority was not undermined in the same manner as that suffered by senior Civil Servants. Indeed, a new breed of generals, from conservative religious families, had replaced the Sandhurst-trained generation, which was dismissed *en masse* as a result of the catastrophe in East Pakistan. Subsequently, Zia emerged as the most important member of the new hierarchy. One of the first changes made by Zia, after his appointment as Chief of Army Staff, was to upgrade the status of the maulvis attached to each army unit. Hitherto they had been regarded as comic figures which the military élite tolerated as a gesture to religious obligation. Zia integrated these religious figures into the everyday ethos of the military and made it compulsory for them to go into battle with the troops.[61] This initial gesture was a harbinger of things to come. Thus, when the military-bureaucratic apparatus regained power in 1977, it was the religiously inclined generals who were dominant. The secular Civil Servants, whose dominance in the fifties and the sixties had played such an important part in ensuring that a theocracy was not implemented, had been removed by the administrative reforms.

Second, domestic political developments were interpreted by the military élite as providing favourable signals for creating a mass support base on religious issues. The PPP's economic policies had hurt, and consequently politicised, the urban *petite bourgeoisie*. Their political muscle was evident in the PNA Movement (see part two). Their power lay in the important role played by them in the urban economy, reflected in the table below, where the size of the commercial trade sector provides a rough indicator of magnitude.[62] The main support for the PNA's slogan for the creation of an Islamic social order, Nizam-e-mustafa, came from the urban lower middle class. In his first speech after the coup, Zia noted with approval the Islamic component of the opposition movement: "The spirit of Islam, demonstrated during the recent movement, was commendable . . . Pakistan will continue to survive only if it sticks to Islam. That is why I consider the introduction of the Islamic system as an essential prerequisite for the country". Subsequently, the military had hoped to utilise this constituency, to develop support for its theocratic system. However, as we noted above, even this potential constituency was not enamoured with Zia's Islamisation programme. This support was not forthcoming, partly because the religious parties[63] were part of a civilian alliance for the return of democratic rule. Thus, instead of canvassing for the theocratic order to be implemented, they remained opposed to the retention of power by the military. Consequently, the military was not able to get religious leaders to lend their authority for the theocratic programme initiated by them.

Finally, the third factor favouring the military's utilisation of Islam was external. The wave of Islamic fundamentalism, in part an ideological by-product of the '74 oil boom, was a source of support to Zia. Saudi Arabia, a major aid donor, enthusiastically endorsed the Islamisation process, providing both financial and intellectual assistance.[64] The Saudis not only provided money for the Zakat fund, but also participated in the committees set up to define the specifics of a fundamentalist order.

The Islamisation process represents a distinct shift in the ideological paradigm within which the state operates. It marks a departure from the conception of society held by the Muslim élite, which led the Pakistan Movement. Their perception of society symbolised a different form of the Islamic

Table 1: *Labour force by major occupation groups (% of total).*

	Urban	Rural	Combined
Agriculture, forestry and fishing	6.2	72.1	54.8
Mining and quarrying	.2	.1	.2
Manufacturing	25.7	9.3	13.6
Electricity, gas and water	1.2	.2	.5
Construction	6.4	3.4	4.2
Commercial trade	25.9	5.8	11.1
Transport and communications	10.3	2.9	4.9
Financial services	2.3	.1	.7
Community, social and personal service	21.3	5.7	9.8
Other	.5	.4	.2

Source: Economic Survey, 1977-78. Government of Pakistan, Islamabad.

response to the modern age. They were the intellectual descendants of Sir Syed and Allama Iqbal, both of whom evolved a flexible interpretation of Islam, which made it compatible with nineteenth-century Western liberalism. This was done by separating out the principles from the letter of the law, disengaging the 'spirit of religion' from the social context of seventh-century Arabia.[65] This view of religion necessitated the rejection of specific punishments and measures contained in the Quran and the Hadith, on the grounds that they were meant to be applied only to the particular social formation in which the prophet and his immediate descendants lived. This approach is one in which the delineation of what is good and desirable is made, and such positive attributes are shown to be compatible with the spirit of religion 'properly understood'.[66] Such an approach to religion is in direct contradiction with the fundamentalism preached by the Zia regime. In the latter concept, that which God commands *is* good, rather than God sanctions what can morally be shown to be good. With these conditions, the original Islamic state under the prophet Mohammad represents the ideal society. Thus, specific measures such as stoning to death and hand amputation are necessary, because they are universally valid commands of God.

The liberal Muslims were forced on to the defensive by the fundamentalist onslaught. At one level they could not question the severe punitive measures and sexual repression, since this was backed by the authority of the Sharia. To question them would raise serious issues regarding the nature of religious precedent. No political party in Pakistan can publicly debate such 'subversive' issues. The only option is to insist on a secular state in which Islam can be referred to in general terms, and not derived from the specifics outlined in the Sharia. Fortunately for them, the process of political liberalisation, which began in 1985, eased the religious fervour evident since

1977. Since the Islamisation process failed to generate popular support for the regime, the government concentrated on creating an institutional structure, which could incorporate civilian participation under a military umbrella. This quest involved a diminution, though not abandonment, of the Islamisation programme, since civilian groups entering Parliament had little enthusiasm for a theocracy.

Between 1977 and 1985, however, the fundamentalist view dominated. Its idiom contained the blueprint of Utopia. The ideal society, however, does not consist of attaining a vision such as that of classless bliss and the 'overcoming of alienation'. Utopia had already been achieved in seventh-century tribal Arabia. The fundamentalist dream is to recreate, as faithfully as possible, a similar social structure thirteen centuries later. It is not difficult to see why the fundamentalist paradigm represents a religious attack on reason unknown since medieval Europe.

Footnotes:

1 There are obvious difficulties in the conceptualisation of a totalitarian state. The definition in the text is a modified version of the one given by Friedrich and Brzezinski in *Totalitarian Dictatorship and Autocracy*, (second edition, Massachusetts, 1965) p. 22. Various methodological problems pertaining to the characterisation of totalitarianism are discussed in L. Shapiro: *Totalitarianism* (London, 1972) and Barber, Curtis and Friedrich: *Totalitarianism in Perspective: Three Views*. (Massachusetts. 1969).
2 For elaboration of this point see A. A. Maududi: *The Process of Islamic Revolution* (Lahore, 1955)
3 Interview with BBC, 15.4.78.
4 Zia's speech on Pakistan Day, 14.8.77.
5 Zia's speech in *Dawn*, 3.3.85.
6 See K. Bahadur: *The Jamaat-e-Islami of Pakistan*, Chapter 4 for discussion of this point.
7 Sharia refers to Islamic law based on the Quran and Hadith, i.e., the actions and sayings of the prophet. The Sharia was interpreted in the early days of Islam by four jurists.
8 Zia's creation of a non-party theocratic state headed by a despotic president is based on Maududi's conception outlined in: (i) The *Process of Islamic Revolution* and (ii) *Islamic Law and Constitution*.
9 See C. J. Adams: 'The ideology of Maududi' in P. E. Jones(ed): *South Asian Politics and Religion*.

10 A. A. Maududi: *Islamic Law and Constitution*, p. 154.
11 The Offences against Property (enforcement of Hadud) Ordinance, 1979.
12 The Zina Ordinance, 1979.
13 The prohibition (enforcement of Hadud) order, 1979. The Quran does not prescribe a penalty for consuming alcohol Punishment was introduced by the Caliph Abu-Bakr who instituted 40 lashes. Caliph Omar increased the penalty to 80.
14 The law of evidence, 1984. A passage from it reads: "Barring cases of Hadud, Qisas and Diyat which would be covered by respective laws, in other matters 2 men, or 1 man and 2 women, would be required to give evidence".
15 In cases of murder where retribution cannot be applied, or the victim leaves no adult relatives, the state will intervene to punish the offender (taazir). In taazir cases, evidence from all parties is accepted on an equal basis.
16 Article 25 of the '73 Constitution prohibited discrimination on the basis of sex.
17 The statement evoked a sharp response from the Women's Action Forum. See *Dawn*, 16.3.85. Zia's statement also contravenes Article 91 of the '73 Constitution, which lays down that a woman is eligible to be a prime minister.
18 The limit for men was 25.
19 FEER. Asia yearbook, 1979. p. 72.
20 FEER. Asia yearbook, 1982. p. 88.
21 ibid. p. 87.
22 Asia yearbook, 1983. In the same year, Israr Ahmed, a cleric close to Zia, declared on state television that women should not mix with men, and should stay at home. The official tendency has been to limit women's public participation such that they do not come into excessive contact with men. Thus, there have been proposals for separate women's universities, separate bank branches or counters for women, female medical doctors to look after women only and so on.
23 FEER, AY, 1985. Also see *Jang*, 16.8.84.
24 For details see A. A. Maududi: *Islamic Law and Constitution*, pp. 140-60.
25 Zia's television address. 30.8.79.
26 *New York Times*, 20.1.80.
27 ibid.
28 In 'Islam ka nazariya siyasi' (Delhi, 1967) Maududi argued "there is no place in Islam for candidature or election canvassing... Islamic mentality hates the idea of several candidates contesting for the same post". p. 86.

29 Zia's television address. 30.8.79.
30 *Dawn*, 2.10.77.
31 *Jang*, 28.3.78.
32 See last chapter.
33 Of course, the analogy with the Soviet Union should not be carried too far. There are obvious differences.
34 For a discussion of Jewish and Christian economic thought see A. Gordon: *Economic Analysis before Adam Smith.* (Macmillan 1975).
35 The intellectual lineage was sustained by the Christian gospel writers, who defined man's economic role as one of 'stewardship of God's resources'.
36 There are, of course, exceptions to the mainstream of Greek thought on economics. For example, the Sophists (sixth century B.C.) conceived of economics as a technology. Its techniques were to be taught and mastered without reference to the desirability of ends, a view shared by modern neo-classical economists.
37 For comparative perspectives, see E. Roll:*History of Economic Thought.*
38 See, for example, Aristotle's treatment of economics in the *Nicomachean Ethics* and the *Politics.*
39 For further discussion of the issue see Polanski, Arensberg and Pearson (eds): *Trade and Markets in the Early Empires.*
40 Solon, for example, wrote off substantial debts to maintain stability.
41 A. Gordon: op cit, p. 96.
42 "Those who swallow riba cannot rise save as he ariseth whom the devil hath prostrated by his touch . . . Allah permits trading but forbids riba . . . as for him who returns to riba such are rightful owners of the fire".
43 A. Rasheed: *Pakistan Leaps into the Unknown.* Euromoney. December, 1983.
44 ibid.
45 State Bank Annual Report, 1980-81.
46 The argument that Islam's redistributive principles imply a welfare state, has been made by the Federal Minister for Finance and Economic Affairs, Ghulam Ishaq Khan. In his opening address to the Annual Meeting (1984) of The Pakistan Society of Development Economists, he argued that trusteeship of God's resources implies an economic system which cannot allow wealth to be concentrated in a few hands. If the initial distribution is skewed, Islam prescribed redistribution, argued Ishaq elsewhere (Welcome address at International Seminar on Monetary and

Fiscal Reform, Islamabad, 1981) A similar view is expressed in M. Nazeer: *The Islamic Economic System*. PIDE. 1981.
47 Calculated from figures issued by the Central Zakat Administration in Economic Survey, 1983-84.
48 The two-nation theory formed the basis of the pre-Partition demand for the creation of a separate Muslim state in the Indian subcontinent.
49 Television address. 15.8.77.
50 This initial dissatisfaction was stressed by a number of junior officers interviewed by the author.
51 See speeches of Zia reported in *Jang* 7.7.77 and 20.8.77.
52 Zia repeated this in an interview on Britain's Channel 4 television in March '85. Kakul address is reported in *Pakistan Times*, 14.4.78.
53 Middle-class conservative urban groups, from which category these officials came, provide the main class base for the religious parties in Punjab and Sind. For further discussion see A. Hussain: 'Pakistan — the Crisis of the State' in Asghar Khan(ed): *Islam, Politics and the State*. Hussain suggests that the Jamaat-e-Islami consciously pursued a policy of infiltration into the army.
54 The cost of the operation was an estimated quarter of a million rupees, a substantial amount for the period. For more details on the Jamaat see A. A. Khan: *The Jamaat-e-Islami of Pakistan*.
55 The main conclusions of the commission were verified by the author in separate interviews with ex-ministers who have read the report.
56 The commission's report would have been published, along with the White Papers against Bhutto, if it did not contain such a damaging conclusion for the army.
57 On 20 August 1978, Zia issued a directive that school textbooks must conform to Islamic ideology — a euphemism for rewriting history.
58 A campaign was launched in 1978 to convince the public that Jinnah wanted a theocratic state. See, for example, Zia's statement in *Dawn*, 25.12.82. In his television address on 23 March 1985, Zia referred to the Muslim League leader as Hazrat Jinnah; Hazrat is normally used as a religious title.
59 This is confirmed by all major biographies of Jinnah. See, for example, H. Bolitho, op cit, and Wolpert: *Jinnah of Pakistan*.
60 M. A. Jinnah: Speeches and Writings. Vol. 1. p. 5.
61 Stephen Cohen, op cit, p. 39.
62 Obviously there are problems in equating lower middle-class segments with aggregate figures for the urban retail and

wholesale sector. It does, however, give a reasonable indication of relative magnitude.
63 The Jamaat was the only exception. It backed Zia's theocracy, but did not have sufficient mass support to mobilise opinion in its favour.
64 EIU, Second quarter, 1983. Report on Pakistan.
65 For a discussion of both writers see: (i) W. C. Smith: *Modern Islam in India* and (ii) A. Ahmed: *Islamic Modernism in India and Pakistan.*
66 Such attempts to make religion compatible with modern developments are not confined to Islam. For the response of Christianity to modernism see, for example, R. H. Tawney: *Religion and the Rise of Capitalism.*

Chapter Three

Economic Developments

The most significant economic development between 1977 and 1985, has been the dramatic growth of remittances from the Middle East. The sharp rise is illustrated in Figure 1 below. From the graph one can see how the sudden jump in remittances coincided with the first year of the Zia Government. The rupee value of remittances also registered a sharp rise between 1982 and 1985, on account of the delinking of the rupee from the dollar. In the three-year period, the rupee declined by 52%. This led to a substantial increase in the rupee value of remittances, since the same dollar amount remitted could be exchanged for more rupees. By 1984, remittances constituted the largest single source of foreign exchange earnings. They were four times greater than net aid inflow to Pakistan. Not only did they provide 40% of total foreign exchange earnings, but they also financed 86% of the trade deficit.[1] Their volume, $3.2 billion, was substantial in relation to the size of the economy. The value of remittances was approximately equal to 8% of the GNP.

The crucial aspect of the migratory flows to the Middle East lies in the class background of migrants. The majority of the migrants are unskilled. The dominance of the urban poor among them is reflected in the prevalence of production workers as the major occupational category in Table 1.

The provincial composition of the migrants, documented in Table 2, also reveals interesting variations of impact. The most widespread migration has emanated from the Punjab. Urban centres such as Lahore, Faisalabad, Pindi, Sialkot, Gujranwala and Jhehlum have provided the bulk of the migrants. Similarly, a substantial flow of unskilled labour from the NWFP has gone to the Gulf. Sind, however, has contributed a disproportionately small number to the total. Since a large proportion of migrants from Sind come from Karachi, the effect on the troubled interior of Sind has been minimal. Punjab is the only province whose share of the migrant population

The Political Economy of Pakistan

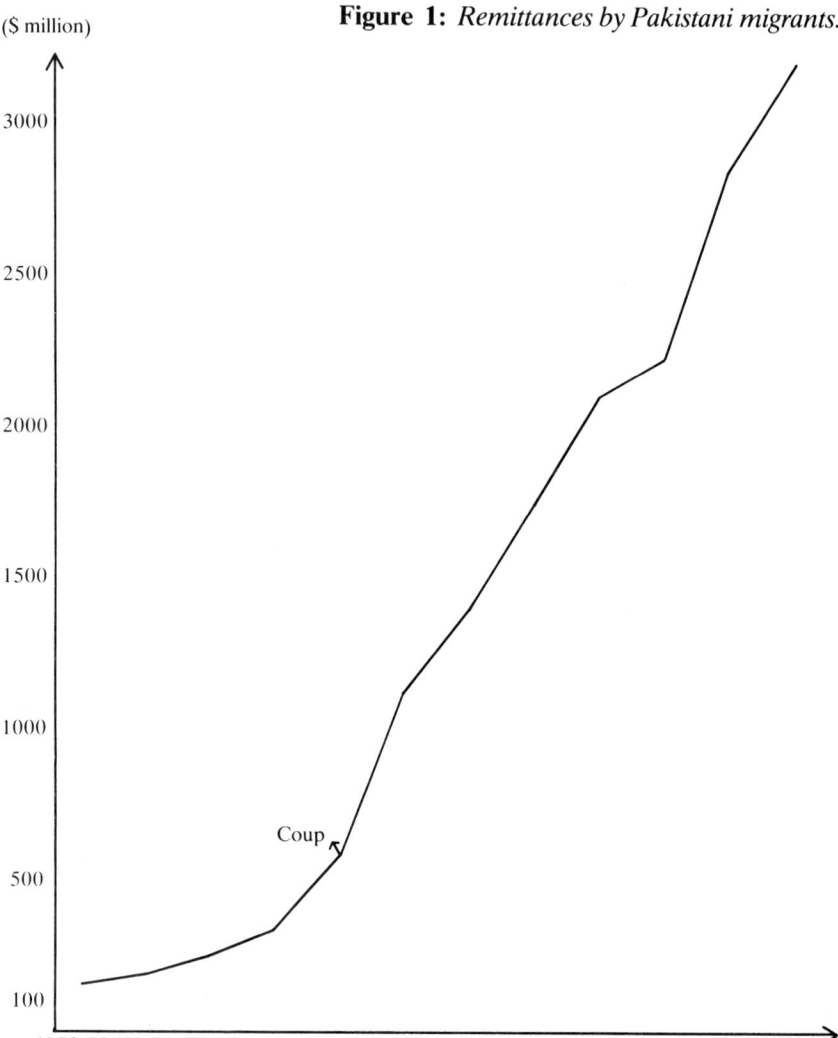

Figure 1: *Remittances by Pakistani migrants.*

Source: State Bank of Pakistan.

exceeds that of its proportion in the national population.

The most favourable consequence of migration has been the decisive impact on the living conditions of the poor. Approximately ten million people, 11% of the total population, have benefited directly from the exodus to the Middle East.[2] The vast majority of the beneficiaries come from low-income households. On average, their salaries increased eightfold.[3] The increased family incomes from remittances have had a pronounced egalitarian impact, in both the urban and rural areas. There is, perhaps, no historical parallel of remittances having resulted in such a rapid and wide dis-

Table 1: *Occupational composition of migrant population (% of total).*

Professional and technical	4.2
Clerical and administrative	1.6
Sales	5.6
Production workers	78.9
Service sector	4.7
Agriculture	4.8

Source: Gilani, Khan and Iqbal, 'Labour Migration'. PIDE. Research report # 126.

Table 2: *Provincial composition of migrant population compared with provincial composition of national population.*

Province	National population (%)	Migrants (%)
Punjab	56	70
NWFP	13	12
Sind	23	14
Baluchistan	5	4

Source: Gilani et al 'Labour Migration'. PIDE. Research report # 126.

tribution of benefits among the poorer sections of society. It is true, of course, that the record on income distribution of the four fast-growing Asian economies — Taiwan, Singapore, Hong Kong and South Korea — has been reasonable.[4] Such an outcome was achieved in spite of the adoption of neoclassical economic policies which did not specifically pursue distributional objectives. A reasonable income distributional outcome was the consequence of initiating a policy framework of private, export-led growth *after* an initial redistribution of assets; for example, the far-reaching land reforms in Taiwan. In Pakistan, the asset distribution remains greatly askew. Yet, over the last few years, the country has been able to achieve a better distribution of income, through manpower export, without having to undergo the politically sensitive process of asset redistribution. Indeed, the government has reversed attempts to redistribute assets. One of the first acts of the Zia regime was to repeal the land reforms announced by the PPP in 1977.

Manpower export has also been responsible for easing the difficulties of productively absorbing the labour force. During the fifth plan period ('78-83), approximately 33% of the increase in labour force was absorbed by overseas migration.[5] At 3.1%, the population growth rate of Pakistan is one of the highest in the world. The problem is particularly serious since Pakistan is the tenth largest country in terms of population. At the same time, the industrial sector has excessively high capital-output and capital-labour ratios, in relation to the resource endowment of surplus labour and scarce capital.[6] The capital-intensive industrial sector cannot therefore adequately absorb the labour that has been migrating to cities. This internal migration has been caused partly by the mechanisation of agriculture, thereby reducing the capacity of rural areas to employ the rapidly increasing labour force. Whereas the four Asian economies mentioned above have switched from an initial phase of import substitution[7] to a more export-oriented growth, Pakistan has entered its second phase of import substitution. She has to develop downstream industries from the uncompetitively priced output of the recently completed steel mill.[8] The process involves establishing capital-intensive industrial units. In the absence of manpower export, the labour market problems, arising from insufficient demand for labour, would have been far more acute.

Table 3: *Pakistan's terms of trade index. (1975-76 = 100).*

1975-76	100.0	1978-79	126.2	1981-82	89.2
1976-77	108.9	1979-80	111.4	1982-83	89.2
1977-78	105.3	1980-81	97.0		

Source: Federal Bureau of Statistics, Government of Pakistan.

Remittances have led to obvious benefits in the external sector. They eased balance of payments problems in the wake of the second oil price rise in 1979, enabling the economy to absorb the shock far better than it would have otherwise done. Balance of payments problems have been compounded by the recession in the West, which has led to restrictions in export markets and a decline in the terms of trade[9] (see Table 3). In addition, high international interest rates, resulting from the U.S. budget deficit, have increased Pakistan's debt service payments considerably. Since foreign loans have not increased proportionately, there has been a fall in net aid inflow,[10] i.e., gross foreign loans minus debt servicing. In the absence of remittances, the recession would have forced a more severe foreign exchange constraint on development projects. However, in assessing the net impact of remittances on the balance of payments, one must bear in mind that remittances themselves encourage consumer imports, thus exerting pressure on the trade deficit. This deficit has been worsening, not only on account of the growth of protectionism[11] but also because of the link in the value of the rupee to the dollar. The dollar had been rising sharply since October 1980, which in effect meant that the rupee was also rising *vis-à-vis* other currencies. Pakistan's poor export performance was partly related to this appreciation. In 1982, the rupee was delinked from the dollar, although the Pakistan Government had been resisting IMF pressure to devalue, on the grounds of low elasticity of exports and imports, which would lead to the worsening of the current account after devaluation. Remittances have eased balance of payments problems, which have persisted due to the reduced, but still large, trade deficits with imports nearly double the value of exports.[12] In 1978-79, debt servicing as a ratio of export earnings stood at the alarmingly high proportion of 35%. However debt repayments as a ratio of total foreign exchange earnings was 13.5%, since remittances are included in the latter. Without these, Pakistan's debt servicing problems would have been far more serious.

The effect of large-scale manpower export has naturally extended to the political sphere. The urban bias in emigration is of particular relevance, since urban areas constitute the nerve centres of the political system. Both the movements to topple Ayub and Bhutto were based in the cities. Consequently, the political parties currently opposing the military relied critically on mobilising these organised groups in urban regions. Ironically, it was precisely from this category that a large proportion of emigrants came. The classes which the MRD was relying on to be in the vanguard of a national movement against the military, were to become the primary beneficiaries of the Middle East. The damage that this process inflicted on the ability of the political parties to mobilise a mass movement, was acknowledged by MRD leaders.[13]

Indeed, even those who were left behind were reluctant to spoil their chances of migrating by engaging in political activity. Since the Gulf countries adopted a policy of giving short-term contracts to hired workers, there was rapid turnover in the labour market. The rotation and mobility in the job market extended the network of opportunities to a larger number of aspirants than would have been the case otherwise. This led to the formation of expectations, amongst the working class who remained in Pakistan, that opportunities may yet occur to raise living standards dramatically. This effect on working-class psychology was noted by an ILO study: "With such large-scale migration of workers, people feel that with a little bit of luck, it is possible to be among the next batch of emigrants ... the working class has come to believe that it is upwardly mobile".[14] Thus, given the choice of confronting the military in an inevitably violent movement or keeping politically dormant to enhance the possibility of migration, it is not surprising that a large number of people chose the latter.

There were, of course, indirect beneficiaries of the migratory process. After all, remittances injected a demand for goods and services, which led to an expansion of economic activity, particularly in the urban areas. In addition, real wages often rose for those left behind. The emigration had resulted in temporary labour shortages in a number of sectors. An example is the construction sector. A large number of workers went to work on construction projects in the Gulf, creating a temporary shortage of workers. At the same time, the remittances of the emigrants went mostly into real estate, as poor families built houses. This led to a construction boom in the urban areas of Pakistan, increasing the demand for labour in the sector just when its supply had become relatively scarce. Consequently, as a World Bank study documented,[15] the real wages of unskilled and semi-skilled workers rose. Similarly, a study of the labour market suggests that there has been a general rise in real wages of all categories of workers, except government employees.[16] In other words, an average wage earner enjoyed a higher real wage in 1984 compared with, for example, 1971, the year of dismemberment. The rise in real wages of workers in large-scale manufacturing is shown in Table 4 below.

Table 4: *Real Wage Trends in Large-scale Manufacturing, 1976-81.*

	(Percent per annum)
Real Wage Growth	
All Workers	7.6%
Production Workers	6.5%
Non-production Workers	9.2%

Source: Census of Manufacturing Industries, Federal Bureau of Statistics. Various issues.

Although the growth in real wages has been broadbased — wages appear to have risen in agriculture and construction as well as large-scale manufacturing — it has had some adverse consequences for the labour market. Particularly serious has been the decline in the capacity of the industrial sector to absorb labour. For example, total employment in large-scale manufacturing, between 1976 and 1981, *fell* by nearly 55,000 workers, or by 2.2% per year; almost two-thirds of the decline was in the textile sector alone. Since real manufacturing output expanded by 12.3% per year, the fall in employment yielded negative employment elasticity (−0.186) compared with an elasticity of 0.76 in the previous six years.[17] In other words, employers have been effectively shedding labour by adopting capital-intensive techniques in order to regain those profit margins squeezed by an increase of real wages over productivity. In agriculture the number of tractors increased by 500% in the 1973-83 decade, a trend which reinforced mechanisation through the increased use of harvesters and threshers. A similar increase in capital-intensive techniques has been documented for the construction sector.[18] Such developments do not augur well for future employment prospects, which could be particularly bleak in view of work being sought by returning migrants.

Like migration, the weather was another exogenous factor to have had a favourable impact on the economy. An excellent weather cycle, ensuring

Economic Developments

consistent and sufficient water supplies, made a critical contribution to the improved performance in the agricultural sector. Production of the four main crops — cotton, rice, wheat and sugar-cane — reached record levels during 1981 and '82. Consequently, self-sufficiency in foodgrains has been achieved. Indeed, a small exportable surplus in wheat emerged.[19] Bumper crops of sugar-cane led to the decontrol and derationing of sugar by the government.[20] Although good weather was crucial, it was complemented by appropriate policies to encourage farmers. Greater incentives, by way of more remunerative prices for output, have accompanied increased availability of inputs, especially fertiliser. Input/output price adjustments have been co-ordinated through the establishment of the Agricultural Prices Commission. In addition, agricultural credit expanded rapidly between 1978 and 1983. For example, disbursements of Rs.6.3 billion in 1983 were more than double the level of lending in 1980.[21] However, lending has been confined to large- and medium-sized farmers.[22] Small farmers remain more or less excluded from the credit markets, the official network of extension services and the private organisations for the distribution of inputs.[23]

Table 5: *Yield per acre of agricultural crops. (maunds per acre).*

	1972-73	1982-83
Sugar-cane	405.5	386.8
Cotton (lint)	3.8	3.9
Rice	17.1	18.9
Wheat	13.5	18.5

Source: Ministry of Food, Agriculture and Co-operatives, 1983.

The scope for a further increase in output is considerable, since Pakistan's per-acre yields in wheat, rice and cotton are well below the world average. Indeed, yields of wheat in the Indian Punjab, where soil composition is similar, are 30% higher.[24] In recent years, the growth in yields has been very disappointing. The increase in output of the principal crops has had more to do with acreage expansion than with yield improvement. As Table 5 indicates, yields in sugar-cane and cotton have not changed much in a decade. While there has been some improvement in rice yields, only in wheat has any progress been made. The major source of output expansion has been increased acreage.[25] The impressive agricultural performance has helped the economy to sustain a respectable average annual growth rate of 6.2% in real GDP between 1977 and 1986. The impressive macroeconomic performance is reflected in Table 6 below. In the five-year period 1978-83, the Gross Domestic Product showed a steady increase, the country's output of goods and services rising by more than 6% each year.

The improved performance, across virtually all sectors of the economy, is shown in Table 6.

Table 6: *GDP growth by sectors, 1978-1983.*
(annual growth rates in constant 1960 prices).

	1978-79	1979-80	1980-81	1981-82	1982-83
Gross domestic product (at factor cost)	4.9%	7.3%	6.4%	5.6%	6.2%
Agriculture	3.5	6.7	3.8	3.3	3.5
Manufacturing	4.8	10.1	10.2	11.9	9.3
Mining and quarrying	4.2	13.1	13.2	7.4	6.9
Construction	5.5	11.5	4.2	2.2	0.7
Electricity, gas and water	9.8	12.1	10.9	4.6	7.8
Transport and communication	8.1	6.7	8.0	6.4	7.6
Public administration and defence	5.3	6.2	10.6	1.6	5.6
Trade	4.8	7.3	6.5	7.7	7.1
Other services	4.0	9.2	7.7	3.8	6.6

Source: Ministry of Finance, Islamabad.

It is perhaps, worth stressing that the growth in domestic incomes of 6% is likely to be a gross underestimate. Two developments suggest domestic income has been growing at an even faster pace in recent years. First, drug production has increased substantially — the annual value of the trade is equal to approximately 8% of Pakistan's GNP — but remains unaccounted for in official statistics, due to its illegality. Second, the multiplier effects of this drug income, as well as the receipt of remittances through unofficial channels have contributed towards the growth of the 'informal sector' in urban areas. Again, official data on the growth of this sector is inadequate.

The Gulf boom, supported by an adequate domestic macro-economic performance, has led to a fundamental structural change in Pakistani society. As we stated above, the prosperity has been spread across a wide social spectrum. Not only did the economic boom help sustain the Zia regime, but it also simultaneously undermined the ability of the opposition to mobilise a popular movement against the military. Such movements have historically been based on the support of urban working class and lower middle class groups. The MRD's attempts to topple the regime failed, however, in key cities such as Karachi and Lahore, as well as other urban centres in Punjab. Political parties in Pakistan may well have to resign themselves to the reality that, as long as the Gulf boom continues, it may not be possible to mobilise effectively the key urban centres. Without the committed support from urban areas, the likelihood of launching a successful movement is remote. It is a predicament which may continue to plague Benazir Bhutto's PPP in particular.

The government's inability to meet its objective of raising domestic resources is related to the pattern of conspicuous consumption, encouraged by remittances and corruption. The Gulf-induced increase in urban wealth is visibly manifest in a glut of imported consumer durables. Since the pattern of migration to the Middle East, unlike that to Europe, has been one in which only male members go to work abroad leaving their families behind, they remit most of their earnings. The expenditure pattern of the recipient families does not indicate, as Table 7 below shows, a particularly high propensity to consume. Nevertheless, the components of consumption expenditure are important in setting social standards. Due to easier access to foreign goods, the remittance recipient families have demonstrated a visible penchant for imported luxury consumer goods. Naturally, the 'demonstration effect' of the flood of video recorders, cars and so on, has distorted the consumption priorities of a country, the majority of whose population is among the poorest in the world. In addition, there have been serious inhibiting effects on the long-term growth of the economy due to the adverse impact on domestic savings. This damage has been lamented by the State Bank on several occasions.[26]

Table 7: *Remittance spending patterns.*
(average across migrants).

	% of total expenditure
Consumption	63.09
Real estate	21.68
Savings	12.05
Residual	3.18
	100.00

Source: Gilani, et al. PIDE. Research report # 126.

The 'demonstration effect' of conspicuous consumption has been bolstered by the growth of the drugs trade. The volume of the trade is such that it has had a considerable impact. Since 1980, when there was a crop failure in the 'golden triangle' of the Far East, Pakistan has emerged as the single largest exporter of heroin and hashish to the West. The narcotics trade brings in an estimated $3 billion annually,[27] which may explain why the government condones, if not actively participates in, the trade. Such illicit flows have led to a rapid growth in the black economy, which public sector financial institutions have attempted to accommodate by issuing bonds, which permit illegally acquired money to become legitimate.[28]

Adverse macro-economic consequences have been generated by a social ethos which places pressures of conspicuous consumption among precisely those classes that can afford to save. The resultant effects on the domestic savings rate has severely constrained the development process. Accordingly, the Planning Minister, Mahbub-ul-Haq, advocated a consumption tax to curtail the consumption orientation of society.[29] The causes and effects of the consumption boom were summarised by the State Bank: "Conspicuous consumption on the part of those elements of society who have become rich in recent years through hoarding, blackmarketing, profiteering, smuggling and corruption has exercised a strong demonstrative effect on other strata of society and the lifestyle we have adopted has seriously eroded the savings base".[30] The fall in the domestic savings rate is illustrated in Figure 2 below.

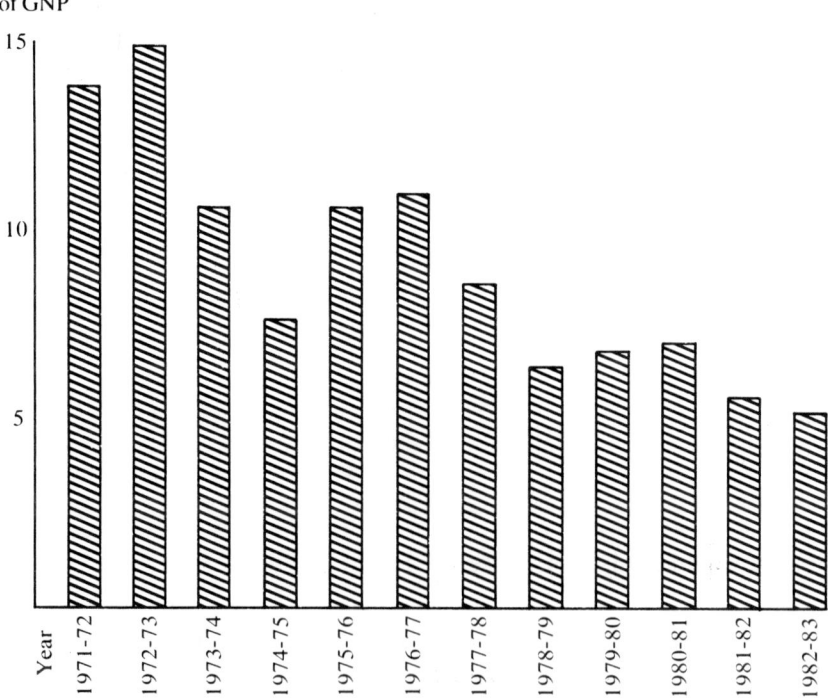

Figure 2: *Gross Domestic Saving as proportion of GNP. (%).*

Source: Calculated from Pakistan Economic Survey, 1983-84. (Government of Pakistan, Islamabad).

Economic Developments

The fifth plan (1978-83) targeted an increase in domestic savings from 7.8% of the GDP in '77-78, to 12.5% by '82-83. The domestic savings rate fell, however, to 5.4% by '82-83. The inability to raise rupee resources resulted in the abandonment of fifth-plan targets in favour of a more modest interim rolling plan. An ambitious sixth plan, with an enormous targeted outlay of Rs. 490 billion, was announced in 1983. In less than two years, this plan's targets were also abandoned, due to the failure in raising domestic resources.[31] An indication of the constraint imposed by the failure to raise domestic resources is provided by the international comparisons of Figure 3. For example, in comparison to Pakistan, the savings rate of Singapore and India are greater by 800% and 400% respectively.

The fall in the savings rate is also related to the measures used in the Islamisation of the economy. The introduction of Islamic banking has led to uncertainty in the financial markets. Indeed, theoretically, those who deposit their money under Islamic banking can suffer losses through the profit and loss accounts.[32] The imposition of Zakat, a 2.5% Islamic welfare tax on savings deposits, has also provided a disincentive to hold cash balances. Consequently, people have been inclined to transfer their savings to other sources, such as real estate.

Figure 3: *An international comparison of Pakistan's savings performance.*

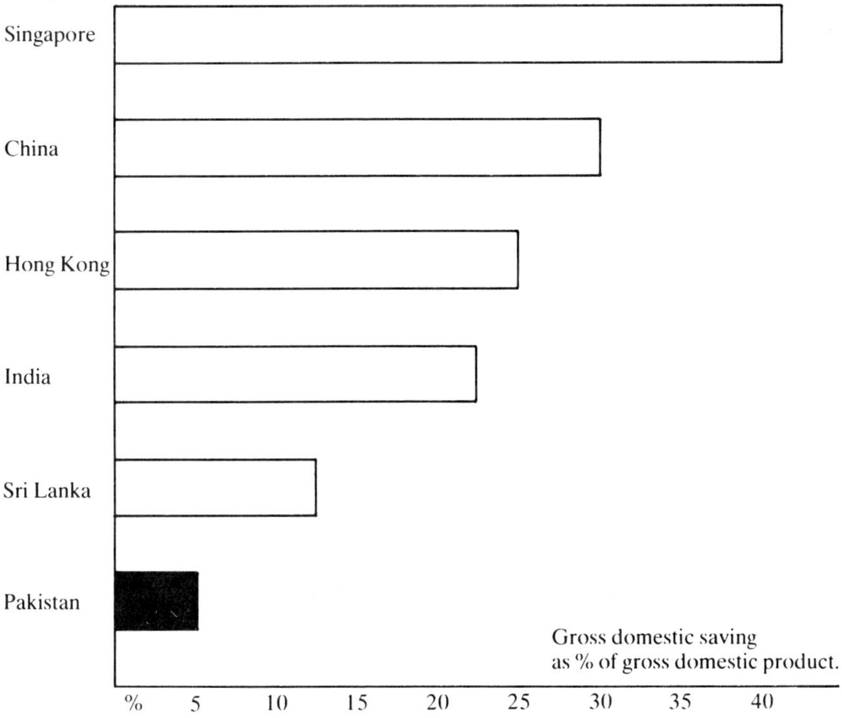

Source: World Development Report, 1984. (World Bank, Washington).

The government's inability to raise domestic resources implied an increased reliance on foreign loans, in order to implement the development plans. However, a harsh international environment of rising debt service charges and reduced lending to developing countries meant that Pakistan had to confront a fall in net aid inflow. American aid after the Afghanistan crisis mitigated the effect of reduced net lending. Aggregate foreign loans for development have, none the less, been declining, a trend illustrated in Figure 4. Foreign loans fell short of fifth-plan targets. The consequent recourse to additional funding from the World Bank entailed the adoption of stringent conditions, as part of the structural adjustment loan (SAL). The critical feature of this programme was the exhaustive monitoring of policies by the World Bank, agreed to by the government in the Letter of Development Policies accompanying the formal loan documentation. The Bank laid down detailed measures for the agricultural, industrial and energy sectors as

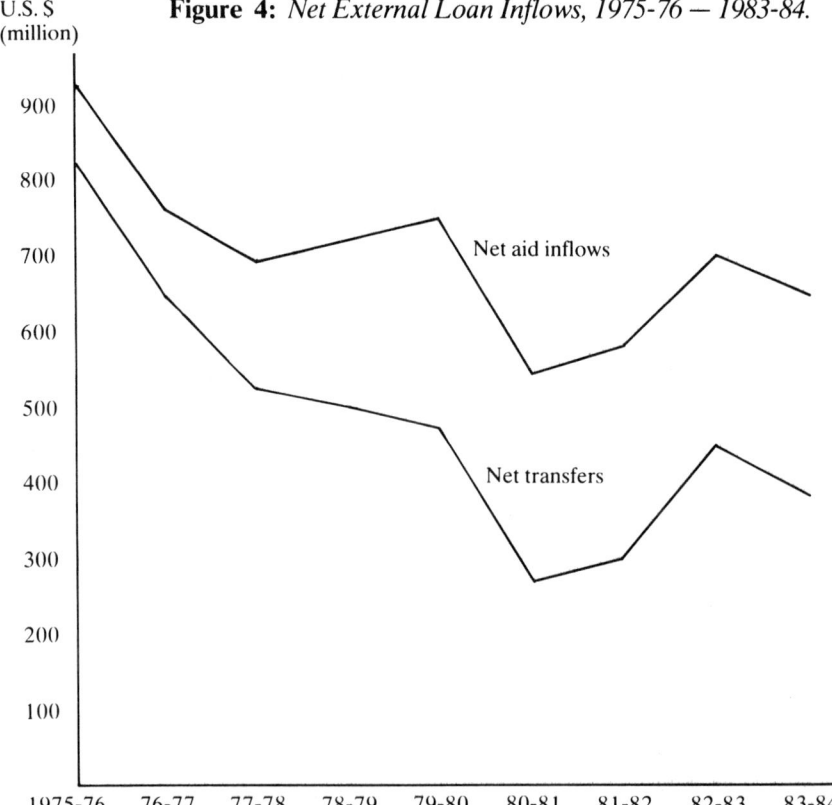

Figure 4: *Net External Loan Inflows, 1975-76 — 1983-84.*

Source: Report on Pakistan, World Bank, 1984.
Note: Net aid inflows are defined as disbursements — amortization.
Net transfers are defined as disbursements — amortization — interest.

well as policy guidelines for public sector enterprises. In effect, SAL implied that the basic outlines of economic policy were being formulated and monitored by the World Bank. The scale of the Bank's intrusion was resented in Islamabad. Thus, the government decided in 1983 not to proceed with the second instalment of the SAL, in order to avoid the explicit and monitorable commitments. Instead, an agreement was reached, whereby the general direction of the SAL policy framework was to be followed.

The ambitious sixth plan, which was launched at a time when both the savings rate and net aid inflow were falling, ran into immediate resource constraints. In the first year of the plan, foreign capital inflows were 20% short of the plan target of $1,070 million.[33] The annual development plan for 1983-4 was Rs. 34 billion. However, only Rs. 29 billion could be raised, leading to a 14% deficit in the first year of the plan.[34] Consequently, the plan had to be replaced by a list of priority projects which conformed to a more realistic assessment of resource availability.

Poor planning was also responsible for the shortages in the energy sector that have persisted since 1980. Insufficient public investment in infrastructure meant that deficiencies in this sector emerged as one of the major constraints on industrial development in Pakistan. Since 1980, both industrial and domestic consumers have had to face constant power supply interruptions, because of rationing of electricity. A Government of Pakistan study has indicated that load-shedding during peak periods of demand is likely to increase, if present trends persist.[35] Faced with an energy crisis of its own making, the government had to respond by increasing allocative priority to the energy sector in the sixth plan. However, even if the sixth plan's energy programme were fully implemented — an unlikely event — shortages of energy are expected to continue up to 1990.[36]

Inadequate public investment in infrastructure occurred precisely at a time when demand for social overhead capital was increasing rapidly. For example, remittances led to patterns of expenditure which imposed considerable demands on the infrastructure. The consequent construction boom required the adequate provision of public utilities, such as electricity. Table 8 documents the effects of the growth in the construction sector on electricity consumption. The share of domestic consumption of electricity rose from 10% of the total in 1970, to 30% in 1984. However, while the demands were growing, constraints on supply were being imposed by cuts in the public sector investment programme. The emphasis, since 1977, had reverted to the centrality of the private sector within the economic structure. The public sector was, in the main, confining manufacturing investment to the completion of existing projects, such as the steel mill. It was no longer to play the major role in domestic capital formation, as it had done under the PPP. Public sector investment in infrastructure also suffered. While energy supply was increasing by 11%, the rate of domestic demand expansion was an estimated 24% per annum.[37] Gas consumption increased by 21.3% in

Table 8: *Use of Electricity by Economic Groups. (% of total sales).*

	1969-70	1976-77	1983-84
Agriculture	26.6	25.68	16.74
Industry	45.7	42.09	36.94
Commercial	3.4	4.5	8.24
Domestic	10.2	14.31	30.29
Public lighting	14.1	12.62	6.92
Other	–	.79	.89

Source: Pakistan Economic Survey, 1983-84.

1980, whereas the supply response was being hindered, partly by the government's maintenance of an extremely low producer price for gas.[38] This acted, naturally, as a disincentive for investment.

The inadequacy of public sector investment in infrastructure, particularly the energy sector, is reflected in Table 9, which shows a 22% decline in *per capita* investment in electricity and gas between 1977 and '82. The effects of poor planning in the energy sector became visible irritants in the form of constant power shortages Urban areas have been subject to regular power cuts, which distribute inadequate supplies by restricting availability.[39] More significantly, private sector investment has been hampered by insufficient provision of infrastructure, a failure publicly acknowledged by the Planning Minister.[40] Existing industry has also suffered, particularly in Karachi, where a fuel adjustment cost was levied on industrial consumers in 1977. In 1983 alone, there was a 58% increase in the cost of power to industrial consumers.[41]

Infrastructural deficiencies were not the only cause for poor private investment in industry. Although, with the resumption of military rule, the industrialists regained some of the influence they had lost under the PPP, their response to government incentives was cautious. After the coup, the emphasis of economic policy had shifted. The government reverted to the sixties' formula of a more explicit alliance with the dominant classes in agriculture and industry. In the agricultural sector, the '77 land reforms were cancelled to eliminate insecurity among landlords. In the industrial sector, the rehabilitation of private entrepreneurs was evident in policy formulation. Both five-year plans placed considerable emphasis on the revival of private investment, which had plummeted after arbitrary nationalisations under the PPP. The public sector's role as the dominant investment sector was curtailed. Its investment activity was confined mainly to the completion of ongoing manufacturing projects and infrastructure. Accordingly, stimulation for the pivotal role assigned to the private sector was provided by a host

Table 9: *Per Capita, Public Gross Fixed Capital Formation. (Cost level 1959 60).*

	Four year periods		
	1974-75 — 1977-78	1976-77 — 1981-82	% change
Manufacturing	62.4	62.0	− .6
Electricity and gas	51.7	40.3	−22.0
Government enterprises	17.9	15.8	−11.7
Autonomous and semi-autonomous bodies	180.9	182.0	+ .6
Railways	11.4	10.1	−10.5

Source: Calculations from Economic Survey, 1981-82 in M. Hasan's 'State of Economy'.

of incentives. Two broad categories of inducements were offered. The first set of measures was designed to raise post-tax profits. These included tax holidays and accelerated depreciation allowances. The second set of incentives consisted of measures which facilitated utilisation of capital, such as duty-free imports of capital equipment and credit availability at low rates of interest.[42]

In spite of such inducements, the private sector investment response was poor, especially in manufacturing. Private investment did not compensate for the cut in public sector investment. Thus, a smaller proportion of national income was being set aside for capital formation, as fixed investment fell from 18.7% of the GNP in 1976/77 to 14.8% in 1982/83.[43] Private investment in large- and medium-scale industry was greater in 1972 than in 1981.[44] The composition of private investment also reflected important changes. Whereas investment in manufacturing was twice as large as that in housebuilding in 1972/73, ten years later real estate acquired the most prominent position in private investment. These trends, reflected in Table 10 were a source of considerable disappointment for the government's strategy.[45]

The reasons for private sector reluctance to invest in long-term projects, despite generous fiscal incentives, are complex. Non-economic factors have acted as an important disincentive. Two phases of political uncertainty were responsible for a cautious response by private capital. First, between 1977-79 there was considerable uncertainty regarding Bhutto's future, and the related issue of whether the military would transfer power. The uncertainty was sustained by the Soviet invasion of Afghanistan, shortly after Bhutto's

Table 10: *Sectoral Share in Private Fixed Investment. (% of total).*

	1972-73	1982-83
Agriculture	16.4	21.0
Manufacturing	27.3	26.8
Services	11.9	11.7
Construction	13.9	29.1
Electricity and gas	3.0	—
Transport and communication	26.0	10.5
Financial institutions	.9	.5
Mining and quarrying	.5	.3

Source: Pakistan Economic Survey, 1982-83.

execution. In this environment, private capital was naturally reluctant to invest in units which could face nationalisation in the event of transfer of power. By 1982/83 however, private sector confidence in the permanence of military rule was reflected in a sharp rise in applications to establish industrial units. This certainty was disturbed by a second phase of political events, which started in 1983. Two simultaneous developments — the movement against the military in Sind, where a large proportion of industry is situated, and the announcement of a schedule to induct civilians into government — led to a sharp decline in investment activity. Uncertainty over the mode of elections and who would return to power, hindered private investment.[46]

Economic factors have also been partially responsible for the limited private sector response. One important change from the Ayub era was the state monopoly over financial institutions. In the sixties, financial and industrial capital had merged to create the much publicised concentration of wealth among twenty-two families. Much to the annoyance of industrialists, the Zia regime did not denationalise banks acquired under the PPP. Consequently, the state retained monopoly control over domestic banks. Further, Islamic reforms increased the power of banks to intervene, a tendency reinforced by the new company ordinance announced in late '84. The private sector has resented the excessive financial and administrative controls.[47] Industrialists complain that such extensive controls have increased the inefficiencies of the system, as well as fuelling corruption.[48] Tension with the government also arose over the scale and terms of denationalisation. Only a small fraction of the major nationalised units were given back.[49] Denationalisation met with little success, as the terms offered were not acceptable to previous owners. They were, for example, unwilling to take over the liability for losses, which these units had been incurring since nationalisation.[50] Indeed, industrialists were sceptical about the sincerity of the denationalisation policy. They felt that nationalised industries were being retained because they provided ex-military officials with another avenue for extending their power and wealth. None the less, the environment for private industrial development is favourable. Sanctioning procedures have been simplified, imports of industrial raw material and equipment have been made easier, and a number of businessmen have been incorporated into the policy-making arena. This led to a revival of private investment in industry — particularly in the small- and medium-scale sectors — after the depressed conditions of the 1970's. Although the large industrial families remained cautious, the period 1978-85 witnessed a favourable response from smaller entrepreneurs to the incentives offered by the government. As a consequence, the growth of the private sector under Zia has been more diverse, compared with the Ayub era when the 'twenty-two families' emerged as a symbol of inequity.

Another aspect of development, however, showed unfortunate similarities with the pattern established in the sixties. Allocations to the social sectors, between 1977 and 1985, suffered at the expense of defence and debt service commitments. Pakistan has one of the worst records, among developing countries, as far as the provision of social services is concerned. In spite of this, the share of expenditure on education *fell* from 2.1% of GNP in 1976/77 to 1.5% in 1982/83.[51] The fifth plan allocated Rs. 10.3 billion for the development of education. However, just over half this amount — Rs. 5.5 billion — was actually spent.[52] The poor performance in education is reflected in Table 11 below. The lack of serious commitment to education has meant that Pakistan has one of the worst literacy rates in the world.[53] Such neglect has an adverse impact on the development process, since investment in human capital is one of the primary inputs responsible for raising the rate of economic growth in developing countries.[54]

Poor allocation for the education sector has resulted in Pakistan having one of the fastest rates of population growth in the world. A population of 88 million is currently growing by 3.1% every year.[55] There is emphatic evidence for the inverse relationship between population growth and education; "more education for women is one of the strongest factors in

Table 11: *Education Enrolment and Literacy Rates.*

	Pakistan	Average for LDCs*
Primary education		
(% enrolment of those eligible)	56	94
Secondary education	17	34
Higher education	2	4
Adult literacy (% of population)	21	37

Note: *LDC refers to less developed countries.
Source: World Development Report, World Bank, 1984.

reducing fertility ... In all countries women who have completed primary school have fewer children and everywhere the number of children declines regularly, and usually substantially, as the education of mothers increases above the primary school level".[56]

Even the allocations for direct control over population, through family planning programmes, have fallen since 1977. In 1976/77, Rs. 202 million were spent on population planning. The figure fell, even in nominal terms. By 1982/83 Rs. 177 million were being spent on population control.[57] Under the fifth plan, Rs. 1.8 billion were earmarked for population welfare, but only 38% of the sum targeted was spent.[58] Even the crude birth rate, which had declined in the seventies, has risen again.[59] The combined effect of government neglect, religious impediment and the subordinate social status for women, implies that Pakistan's population will double itself in less than twenty-five years. Similar government nonchalance is evident in the health sector. Only five countries in the world spend less than Pakistan on health.[60] Official acknowledgement of the problem has not altered priorities: "Our past record in respect of provision of educational and health facilities is perhaps the least satisfactory part of our development performance".[61] The appalling allocations for the social sectors are a reflection of political representation in Pakistan. Public policy is formulated by, and in the interests of, a tiny élite which defines priorities and appropriates resources accordingly.

The squeeze on the social sectors has been caused by defence allocations. As Figure 5 illustrates, the government devotes nearly 30% of central government expenditure to defence. No military government in the world allocates such a large share of central government resources to defence.[62] A disproportionate share of resources is diverted from the productive and social sectors, adversely affecting both economic growth and social welfare. Outlays on defence and debt servicing exceed 50% of current budgets. Accordingly, a recent review of the economy concluded that "the pre-emption of a high fraction of available resources by defence and debt servicing has constrained the development of some major services provided by federal and provincial governments ... the allocations have fallen far short of what is needed for a reasonable rate of progress in the social sectors".[63] As Tables 12 and 13 indicate, defence expenditure distorts Pakistan's economy more than in any of the economies of South Asia. These distortions have been accentuated by recent developments. The army added 30,000 men to its ranks in 1981 alone, an increase equivalent to two divisions.[64]

Pakistan, in 1985, is about to enter a second phase of industrialisation. The heavy capital-intensive projects, undertaken by the PPP, have begun. The output of these basic industries, such as the steel mill, has to be absorbed by investment in downstream engineering units. The development of the domestic capital goods sector will require substantial investment. This imposes an urgent need to raise domestic resources by curtailing the con-

Economic Developments

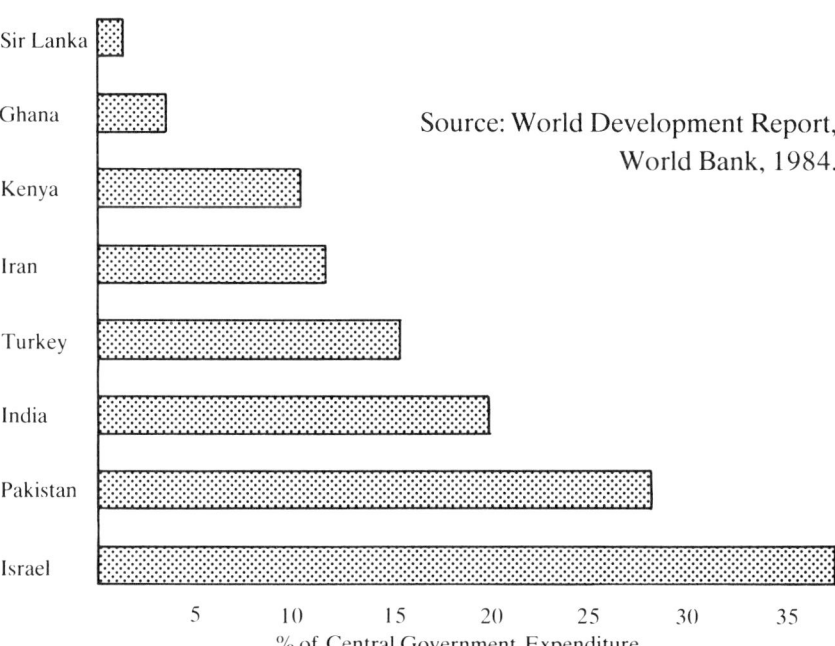

Figure 5: *Defence Expenditure as % of Total Central Government Expenditure.*

Source: World Development Report, World Bank, 1984.

sumption orientation of society. The downstream industries are capital intensive and thus not likely to absorb much labour. The prospects for productive employment of a large proportion of the rapidly growing labour force appear to be bleak, particularly since migration to the Gulf has slowed down considerably. Further, capital intensive methods continue to be promoted in both agriculture and industry. It seems unlikely that the resultant increase in growth, and employment, will be large enough to offset the direct loss of employment opportunities entailed in capital intensive processes. Indeed, it is imperative that simultaneous improvements be made in the abysmal social sector allocations, to contain the growth in the labour force, as well as to provide the necessary health and educational amenities. The

Table 12: *Military Expenditure as % of GNP, South Asia.*

Pakistan	6.9%
India	3.3
Bangladesh	1.5
Sri Lanka	.8
Nepal	.7

Source: The Military Balance, 1982-83. IISS. London.

Table 13: *Defence Spending and the Economy.*

	Population (million)	Armed Forces (manpower in thousands)	GNP (billion $)	Military expenditure – Milex (billion $)	Milex per person ($)	Milex as % of GNP	Milex as % of Govt. spending
Pakistan	88.9	478.6	27.3	1.89	21.2	6.9	28.1
India	688.6	1,104.0	157.8	5.26	8.0	3.3	17.3
China	1,024.9	4,000.0	568.0	11.8	10.0	2.0	20.7
Indonesia	156.0	269.0	67.66	2.69	17.0	3.3	12.3
Bangladesh	93.0	77.0	10.4	.153	1.64	1.47	10.9
Sri Lanka	14.9	16.4	4.07	.029	1.94	.07	

Source: The Military Balance, 1982-83. International Institute for Strategic Studies, London.

Economic Developments

answer to appalling educational facilities does not lie in cutting corners through the use of mosques as schools. This strategy, the outlines of which are contained in the sixth plan, will strengthen the tendencies, already much in evidence, to create a theocracy.

Footnotes:

1 Pakistan Economic Survey, 1983/84.
2 The figure of ten million includes dependants.
3 Calculated from a random sample of 500 migrants. A World Bank study, in the early days of migration, put the average rise in income at 650%.
4 Perhaps Korea has the least impressive record.
5 ILO: Impact of Return Migration on Domestic Employment in Pakistan, 1984.
6 As we noted in part one, the government effectively subsidised the use of capital in the sixties, through an artificially high exchange rate.
7 During their import substitution stage, these economies achieved impressive rates of saving and investment, which were gradually channelled into export industries.
8 On average, the price of the steel mill's output exceeds world prices by 25%.
9 Although the terms of trade effect is not so large as in parts of Africa, it is none the less substantial.
10 Between 1976 and 1981, net aid inflow fell by 30% in real terms. See the statement of Finance Minister Ishaq on 6.5.81 in the *Pakistan Times*.
11 A trade restriction which particularly affects Pakistan's important textile exports is the Multi-Fibre Agreement (MFA), which imposes quotas on specific items.
12 PES, 1983/84, p. 144.
13 Interviews with the author.
14 ILO-ARTEP, op cit, p. 10.
15 Home remittances in Pakistan. World Bank. 1982.
16 See Meekal Ahmed and M.Irfan: "Real wages in Pakistan, 1970-84". *The Pakistan Development Review*. Autumn-winter 1985. Islamabad.
17 ibid. p. 430.
18 M. Irfan: Consequences of out migration on domestic labour market. 1984 (Mimeo).

19 Agricultural Production Statistics. Ministry of Food, Agriculture & Co-operatives. 1983.
20 Sugar was previously rationed through government depots.
21 Monetary Survey, 1984, State Bank of Pakistan. p. 15.
22 By large we mean holders of land in excess of l00 acres; medium refers to 50-100 acres.
23 The distribution of inputs, such as pesticides, is undertaken entirely by the private sector in Punjab and Sind. The government has also encouraged the spread of private distribution networks in NWFP and Baluchistan. Small farmers lack the market power to utilise this network effectively.
24 Per acre yield in Pakistan is 18 maunds, while in India it is 25.
25 World Bank report on Pakistan, 1982, p. 156.
26 See, for example, the Annual Report of the State Bank, 1980-81, p. 5.
27 Figure quoted in the *Sunday Times*, London, 31.3.85. and by the *Economist*, London, 10.4.85. By the nature of the trade these estimates are likely to be speculative
28 Senior public sector bankers, in interviews with the author, gave examples of schemes to attract illicit funds into the mainstream banking channels. The NDFC issued a bond in '83, the purchase of which does not require registration of name or address.
29 See his statement in *Dawn*, 6.1.85.
30 State Bank Annual Report, 1979.
31 It has been replaced by a more modest rolling plan.
32 Uncertainty over the structure of the financial system persists, since further reforms were announced in 1985.
33 Pakistan. Recent Economic Developments, World Bank, 1984.
34 ibid. Also see report in *Dawn*, 30.5.84.
35 Commissioned by the OGDC in 1980/81.
36 On account of lag effects, since current investment will yield output later.
37 WAPDA figures quoted in *Dawn*, 6.1.85.
38 Average consumer price of gas was only 25% of fuel oil energy equivalent.
39 Even the first television address of Prime Minister Junejo could not escape the power cuts. See *Dawn*, 19.5.84.
40 *Herald*, Karachi. June 1984.
41 *Herald*, Karachi. February 1984.
42 For details see A. R. Kemal: Incentive structure of manufacturing industries of Pakistan. PIDE, 1984.
43 Calculated from PES, 1983/84, p.35.
44 In real terms. See, World Bank, op cit, 1982. p. 168.
45 This disappointment was reflected in public complaints by

officials. For example, see the statements of Federal Production Minister in *Dawn*, 2.3.83 and 23.2.84. The Federal Planning Secretary complained that private sector investment was low and confined mainly to the service sector. *Dawn*, 7.3.84.

46 The 'wait and see' policy among private entrepreneurs was evident in public statements. See, for example, *Dawn* 11.11.84 and 1.10.79.
47 In 1981, a West German economist, Dr Schiller, was appointed by the government to ascertain what needed to be done to mobilise the private sector. Nearly all the representatives of the private sector stressed the need to lessen bureaucratic controls.
48 ibid.
49 The '76 nationalisation of small, agro-based units was undone in '77. But the major units were left in the public sector. In 1978, three ghee units were denationalised. In 1984, two sugar mills and a paper mill were sold off. Denationalisation has remained patchy and hesitant.
50 *Pakistan and Gulf Economist*, 6.1.84. The government has also dragged its feet over a more stringent labour policy demanded by the industrialists.
51 Calculated from PES, various issues.
52 ibid.
53 According to UNESCO's definition, which requires a minimum of reading and writing, Pakistan has a literacy rate of 8%. FEER, 12.4.84 has a related article.
54 The dramatic impact of human capital investment in the Far East, for example, is analysed in E.Lee (ed): *Export led industrialisation and development.* ILO. 1981.
55 In the 1951 census, the population growth rate was 1.7%. The population more than doubled in the first 25 years, rising from 32.5 million to 65.31 million in 1972.
56 World Development Report, World Bank. 1984. p. 109.
57 Family Planning Association of Pakistan, *Dawn*, 2.10.83.
58 ibid.
59 ibid.
60 WDR.WB. 1984. p. 268.
61 State Bank Annual Report. 1982/83. p. 7.
62 WDR.WB. 1984 p. 269.
63 Pakistan: recent economic developments. WB. 1982.
64 The Military Balance, IISS, London. 1982/83.

Chapter Four

Ethnic Conflict

The two recent, vivid symbols of Pakistan's tortured political history are the execution, by the military, of its only democratically elected leader and the dismemberment of the country after the army's refusal to transfer power to the Bengalis. Each stigma is an epitome of the two primary levels of political conflict in Pakistan. The first consists of the struggle to create a democratic government. The second represents the conflict between ethnic groups, over the distribution of power between the centre and the provinces. Both domains of political struggle are inseparably linked, the connection being provided by the military. There is an overwhelming dominance of Punjabis in the army. Thus military rule not only, by definition, subverts the democratic process, but it is also accompanied by Punjabi hegemony over the other ethnic groups.

In part one, we traced the origins of ethnic conflict in Pakistan. A brief recapitulation follows.

Soon after the creation of Pakistan, the military and the bureaucracy acquired effective supremacy of power over the state, at the expense of civilian representatives. The ethnic composition of this nucleus of power reflected the preponderance of Punjabis in the military, and North Indian immigrant supremacy in the civil service. The appropriation of power, by the military-bureaucratic apparatus, entailed the denial of power to the élite of the majority ethnic group, the Bengalis. The class background of the Bengali élite could not overcome the inferior status accorded to their ethnic group. Ethnic hierarchies existed within classes. Ethnic allegiance provided the basic unit of political organisation. Accordingly, political parties were based on regional lines. No political party could claim support across the nation. In West Pakistan, the four provinces were merged into one unit, a fusion resented by all except the Punjabi-mahajjir élite. The struggle against a strong centre was led, up to 1971, by the Bengalis. The only way the Bengalis could end Punjabi domination was through a democratically elected government in which, by virtue of their majority, they would emerge as controllers of the central government. Thus, their campaign for democratic rule was intricately linked with the struggle to eliminate the supremacy of a minority ethnic group. At the same time, the demand for democratic government in West Pakistan was led by regional élites excluded from power. In NWFP and Baluchistan, respective upper classes led the NAP's demand for democratic rule. Indeed, the initial leadership of the PPP was provided, in large measure, by Sindhi landlords.

In 1977, after the resumption of military rule in the truncated Pakistan, the struggle for democratic rule again became synonymous with the movement against ethnic domination. There were, however, important differences in regional structure. The Punjabis were now the major ethnic group. Moreover, those regional élites denied access to power had to confront the army in a situation which was, militarily, far more vulnerable than that of the Bengalis. The logistical problem of containing a civil war across India had been a critical factor favouring the Bengalis. The remaining areas of Pakistan were physically contiguous, hence containment of internal rebellion did not pose a serious threat for one of the largest armies in the Third World.[1]

The growth and intensity of Sindhi nationalism under Zia is symbolic of the persistence of ethnic struggles as a primary source of political conflict in Pakistan. The ferocity with which Sind erupted in 1983 was perhaps the most ominous legacy of Bhutto's hanging. Bhutto was the first Sindhi to hold such an important political post. Under him, both substantive and symbolic measures were undertaken to rectify past discrimination against Sindhis. Preference was given to Sindhis for government jobs in Karachi, as well as in other parts of Sind. Perhaps no less significant were cultural achievements, such as the compulsory teaching of Sindhi in schools. Thus, Bhutto's trial was perceived in Sind to be motivated by the Punjabi élite's intolerance of competing claims to power from other regions. The nature of the Supreme Court judgement did little to assuage the sentiment. The verdict of the seven-member bench was split along ethnic lines. Four judges, all Punjabi, found Bhutto guilty. The remaining judges, all non-Punjabi, acquitted him.

The subsequent replacement and victimisation of PPP workers also fuelled ethnic antagonisms. Sindhi administrators were quite often displaced by Punjabi military officials. From 1977 to 1985, Zia relied, far more than Ayub ever did, on the exclusive support of the military.Unable to create a wider constituency, Zia accordingly distributed the rewards of power to the only institution which supported him. Consequently, military officials were far more visible in the performance of civilian duties. In contrast to the sixties, the network of state officials had expanded rapidly after nationalisation. The growth of state corporations and semi-autonomous 'quangos' increased the avenues of patronage open to Zia. The extensive appointment of military officials to top civilian posts led to what has been described as "the military colonisation of other institutions . . . the military acts as a reservoir or core of personnel for the sensitive institutions of the state".[2] Military intrusion into the Foreign Service, for example, was evident in the fact that 43% of Pakistan's ambassadors in 1982 came from the military.[3] The dominance of the Punjab in the upper echelons of the military is reflected in Table 1. The extension of the army's control over civil society has predictable ethnic connotations. The table illustrates the well-known dominance of the Punjabis in the military hierarchy, a feature which would not be so important, were it not for the fact that army personnel extended their control over civilian institutions during 1977-85. The only other ethnic group to have a fair representation in the army are, of course, the Pushtuns. In addition to their share in army hierarchy, or indeed as an adjunct to it, the Pushtuns have increased their participation in industrial and commercial enterprises. In recent years the Pushtun component of the power élite has expanded at the cost of mahajjirs.

Table 1: *Ethnic Background of Senior Government Officials, 1983.*

President Zia-ul-Haq	Punjab
General Sarwar Khan (MLA* NWFP and Punjab)	Punjab
Lt. General Gilani (Governor Punjab)	Punjab
Lt. General M. Iqbal Khan (MLA* Sind and Punjab)	Punjab
Lt. General K. Arif (Chief of staff to CMLA)	Punjab
Lt. General Rahimuddin Khan (MLA Baluchistan)	Punjab
Rear Admiral Tariq Kamal Khan (Naval chief)	Punjab
Air Marshal Jamal Ahmed Khan (Chief of the air force)	Punjab

Note: *Martial Law Administration.
Source: Biodatas published in *Dawn, Jang* and *Pakistan Times.*

Anger in response to the political victimisation of Sindhis, which was inherent in the efforts of the military to suppress the PPP, was fuelled by frustrations generated by the distributive impact of migration to the Gulf. As chapter three showed, the Sind interior had a disproportionately low share of emigrants. Thus, as has been the case since the creation of Pakistan, non-Sindhis in Karachi were the primary beneficiaries of economic prosperity in the province.

The scale of resentment in Sind surfaced in 1983. In August of that year, what MRD launched as a national movement against the military government turned into a violent regional struggle. Not only was the protest movement confined to Sind, but its character was also unlike any previous uprising. For the first time in Sind's history a protest movement was not limited to the urban centres. Far-flung rural areas[4] participated in an unrelenting series of riots which took the army four months to quell, even though

Sind had been isolated since the envisaged national movement failed to gather momentum elsewhere. The scale and ferocity of the rioting were disturbing enough, but the demands for a separate Sindhi nation-state were more ominous indicators of how swiftly the situation had deteriorated.[5] The wide social base of the movement revealed the depth of regionalist sentiment. Although in a number of areas the initial impetus was given by landlords, the movement was spontaneously joined by radical students and groups of peasants and workers. Indeed, sections of the MRD were disturbed by the swift radicalisation of the process.[6]

There were four principal political forces responsible for mobilising support in the '83 Movement. A major part was played by the PPP, which is led by landlords in Sind but commands support across a wide spectrum of Sindhi society. However, the party to have emerged as a serious force in Sindhi politics was the Sindhi Awami Tehrik (SAT). The party is led by R. B. Palejo, a one-time 'Maoist', who now combines Sindhi nationalism with a socialist platform. SAT draws its support from students, workers and peasants. It also has close links with Baluch student and labour unions. The third organisational force was provided by a cluster of small parties and groups; the most prominent amongst them was the Sind Hari Committee and the Jiye Sind Group. Jiye Sind represents hard-core Sindhi nationalists in the intelligentsia and is led by the veteran advocate of the rights of Sindhis, G. M. Syed. Finally, a significant role was played by religious leaders, who exercise considerable influence in rural Sind.

The role of the above groups was evident in each of the main areas of conflict during the '83 Movement. The most persistent resistance occurred in: (i) Nawabshah District (Sukkur Division), where the movement was organised by the local PPP leadership; (ii) Hala (Hyderabad Division), where the most potent figure was the Pir of Hala, who mobilised his religious followers (murids) — the Pir of Hala was also the vice-president of the PPP; (iii) Khairpur District (Sukkur Division), where the murids of the Pir of Ranipur led the movement; (iv) Dadu District (Hyderabad Division), where the most active elements were radical left-wing organisations such as Sind Awami Tehrik and Sind Hari Committee.

It is not surprising that the struggle was concentrated in the Sukkur and Hyderabad divisions of the province. There are approximately eleven million Sindhis in Pakistan, 92% of whom are concentrated in the Sukkur and Hyderabad regions.It is worth reiterating that the '83 Movement received no support from Karachi, the largest city not only of Sind but also of Pakistan. Karachi has a population of seven million, only 15% of whom are Sindhis. The efficacy of the Sindhi Nationalist Movement is severely hampered by the demographic distribution of Sindhis. Without mass support in Karachi, it is unlikely to seriously destabilise the military regime. In addition, the Sindhi Movement appears to suffer from organisational fragmentation and the concomitant lack of a unified leadership. This was all too obvious in the '83 Movement. No single figure emerged, who was accepted as the leader by all participants. There was little evidence of joint action or of a collective common platform. The splits were due to ideological schisms, as well as the result of historical grievances, still unresolved amongst the participants.

The '83 Movement was more a spontaneous outburst of Sindhi resentment than an organised, cohesive nationalist struggle. The parallels with East Pakistan ought not to be exaggerated. The Sindhis almost constitute a minority in their own province. The current phase of the struggle in Sind has determined the agenda for political reform — the 'resolution' of the problem lies in greater participation in government and a more equitable share in the economic progress of the province. This states the obvious but also emphasises that the interests of Sindhi nationalism are inextricably linked to a return of democratic rule. Indeed, the demise of democratic government provided a critical spur to the growth of the Nationalist Movement in Sind. The PPP's rule had begun to rectify discrimination against Sindhis. In the limited span of five years, measures had been taken to increase Sindhi participation in government, as well as to promote the Sindhi language. The removal of the first government favourable to Sindhis, and its replacement by a Punjabi-Pushtun dominated army, fuelled ethnic antagonism in the province. The removal of PPP appointees and the suppression of the party had obvious ethnic connotations, since Sindhis were inevitably bearing the brunt of the repression. These discriminatory actions were accompanied by a particularly insensitive pattern of land allocation. The bulk of the newly irrigated lands in the fertile northern districts of Sind were distributed among retired military officers and members of the Civil Service. Most of these officials were Punjabis. These 'settler colonies' became, not unnaturally, potent symbols of Punjabi/army exploitation. Ethnic hierarchies implicit in military rule, and the consequent organised manifestations of growth in Sindhi consciousness, have provoked a qualitative shift in the ability of Sind to act as a catalyst for protest movements.

The articulation of regional aspirations was formalised in the demand for a Confederation, outlined by the ex-governor of Sind, Mumtaz Bhutto. The essence of the proposals, reproduced below, are almost identical to the Awami League's six-point programme, which formed the basis for the Regional Autonomy Movement in East Pakistan. The Confederation proposal consists of the following principal demands:[8]

1. The Confederation shall consist of the centre, which shall be known as the federation, and the provinces, which shall be known as states. (The term provinces is normally used in dominions and must be dropped.)

2. The states must be recognised as 'autonomous and sovereign'. They shall co-exist and federate to form the Confederation and shall surrender a part of their sovereign authority to federal institutions.

3. The authority and power to be surrendered by the states to the federation shall be restricted to the following subjects:
(i) Defence.
(ii) Foreign affairs.
(iii) Currency.
(iv) Interstate and international communication, including telecommunications.
(v) Economic co-ordination and interstate movement of goods, including the power to arbitrate in disputes between states.
(vi) Election of federal legislature.

4. The Confederation shall have a parliamentary, democratic system. Elections to the federal and state legislatures shall be held by adult franchise and for a term of five years. The federal and state governments shall be responsible to the federal and state legislatures respectively.

5. The office of Prime Minister shall rotate among the states.

6. The states shall have all authority and power which has not been expressly and by mutual consent surrendered to the federal government, including the power to enter into agreements of a commercial nature, and for the purpose of development of the states, with foreign countries provided it is not incompatible with the foreign policy of the country.

7. There shall be one and the same flag for Pakistan. As a mark of their 'autonomy and sovereignty' the states shall also have their own flags.

8. In the event of any subversion of the constitution and the overall democratic set-up, usurpation of powers of the federal government and/or interference with the 'autonomy and sovereignty' of any state or states, by the armed forces or any individual or agency being a part of the Confederation, the state or states concerned shall have the power to separate from the Confederation and declare Independence. In such an event the state or states concerned shall be at liberty and shall have the power to appeal to the international community and/or the United Nations to provide it all the protection and aid necessary to preserve its sovereignty and independence under the provisions of international law and the charter of the United Nations . . .

The Confederation proposals are unrealistic, not only because the provinces of Punjab and NWFP will not support its provisions, but also on account of the ambiguity as to who would implement such a scheme. In a democratic dispensation, a Confederation cannot be brought about through constitutional changes, since the required majority in Parliament is likely to prove elusive within the parameters of Pakistan's demographic distribution. Under military rule, the only option is an armed struggle — the success of such a course of action requires external assistance, which is not likely to be forthcoming in the current geo-political situation. None the less, these proposals may well acquire value as symbols of Sindhi alienation, similar to the role played by the six-point demand of the Awami League.

A section of Sindhi landlords, who had supported the '83 Movement, participated in the '85 elections. Their decision was partly influenced by the government's decision to set up a tribunal to investigate violations of the '72 land reforms.[9] The military was well aware of the fact that almost all of the sixty-four major landowners had circumvented the PPP reforms. The timing of the tribunal announcement was designed to exert pressure on recalcitrant landlords to participate in, and thus extend legitimacy to, the '85 elections. It is, unlikely, however, that their co-operation will dampen the more strident nationalist tendencies.[10]

In contrast to Sind, a substantial section of the Pushtun élite of NWFP is well integrated into the Pakistani power structure. The primary source of incorporation is the army. Recent developments in the province have been determined largely by the Soviet intervention in neighbouring Afghanistan. With it has evaporated much of the support, within NWFP, for a larger Afghanistan — referred to as Pushtunistan, which would combine Afghanistan with the NWFP and the Pushtun regions of Baluchistan Province. Support for Pushtunistan within the NWFP has always been exaggerated by the central government. None the less, for those who supported it, the creation of such a state was ultimately based on getting military support from the Soviet Union. However, the '79 Russian intervention in a Pushtun country provoked, by and large, a mixture of fear and anger which was not conducive to future collaboration. Ironically, Soviet activities in Afghanistan may have contributed towards a greater integration of the NWFP with the rest of Pakistan. Further, the massive flow of Afghan refugees, whose permanent abode in Pakistan looks increasingly certain, has also meant that a substantial proportion of the population which would have been part of 'Pushtunistan' now resides in NWFP. After the invasion, the Afghan population is approximately fourteen million, whereas the population of the Frontier Province, inclusive of refugees, is nearly sixteen million.[11] The effect of recent events was summed up by a former Chief Minister of Baluchistan, in an interview with the author: "A *de facto* Pushtunistan has already come into being . . . most of the three million refugees that Pakistan claims have come from Afghanistan will not go back. History shows that migrations from the north to the south are never reversed . . . today, and this is claimed by Pushtuns themselves, there are only two non-Pushtuns in a senior capacity in the Frontier Administration. All the rest are Pushtuns. The bureaucracy is Pushtun. On top of that, Pushtuns are not that unhappy because there is nothing in the frontier that the Punjabis have usurped . . . the Pathans control the frontier".[12]

Economic developments have also had a corrosive effect on possible regionalist aspirations. Not only have Pathans been prominent in the enriching migratory process to the Gulf, but internal migration has also provided an avenue for employment. There has been a substantial migration of Pathans to Karachi, where they dominate the privately owned transport sector. Indeed, there are more Pathans in Karachi than in any city of the NWFP.[13] Further, the primary economic beneficiaries of the drugs trade, an estimated $3 billion, are groups in the Frontier Province. Government officials are not innocent about the political advantages they derive by not clamping down on narcotics dealers and cultivators.[14]

In addition to the above factors, the assimilation of Pathans within Pakistan is helped as stated earlier, by the fair degree of representation that they have in the Administration. Indeed, some partisan splits within opposition groups have had distinct ethnic connotations. In 1979, the Pathan leaders split with their Baluch partners in the NAP. The Baluch leader, Bizenjo, formed the PNP as dissension occurred over Pushtun leaders' backing for the Pakistan government's support of Afghan guerrillas. The objection of the Pathan leader Wali Khan to the use of the emphatic term, nationalities, to describe ethnic groups, also contributed to the split. He suggested the milder characterisation of ethnic groups as "distinctive cultural and linguistic entities."[15]

Developments in the NWFP have, of course, been shaped almost exclusively by the Afghan crisis. The magnitude of the influx is indicated in Table 2 below. It is worth emphasising that the figures underestimate the numbers concerned, since a substantial body of young male refugees are unregistered. In addition, there are a number of refugees in Karachi who are not accounted for in the figures *below*.

The Pushtun refugees from Afghanistan have been wary of involving themselves in Pushtun nationalism. In Pakistan this involves conflict with the central government, which has been the prime benefactor of the refugees. It is not surprising, therefore, that the refugees have steered clear of activity which would antagonise the Pakistan Government. Indeed their struggle against the Soviet-backed Afghan regime has emphasised religion, not ethnicity. The emphasis on Islam has, ironically, enabled the Pakistan Government to achieve by accident what it has previously failed to obtain by design — the dampening of ethnic nationalism through religion. The guerrilla groups are perhaps ideologically closer to the central government than any substantial group within Pakistani society.

Table 2: *Afghan Refugees in Pakistan.*

Region	Population	Camps
NWFP and Tribal Areas	2,047,081	179
Baluchistan	727,173	60
Punjab	91,552	10
Total	2,865,806	249

Source: Chief Commissioner for Afghan Refugees, Islamabad, 1984.

In an earlier chapter we emphasised the immediate benefits accruing to the Zia regime from the Afghan crisis: international support, aid inflows, mitigation of provincialism. One needs to supplement this by taking the long-term consequences into account. In doing so one must distinguish between the effect on the central government and the costs borne by the local population. It is true that, by and large, the host population has reacted with considerable graciousness and accommodation to this large influx of refugees. This hospitality and lack of friction was helped considerably by ethnic affinity with the migrants. However, the longer the refugees stay in Pakistan and, concomitantly, the longer the war goes on, the patience of the host community is put under increasing strain. The growing tensions were evident during the author's research trip in 1986. Two menacing effects on Pakistani society appear to be commonly associated with the refugees. The first is the militarisation of civil society due to the large influx of arms. Sub-machine-guns and automatic rifles are easily available on the black market. These relatively sophisticated weapons were used, for example, in the ethnic violence which flared in Karachi in 1986. In some cases the rioters were better armed than the police. The easier access to arms has been a dangerous side effect of the Afghan crisis, and has particularly ominous implications for the future level of violence in civilian conflicts within Pakistan. The second feature commonly associated with the Afghan development is drugs. The involvement of some refugees has led to exaggerated popular association of refugees with drug smuggling. Indeed in situations such as these it is not uncommon for refugees to become scapegoats for most social ills. The growth of the drugs trade has not only created a substantial community of addicts within Pakistan but has also contributed to an insidious debasement of public morality. The association of some refugees with this development has contributed to an increasingly hostile climate of opinion against them. The association of refugees with drugs was evident in police raids of Karachi's Sohrab Goth Market in 1986. This part of Karachi had a large number of unregistered refugees, most of whom were non-Pushtun. After the anti-smuggling raid the refugees, mostly of Turkic and Tajik origin, were moved to transit camps. The incident reinforced popular prejudices against refugee involvement with drugs. However, the most pernicious source of tension between the refugees and the host population is the increasing fear that a substantial number will not return to Afghanistan, as well as the resentment felt towards the refugees for being the cause of sustained military conflict in NWFP. The war is enveloping the host population at two levels. First, Afghan planes encroach deeper and deeper into Pakistani territory in 'hot pursuit' operations against the guerrillas. Second, the Afghan Secret Service, KHAD, has been pursuing a policy of destabilising civilian life in Pakistani cities such as Peshawar. This is done through frequent planting of bombs across the city, with the obvious intention of creating a rift between the host population and the refugees. It is quite evident that such rifts are widening and will continue to do so the longer the war goes on, and the more weary the host population grows.

Within Pakistan the pressure for a settlement with the Afghan Government is growing. The initial fear that the Soviets may go beyond Afghanistan and cross the Pakistani border has subsided. As the threat of Soviet invasion subsides and is perceived to be virtually non-existent, there has been a noticeable shift in sentiment against the United States for appearing to have an interest in prolonging the war. The offer of a cease-fire, made by the Afghan Government in December 1986, acted as a catalyst for this change in perception among sections of the population and the press. The Zia Government increasingly runs the risk of being perceived domestically as having surrendered the right to reach a swift settlement on account of ultimate authority resting in Washington. Howver, there is a fear of retaliatory action if the Pakistan Government does not reach an accord with Afghanistan. Sources within the Pakistan army concede that there is little likelihood of breaking the stalemate on the battlefields. The Mujahadeen are incapable of toppling the Afghan regime, but have the capacity to sustain a war of attrition. In such circumstances, the refugees may find that some of the hospitality could turn sour. A recognition that they might have overstayed their welcome was also evident among refugees interviewed by the author in late 1986. Although there appears to be considerable sympathy regarding the refugees' predicament, the host population is increasingly wary of the costs of a war which is not of their own making. Pakistan has been embroiled, for eight years, in a war in which its population does not participate. The government was not responsible for starting it, but is under domestic pressure to play an active role in assisting its termination. The much-quoted parallels with Palestine and Lebanon may be exaggerated but there is little doubt that violence within Pakistan will escalate as tensions with refugees mount.

Conflict among refugees is also a source of worry for the government. The large majority of refugees are Pushtun (90%). The tensions with refugees of different ethnic origin — Uzbeks, Tajiks, Turkics — have surfaced periodically. In July 1985, for example, violence flared among refugees in Quetta. As a result of the political unrest, unregistered refugees were forced to register; some were sent to Punjab (Mianwali) and unregistered refugees were barred from entering Quetta. The recurrence of such trouble could complicate a potentially explosive situation for Pakistan.

In Baluchistan, particularly since early '79, attitudes of some groups have hardened. There have been open declarations by prominent Baluch leaders to the effect that accommodation with the central government is not possible and, consequently, their aim is to create an independent Baluchistan.[16] "Under Ayub and Bhutto we fought an internal war. We took it as an internal conflict between the government and the people of Pakistan ... we thought of ourselves as the people of Pakistan and we were loyal — but now the situation has changed altogether. We have declared that there is no room for us in Pakistan and ours is a fight for independence".[17]

The dilemma for those advocating independence lies in the increasing chasm between intention and possibility. Ironically, the defiant declarations of emancipation are being made in a political environment where the military possibilities of achieving these objectives are rapidly diminishing. The likelihood of defeating the Pakistan army through a guerrilla struggle in Baluchistan have always been remote. The terrain limits activity to specific areas, and the tiny population of Baluchistan, 5% of the national, is neither large nor well equipped enough to defeat a huge, modern army. Already the Baluch have paid a heavy price for their confrontation with the army in the seventies. The decisive military defeat was followed by a substantial inflow of central government funds to develop infrastructure in Baluchistan.[18] This expansion was primarily motivated by military strategy.[19] The recently constructed network of roads and communications has considerably improved the army's mobility and access to hitherto remote areas.[20] The second motive for improving infrastructure is to facilitate exploration of Baluchistan's mineral resources. Of particular importance are the ore deposits at Saindak which, according to a U.N. study, are likely to yield not only copper but also gold, silver, pyrite and magnetite.[21] The prospect that the output of these deposits will be used for industrial development outside Baluchistan has revived Baluchi bitterness over the use of gas from the Sui fields for the benefit of provinces other than Baluchistan.[22] These sentiments are reminiscent of East Pakistani bitterness over the use of jute revenues for industrial development in West Pakistan.[23] One source of bitterness is the claim that the royalty rate of gas to the Baluchistan State Treasury is 12.5% of the well-head price, whereas the rate for provincial share is 45% in countries such as Canada.[24] Anger over economic exploitation reinforces the sense of alienation from Pakistani nationhood prevalent in Baluchistan. Baluchis have been, by and large, excluded not only from the central government but also from positions of authority within Baluchistan.[25]

In spite of hardening attitudes among some of its leaders, Baluchistan has been politically docile under the Zia Administration. This uncharacteristic silence has been due to a combination of external developments and internal dissensions. The Afghan crisis, and the toppling of the Shah of Iran, have enhanced the geo-political significance of Baluchistan. The strategic importance acquired by the province has led to a substantial inflow of resources. In 1982, a special development programme for Baluchistan was launched, funded by the U.S.A., the E.E.C., Japan and Arab countries, particularly Kuwait and Saudi Arabia. The U.S.A.I.D. has financed the ambitious Baluchistan Area Development Programme (BALAD). The influx of resources into the province has been substantial, reflected in rapid infrastructural development: five new airports have been built, a naval harbour is nearing completion at Gwadur, and three fishing harbours are under construction.[26] An extensive road network has been developed. The construction of infrastructure in Baluchistan, particularly along the 400-mile coastline of the province, has been determined primarily by the above mentioned security interests in the wake of developments in Iran and Afghanistan. These interests were evident in a report recommending U.S. assistance for infrastructural development in Baluchistan, since it "would be politically less provocative because while it would have a clear cut military utility, it could be disguised as economic aid".[27]

Most of the income-generating investment has been concentrated in Quetta and the Pushtun-dominated north — areas which have a relatively well-developed infrastructure and agriculture. The resources being poured into the province appear to have cultivated a segment of the Baluchi élite. As benefiting intermediaries they have actively participated in the development programmes. The magnet of resources has attracted many of the Sardars, a degree of collusion with central authorities unprecedented in the recent history of Baluchistan.

The other consequence of the Afghan crisis — the refugee influx — has also had a deep impact on Baluchistan. In fact, the province has the highest number of refugees as a percentage of local population. Most of the refugees are Pushtun, which has significantly altered the ethnic balance in the province. Out of a population of four million people, one and a half million (nearly 38%) are Pushtun. If one adds the three-quarters of a million Pushtun refugees, then Baluchis virtually cease to be the majority ethnic group in their own province.

The third external influence on the province has been migration to the Gulf. Like other provinces of Pakistan, Baluchistan has benefited from the process (see chapter on the economy). The Mekran region of the province has been the primary recipient of Gulf remittances. Not surprisingly, the flow of money has contributed towards an expansion of local consumer demand.

These external influences have combined with internal dissension to mollify Baluch hostility towards the central government. We have referred above to the exercise of patronage by Sardars, who have co-operated with the government's development programme. Differences have widened, however, even amongst those Baluch leaders who are in opposition. To a large extent, these differences reflect the post-mortem analysis of the Baluch uprising of the seventies. Splits have occurred at two levels. The first relates to the extent of regional autonomy and the tactics to be pursued *vis-à-vis* the rest of the federation. The second split reflects ethnic divisions within Baluchistan, evident in growing differences among Baluch and Pushtun leaders. Regarding the former, ex-Governor Bizenjo split from the more militant groups to form the Pakistan National Party, advocating greater provincial autonomy but adhering firmly to constitutional methods within the framework of a federal Pakistan. Bizenjo advocates a revision of the '73 Constitution in favour of extending regional autonomy, citing a clause in the original document that the extent of regional powers was to be revised a decade after 1973. Other former colleagues of Bizenjo, such as Mengal and K. B. Marri, are far less sanguine about the possibilities of *'rapprochement'*. Both consider armed struggle as a necessary instrument to achieve independence either as a separate state or as a far more autonomous unit in a confederal framework. A. T. Mengal is a founder member of the Sind-Baluchistan-Pushtun Front (SBPF), advocating a confederation (see section on Sind). Marri adheres to the belief in the efficacy of guerrilla warfare, although his current following appears to be largely restricted to his tribe. Both Marri and Mengal have been in exile for most of the Zia period, which has not only reduced their immediate potency but has also created a leadership vacuum. On account of this, leadership of strident Baluch nationalism is currently in the hands of the Baluch Students Organisation (BSO). The BSO is particularly incensed by the form of recent development in Baluchistan. A source of resentment is the Hub Industrial Trading Estate, established ostensibly with the intention of creating and encouraging local entrepreneurs. Due to a number of fiscal incentives, such as a five-year tax holiday and exemption from import duty on plant and equipment, Hub has attracted a number of projects. However, the primary beneficiaries have been industrialists from Karachi. The trading estate is only fourteen miles from Karachi and hence an ideal location for the city's industrialists. According to a study undertaken by the Applied Economics Research Centre at Karachi University, only 1% of management at Hub is Baluch. The head offices of all twenty-nine major projects in 1986 were at Karachi. Further, due to the import duty exemptions, the projects are biased towards capital-intensive techniques; hence the employment effect is not particularly large. It is not difficult to see why the industrial estate has become a symbol, among groups such as the BSO, of regional exploitation.

The second source of division among opposition groups in Baluchistan is ethnicity. As mentioned earlier, the province has been subjected to a substantial increase in the Pushtun component of its population due to the Afghan refugee influx. Most of the Pushtun population of Baluchistan is concentrated in the northern areas of the province: Quetta, Zhob, Loralai and Pisin. The demand to merge these Pushtun areas of Baluchistan with the NWFP has been forcefully articulated by the Pukhtunkhwa NAP, led by M. K. Achakzai. Some of the Baluch leaders, such as Bizenjo and Marri, appear to accept the legitimacy of demands for redrawing provincial boundaries. These internal splits have reinforced larger, international factors to produce a relatively docile decade in Baluchistan.

President Zia's observation that "if the Russians come to Baluchistan it will be by naked aggression and that is the only Baluch problem we have to worry about",[28] is both an apt summary of the military balance in Baluchistan and a reflection of the army's attitude to demands for greater provincial autonomy. In 1977, however, General Zia had disbanded the Hyderabad tribunal which was trying Baluch and Pathan leaders for treason. The disbandment was necessitated by the needs of the military government to cultivate all political parties while they eliminated Bhutto. The NDP, a component of the PNA alliance which was being wooed by the military at the time, had insisted on the abolition of the tribunal. At the same time the Daoud Government in Afghanistan was keen to send Baluch refugees, from the conflict in the seventies, back to Pakistan. To facilitate the process, they wanted guarantees of an amnesty from the Pakistan Government in return for commitments on their part that they would not actively support BPLF's guerrilla organisation. The release of the Baluch leaders was followed by negotiations with Zia, during the course of which it became quite evident that the military were not serious about increasing Baluch representation in government. Hopes for the formation of a Baluch provincial government were dashed once it became evident that the military were not going to transfer power. For the Baluch leaders, sustained military rule had only one overwhelming implication — the prolongation of Punjabi hegemony. Relations with the central government were further soured by the hanging of a leader of the Baluch Student Organisation, in spite of a stay of execution imposed by the Baluchistan High Court. Incidently, this judgement by Justice Marri provoked Zia into promulgating a new oath for judges which drastically diminished the powers of the judiciary. Five judges of the high courts, and three of the Supreme Court, refused to take the oath and resigned.

Zia's previously quoted reference to Russian intervention as being the critical factor in Baluchistan is acknowledged by Baluch leaders. However, despite Russian threats of retaliation against the Pakistan Government for harbouring Afghan guerrillas, their options in Baluchistan are limited. They have made it clear to the Baluchis that they have no intention of directly getting involved in their struggle.[29] Historically, the Soviet Union has never backed the Baluch in their confrontations with the central government.[30] At present, the USSR cannot invade Pakistan, since this would involve risking a hostile response from the U.S.A. This implies that armed struggle against the Pakistan army is not a viable option for the Baluchis. The predicament was summarised by a Baluch leader: "What threat can the Baluch pose to such a large army with sophisticated weapons . . . in our fight for independence we know what sort of resistance we will get from the other side. . . it will be ten times more than the last two conflicts. So definitely we are not going to enter into any kind of adventure where we know the result will not be in our favour, unless and until we have outside support . . . Afghanistan by itself cannot pose a threat to Pakistan unless the Russians support them . . . so far the Russians don't feel like aiding the Baluch. There are reasons for it. The Russians will be quite reluctant to Balkanise Pakistan".[31]

Perhaps the only option left for the Baluchis is to participate in a national movement for democratic rule, as advocated by the former Governor of Baluchistan, G. B. Bizenjo. Natural allies are sections of the Sindhi élite. The formation of a Sindhi-Baluch-Pushtun alliance for democratic rule, in April 1985,[32] reflects the continuing synonymity of ethnic and democratic struggles. It is only through a democratic system that the élites of the minority ethnic groups are likely to get any semblance of power within Pakistan.

Centralisation of state power is not an unusual phenomenon in the contemporary world. To a certain extent, such centralisation is inevitable if the state is to play the extensive role that is expected of it in the development process. The concentration of power is inherent in a framework of economic planning and detailed intervention of the state in social and political spheres. The specific circumstances of a nation-state determine the degree to which such centralisation would be desirable. If a centralised system operates in a democratic environment with minimal ethnic diversity, then the centre's dominance is least likely to provoke centre-state tensions. Resentment and hostility to a powerful central government is a function of three critical variables:

(i) Ethnic and linguistic diversity.
(ii) Economic disparity among regions.
(iii) Unrepresentative, authoritarian central government.

The above three conditions usually entail the exclusion from power of some of the ethnic élites.

The combined existence of the above three features in Pakistan is reflected in its violent history of ethnic conflict — the '71 catastrophe, the rebellions of the Baluchis in the sixties and the seventies and the '83 uprising in Sind. Pakistan's quest for national cohesion required an adhesive framework based on an acceptable distribution of economic and political power among ethnic groups. In the absence of such devolution, the recourse to religion as a uniting bond cannot override the coercion explicit in the denial of legitimate claims to power. The inability to absorb the conflict between ethnic élites has already led to the dismemberment of Pakistan. The outcome was a direct result of minority ethnic dominance imposed through military rule. In the truncated Pakistan, it is conceivable that the army can handle, in purely physical terms, the violence generated by ethnic conflict. But the task of effective political integration necessitates the evolution of a mechanism to accommodate the struggle among ethnic groups. In the Pakistani context, such a stable distribution of power requires, at the very minimum, the revival of a genuine electoral process for the formation of representative governments at the central and provincial levels.

Footnotes:

1. Only India has a larger army.
2. S. E. Finer: "Military and politics in the third world", in W. S. Thompson (ed): *The Third World.* p. 84.
3. H. A. Rizvi: "Paradox of military rule in Pakistan", *Asian Survey,* May 1984.
4. Serious rioting took place in Naushero, Warah, Moro, Feroze, Dadu, Thatta Larkana, Nawabshah, Sukkur.
5. See reports in *Dawn,* 17.8.83 — 1.9.83.
6. For example, these fears were expressed in a letter from A. Zuberi, Central Information Secretary NDP, to the MRD leadership. Published in *Herald,* Karachi January 1984.
7. Palejo has been in prison since '79.
8. M. A. Bhutto: "Confederation", mimeo, 1984.
9. See report in *Herald,* op cit.
10. Unless they are given a substantial share in power, which is unlikely, their position could become similar to that of Bengalis who co-operated with central government in the fifties.
11. Calculations based on U.N. population statistics contained in Population and Vital Statistics, Report, New York. 1983, corrected for refugee flows.
12. A. T. Mengal's interview with author. 1985.
13. An estimated quarter of a million Pathans reside in Karachi, which exceeds the Pathan population of Peshawar, the largest city in NWFP. In May 1985 Pathan operators of private transport in Karachi became targets of rioting after a series of accidents.
14. This point was emphasised by a member of the government's Narcotics Control Agency in a conversation with the author, 1984.
15. The immediate cause which brought on the crisis was Mazari's arbitrary dissolution of the central committee of the NDP.
16. Interviews of Baluch leaders in S. Harrison, op. cit. pp. 60-70.
17. Interview with Mengal, op cit.
18. Between 1973 and 1976, the PPP Government built 562 miles of new roads. See White Paper on Baluchistan, 1976. p. 42.
19. Over 50% of the $1.97 billion special development plan for Baluchistan, unveiled in 1980, was devoted to infrastructural development.
20. Military officials, in interviews with the author, stressed the military drawbacks due to poor infrastructure in the seventies rebellion.

21 S. Harrison, op cit, p. 166.
22 Primary beneficiaries were commercial and domestic users in Punjab and Karachi.
23 See part one, chapter two.
24 S. Harrison, op cit, p. 163.
25 For details of poor Baluch representation in government see The Baluch Are Deprived of Jobs in Baluchistan. (Nedae Baluchistan 1. 1. London, 1980.)
26 For details see J. Rashid: "Pakistan and the Central Command". Middle East Report. July-August 1986.
27 F. Fukuyama: "The Security of Pakistan". A Rand Corporation Trip Report, 1980.
28 S. Harrison, op cit, p. 150.
29 Confirmed by Baluch leaders in interviews with the author.
30 The Russian opposition to Baluchi separatism is spelled out clearly in B. Igragimov: *The Baluch of Pakistan.*
31 Interview with A. T. Mengal.
32 Formed by exiled leaders in London. The Pushtun component of the alliance seems to be at variance with developments in Pakistan.

Chapter Five

The Role of the State

The quantitative growth of the state has been an ubiquitous phenomenon. In the industrialised capitalist countries, state power has been used to secure substantial reforms in the economic, social and political spheres. In socialist economies, the state defines the matrix within which the whole society operates. Similarly, in the developing world the state permeates social structures. Increasingly, the state has acquired the pre-eminence in society accorded to it by Hobbes in his conception of a Leviathan.[1] The pervasiveness of the state's intervention raises fundamental issues about its nature. What is the state? What is its relationship with society? Is it primarily an instrument for the ruling classes to maintain their hegemony? Or is the state's role derived from the functional necessities of modern society? Before we examine these issues it is important to emphasise that the state does not consist of static, timeless institutions with a specific immutable relationship to society. Some governments use the power of the state to initiate fundamental reforms, while others use it to maintain or accentuate hierarchies in society. The state may be generally referred to as constituting "the presence of a supreme authority, ruling over a defined territory, who is recognised as having power to make decisions in matters of government and is able to enforce such decisions and generally maintain order . . . the capacity to exercise coercive authority is an essential ingredient".[2]

The extensive role of the state in Pakistan has to be seen in the context of the rapid structural change imposed by the development process. It is obvious that in the long run, economic development produces stable political systems, i.e. rich societies tend to be stable since material resources are, by definition, not particularly scarce, thus mitigating a principal cause of political conflict. In contrast, the *process* of economic and social change is disruptive since it entails breaking society's traditional equilibrium. Consequently there is a readjustment of aspirations regarding a share in political power and material benefits. These claims generate conflicts which the state either accommodates or represses. As we have seen in the preceding chapters, the Pakistani élite has tended to use the power of the state to repress, rather than accommodate, demands on the political system.

Whereas the state may primarily be used to serve the interests of a specific ethnic-class élite, its wide-ranging activities affect all sections of society. The pervasiveness of its impact on the community derives from the infinite variety of functions it performs in a developing country. The state's realm of duties can be divided into three broad categories. First, in the economic sphere the state participates directly in the processes of productive capital formation and the provision of infrastructure and it also affects private sector resource allocation through fiscal and monetary policies. Secondly, in the social sector most contemporary states take responsibility for the provision of mass education, health facilities and population control programmes. Finally, in the political sphere, the coercive component of the state provides a military force capable of fighting external threats and of repressing internal dissent which the political system cannot absorb. Indeed, the success of political institutionalisation lies precisely in the ability of the state to resolve internal conflicts without the use of force.

These functional necessities emanate from the imperatives of organisation inherent in a complex modern society, whether it be socialist or capitalist. The relative weight attached to separate functions naturally differs from country to country. But the failure to recognise the necessity of the state in modern industrialised societies led to the astonishing prediction by Marx that the state would 'wither away' once a communist society was established.[3] Similarly, Lenin's view that the state had to be 'smashed' was based, as Weber pointed out, on a basic confusion between the nature of administrating an industrialised nation and the question of who controls the state apparatus.[4] The issue of the class dominance of a specific state is distinct from accepting the necessity of public institutions for political, economic and social organisation. The failure to discriminate between the two led to the original Marxist-Leninist perspective that the elimination of the bourgeoisie would lead to the disappearance of the state, since the latter is merely an 'instrument of bourgeois rule'.[5]

The relevant issue is not whether the state will continue to exist, but how it can be controlled such that its coercive powers are minimised, while its capacity for reform is utilised. Regulations controlling the powers of the state are particularly important since only the state has the publicly sanctioned authority to use force in a given territorial unit. Thus a central component of the popular demand for constitutional, democratic government in Pakistan consists of an appeal for the replacement of arbitrary and capricious use of state power by a systematic set of regulations. The latter constraint on state power, provided by law, enables the judicial system to function against defined public criteria for measuring the legality of state actions.

These constitutional limits are intended to give protection against arbitrary coercion by the state.[6] Such rule of law arguments are not to be confused with authoritarian tendencies which stress the primacy of obedience to law. The demand for civilian government, as opposed to military rule, is based not only on the grounds that the latter denies representation to the people but also on the fact that martial law undermines the basis of the state's legitimacy.[7] The right to command the state, in the twentieth century, can no longer be sustained on the basis of traditional sources of authority such as hereditary rule of monarchs or divine mission.[8] The legitimacy of the modern state rests primarily on legal authority. It emanates from a code of regulations embodied in a constitution. The requirement of legitimacy is critical: "The domination that characterises the state claims to be legitimate, and must actually be regarded as such by rulers and ruled. The domination is legitimate only if it takes place in accordance with a legal order whose validity is presupposed by the acting individuals".[9]

In the case of Pakistan under Zia, the uninterrupted use of martial law between 1977 and 1986 emphasised the military's illegitimate command over the state. The arbitrary nature of martial law prevented protection against state coercion. The power of the judiciary to review sentences by military courts was abrogated. Thus, there were no limits to what the state could do to repress dissent. This produced a situation where the threat of terror was institutionalised. Fear was instilled by the cumulative effect of continuous martial law, against which there was no legal or physical protection.[10]

The question of whether the military or civilians should exert supreme command over the state is related to the struggle for legitimate government and the denial of supremacy to the coercive and unrepresentative apparatus of the state. There are, however, other issues regarding the state's relationship with society which are distinct from the question of representational legitimacy. One of these concerns the nature of the connection between the economic structure and the state. Hamza Alavi's perceptive analysis[11] has provided the basic framework for a number of studies of developing countries.[12] Alavi's argument is thus summarised: "A weak and underdeveloped indigenous bourgeoisie is unable, at the moment of independence, to subordinate the relatively highly developed colonial state apparatus through which the metropolitan power had exercised dominion over it. However, in addition, given a new convergence of interests of the three competing propertied classes under metropolitan patronage, the bureaucratic-military oligarchy mediates their competing, but no longer contradictory, interests and demands. *By that token* it acquires a relatively autonomous role and is not simply the instrument of any of the three classes ... the superstructure in the colony is 'overdeveloped' in relation to the structure in the colony, for its basis lies in the metropolitan structure itself, from which it is later separated at the time of independence".[13]

Although Alavi provides a general theoretical framework for developing countries, his empirical analysis is rooted in Pakistan. It is surprising, therefore, that ethnic dominance is ignored. Defining the 'nature' of the Pakistani state purely in terms of class overlooks, quite arbitrarily and unjustifiably, other cleavages and hierarchies in society which are reflected in the state. Ironically, if the state had played the role Alavi claims for it, i.e. mediating the interests of the propertied classes, Pakistan would have had a far less disruptive political history. Has the Pakistani state accommodated the interests of the property-owning classes of Bengal or Baluchistan or indeed of Sind? It was precisely on account of the failure to integrate the dominant Bengali classes into the framework of state authority that Bangladesh was created. Similarly, the propertied classes of Baluchistan have been excluded from state power. Except for a brief period under the PPP the Sindhi landlords, too, have had very limited access to power at the centre. Alavi's analysis imposes a partial class framework, which is a poor explanatory device for the political structure being examined, and is therefore analytically deficient.

There are other subsidiary issues worth mentioning. The characterisation of the colonial state as 'overdeveloped' is misleading. The state's interaction with civil society, during the era of foreign domination, was primarily coercive, *not* functionally pervasive. Indeed, the state's intervention in the economic, political or social spheres was minimal. As long as metropolitan military supremacy was enforced and an economic surplus transferred to the colonising power, the government was quite content to relegate autonomous authority to princes and members of other dominant classes for dealing with their subjects. For example, land was granted "to military chiefs who were permitted to realise the revenues, on condition of keeping order and supporting a body of troops for state service when required".[14] The state was not 'overdeveloped'; in a sense it stood outside society. It was not derived from society, but exerted absolute power over it. This legacy of a hierarchical relationship, in which the dominant classes of civil society were subordinate to the state, had important repercussions after Independence. The scale and pace of the development process required a substantial concentration of organisational and financial resources in the hands of the state. Accordingly, there was an exponential increase in its functions. The state channelled domestic and foreign capital, built infrastructure, developed industry and was responsible for the provision of social services such as education. The state did not merely reflect socio-economic reality, it was shaping it. In the process, it was harnessing and creating an indigenous bourgeoisie out of the migrant merchant communities of North India and the Punjab. At the same time, the landowning families of the Punjab were not only directly represented in the upper echelons of the military-bureaucratic complex but were also, not surprisingly, the primary beneficiaries of policies for the agricultural sector. The élite consisted of this combination of refugee and Punjabi industrial and landowning classes. Sections of this élite formulated and executed government policy. Resources at the command of the state were allocated to groups within this élite. For example, the Ayub Government consciously adopted a strategy in which the explicit objective was to transfer resources to the élite. This was done on the grounds that a concentration of income in the hands of entrepreneurs would lead to higher savings and investment and, consequently, higher growth. Accordingly, resources were transferred from the jute growers in East Pakistan to the industrial entrepreneurs in Karachi and Punjab, through mechanisms such as an artificially high exchange rate.[15]

The blatant appropriation of the state's resources for the benefit of a tiny élite produced the political convulsions of the sixties. Unlike Europe, there was no struggle for power between a feudal class and an emerging bourgeoisie, since at no point did a conflict of interest exist. Instead, the struggle was primarily between the propertied classes of the various regions. The property-owning élite of the majority province, Bengal, had been excluded from a share in power and resources. In West Pakistan, a collective opposition to the élite in command of the state incorporated the Sindhi, Baluchi and Pathan landlords, as well as the dominated classes of the various regions. The civil war in East Pakistan forced the military to transfer power to the PPP after Bangladesh had been created. The PPP's reforms were a response to the explosive tensions bred by increasing inequalities and the close association of the state with them. The nationalisation programme was motivated partly by an electoral mandate from the classes who had suffered the consequences of increased inequalities. Another factor, however, was the ethnic background of the monopoly industrialists. The Sindhi landlords, prominent in the PPP, resented the growth of migrant industrialists in Sind. Consequently, there were readjustments of power and influence. The groups to suffer were migrant industrialists and Civil Servants, whereas Sindhi landlords increased their influence over public policies. With the revival of military rule in 1977, the old coalition has re-emerged, with the industrialists regaining some of the influence lost in the seventies.

Finally, the questions of the nature of the state in Pakistan is linked to its religious origins. The state has been central to the recent drift towards a theocracy. The Islamisation programme, unilaterally initiated by the state, has altered three fundamental aspects of the relationship between state and society. First, the conception of a separate but secular state for the Muslims, which Jinnah and the Muslim League advocated, is no longer embodied in the state. In spite of its origins, religion in Pakistan has never been associated with the state. All governments prior to Zia's confined religious beliefs to the private domain. Implicit in such a conception was the notion that the state did not enforce conformity to religious practices. Secondly, this merger of political and religious authority has led to a redefinition of private and public spheres. The attempts to protect a private sphere from state encroachment have been the traditional concern of liberal writers such as Locke.[16] Their anxieties have been revived by recent endeavours to create theocracies. Restrictions on the scope of the state to interfere with the private domain have been eroded by the state's enforcement of a fundamentalist order. A particularly dangerous aspect of the extension of state authority into the private domain are the punishments imposed for acts which do not violate the freedom of any individual. For example, lashes and stoning to death were promulgated as punishments for pre-marital sex and adultery. Prayer wardens were set up with the mandate to 'encourage' and mobilise people into attending prayers at the mosque. Third, the state has become the dominant ideological force in society. It has acquired the role of a vanguard for a fundamentalist vision of Islam. The state's enforcement of conformity to religious ideology, and the encroachment of public institutions into private spheres of activity, collectively constituted a shift, between 1977-85, towards totalitarianism in Pakistan. Military dictatorships, even without divine missions, are bad enough. When they are imbued with the spirit of religious fundamentalism, an atmosphere of ideological oppression suffocates the creative impulses of a society.

General Zia's hold on power has been based on a mixture of repression, fortuitous external developments and substantial economic prosperity for a wide section of the population. The symbols and slogans of the decade — Islam, drugs, the 'Dubai syndrome', the 'Kalashnikov culture', Sind, Bhutto, public lashings — reflect the contradictions of a macabre era. The hypocrisy is crude and has an element of farce. Western culture and values are denigrated, yet $7 billion are acquired from the West in exchange for political allegiance; liquor is banned, but destructive drugs are permitted to be grown, processed, exported and consumed domestically because the revenues are too lucrative; the religious discourse is totalitarian but the implementation is constrained by pragmatic considerations. A regime formed under a self-proclaimed transitory mandate finds itself, a decade later, devising new strategies to prolong its rule. A despondent opposition fears the success of another controlled electoral exercise — the 1990 elections. These elections could provide the institutional mechanism for extending military control up to 1995. For General Zia, the conditions are as favourable as they have ever been since he took over. The opposition, which has launched three movements to topple the government, is perhaps more vulnerable than at any other time. Substantial sections of the civilian élite have been co-opted and have developed a stake in the political structure. For the opposition, refuge in precedent may be a cause for optimism — previous governments in Pakistan have been swept out of power just when their tenure has seemed most assured.

Footnotes:

1. Hobbes, T: *Leviathan.* (Contains a vision of an all-embracing state.)
2. Roberts, K: *Order and Dispute*, p.32.
3. Marx, K: *The Communist Manifesto*, and *A Contribution to the Critique of Political Economy*.
4. Weber, M: *Economy and Society*, volume 2, p. 951.
5. Lenin, V: *The State and Revolution*, p. 17.
6. For details of conceptual issues involved see McLennan, Held and Hall (eds): *The Idea of the Modern State.*
7. Thus military governments quite often promulgate constitutions to deflect this criticism of their rule. But since these constitutions can be arbitrarily changed, their very purpose is defeated.
8. Weber dealt with this issue in considerable detail. See selections in, for example, *From Max Weber*, edited by Gerth and Mills.
9. Kelsen, H: *General Theory of Law and State*, pp. 187-88.
10. The danger of isolating the military by the sole reliance on martial law, and the related pressures of legitimising military command over the state, led to the '85 Constitution and the induction of civilians into government.
11. Alavi, H: "The State in Post-Colonial Societies; Pakistan and Bangladesh" *New Left Review*, 1972.
12. See, for example, Mamdani, M: *Politics and Class Formation in Uganda*. Saul, J: "The State in Post-Colonial Societies: Tanzania". For a comment on the debate see Leys, C: "The Over-developed Post-Colonial State: a Re-evaluation" *New Left Review*, 1973.
13. Alavi: op cit, pp. 154-56.
14. Baden-Powell: *The Land Systems of British India.* Volume 3, p. 332.
15. For details of the mechanism see economy section of the Ayub chapter.
16. Locke, J: *Two Treatises of Government.*

BIBLIOGRAPHY

Adas, M.: *Prophets of Rebellion*
(1979, University of North Carolina Press, U.S.A.).
Aharoni, Y.: *Markets, Planning and Development*
(1978, Bullinger, Cambridge, U.S.A.).
Ahmed, A.: *Islamic Modernism in India and Pakistan*
(1970, Oxford University Press, Pakistan).
Ahmed, I.: *The Islamic State Controversy in Pakistan*
(1985, Unpublished Ph.D. thesis, University of Stockholm).
Ahmed, M.: Bangladesh — *Constitutional Quest for Autonomy, 1950-71*
(1978, Franz Steiner Verlag, Germany.)
Ahmed, M.: *Bureaucracy and Political Development in Pakistan*
(1974 NIPA. Pakistan).
Ahmed, M.: "Factors Which Hinder or Help Productivity" mimeograph
(1978, Asian Productivity Organisation, Tokyo, Japan).
Ahmed, M. and Irfan, M.: Real Wages in Pakistan, 1970-84. *The Pakistan Development Review*
(Autumn-Winter 1985. Islamabad).
Alavi, H.: "The State in Post-Colonial Societies: Pakistan and Bangladesh". *New Left Review*
(July 1972).
Alavi, H.: "The Army and the Bureaucracy in Pakistan" *International Socialist Journal*
(April 1966).
Alavi, H.: *Rural Development in Bangladesh and Pakistan*
(1976, University of Hawaii).
Ali, T.: *Pakistan: Military Rule or People's Power?*
(1970, Jonathan Cape, U.K.).
Ali, T.: *Can Pakistan Survive?*
(1982, Pelican, London).
All India Muslim League: *Official documents*
(National Archives of Pakistan, Islamabad).
Andrus and Mohammed: *The Economy of Pakistan*
(1958, Stanford University Press, US.A.).

Amjad and Ahmed: *The Management of Pakistan's Economy*
  (1985, Oxford University Press, U.K.).
Apter, D.: *The Politics of Modernisation*
  (1965, University of Chicago Press, U.S.A.).
Aristotle: *Nicomachean Ethics and The Politics*
  (1936, Oxford University Press, U.K.).
Asher and Mason: *The World Bank Since Bretton Woods*
  (1974, Holt, Rinehart and Winston, U.S.A.).
Ayub Khan, M.: *Friends Not Masters*
  (1967, Oxford University Press, U.K.).
Ayub Khan, M.: *Speeches and Statements: 1958-64*
  (1966, Ferozesons, Pakistan).
Aziz, K.: *Party Politics in Pakistan 1947-58*
  (1976, National Commission on Historical and Cultural Research, Islamabad).
Baden-Powell, B. H.: *The Land Systems of British India*
  (1892, Oxford University Press U.K.).
Bahadur, K.: *The Jamaat-e-Islami of Pakistan*
  (1983, Progressive Books, Lahore).
Barber, Curtis and Friedrich: *Totalitarianism in Perspective: Three Views*
  (1969 Harvard University Press, U.S.A.).
Baxter and Burki: "Socio-economic Indicators of the People's Party Vote in the Punjab", *Journal of Asian Studies*
  (August 1975, California, U.S.A.).
Berman, H. J.: *Justice in the U.S.S.R.*
  (1963, Harvard University Press, U.S.A.).
Bhatia, B. M.: *Pakistan's Economic Development*
  (1979, Vikas Publishing House, India).
Bhutto, Z. A.: *If I Am Assassinated...*
  (1979, Vikas Publishing House, India).
Bhutto, Z. A.: *The Third World; New Directions*
  (1977, Quartet Books, U.K.).
Bhutto, Z. A.: *The Myth of Independence*
  (1969, Oxford University Press, U.K.).
Bhutto, Z. A.: "Political Situation in Pakistan", *PPP Political Series*
  (1968, P.P.P. Pakistan).
Binder, L.: *Religion and Politics in Pakistan*
  (1961, University of California Press, U.S.A.).
Bolitho, H.: *Jinnah, Creator of Pakistan*
  (1954, John Murray, U.K.).
Braibanti, R.: *Research on the Bureaucracy of Pakistan*
  (1966, Duke University Press, U.S.A.).
Brecher and Abbas: *Foreign Aid and Industrial Development in Pakistan*
  (1972, Cambridge University Press, U.K.).

Burki, S. J.: *Pakistan Under Bhutto, 1971-77*
  (1980, Macmillan Press, U.S.A.).
Burki and Laporte (eds): *Pakistan's Development Priorities*
  (1984, Oxford University Press, U.K.).
Callard, K.: *Pakistan: A Political Study*
  (1957, Allen & Unwin, U.K.).
Casper, J. D.: "The Supreme Court and National Policy Making", *American Political Science Register*
  (March 1976, U.S.A.).
Chaudhry and Herring: "The 1972 Land Reforms in Pakistan and their Economic Implications"; *Pakistan Development Review*
  (Autumn, 1974, P.I.D.E.).
Chenery, H.: *Structural Change and Development Policy*
  (1979, John Hopkins University Press, U.S.A.).
Chomsky and Herman: *The Washington Connection and Third World Fascism* (1979, Black Rose Books, Canada).
Choudhry, G. W.: *Last Days of United Pakistan*
  (1974, C. Hurst, U.K.).
Cohen, S.: *The Pakistan Army*
  (1984, University of California Press, U.S.A.).
Dawn: Daily English newspaper, 1947-1985 (Various issues, Karachi).
Economist Intelligence Unit: Quarterly reports on Pakistan (Various issues, London).
Far Eastern Economic Review
  1970-85. (Various issues, Hong Kong).
Farooqi, M.: *Pakistan: Policies That Led to Break Up*
  (1972, Party Publications, India).
Feldman, H.: "Pakistan — 1973", *Asian Survey*
  (February 1974).
Feldman, H.: "Pakistan in 1974", *Asian Survey* (February 1975).
Fieldhouse, D. K.: *Economics and Empire 1830-1914*
  (1973, Cornell University Press, U.S.A.).
Finer, S. E.: *The Man on Horseback*
  (1962, Pall Mall, U.K.).
Fox. R.: *The Colonial Policy of British Imperialism*
  (1933, Martin Lawrence, U.K.).
Friedrich and Brzezinski: *Totalitarian Dictatorship and Autocracy*
  (1965, Harvard University Press, U.S.A.).
Gankovsky, Y. V.: *The Peoples of Pakistan*
  (1971, Nauka Publishing House, U.S.S.R.).
Gankovsky and Moskalenko: *The Three Constitutions of Pakistan*
  (1978, People's Publishing House, Pakistan).
Gardezi & Rashid (eds): *Pakistan — The Roots of Dictatorship*
  (1981, Zed Publications, U.K.).

Government of Pakistan: *M. A. Jinnah: Speeches and Writings.*
Government of Pakistan: Legislative Assembly Debates, 1972-77 (Islamabad).
Government of Pakistan: *Constitutions*
(1956, 1962 and 1973, Islamabad & Karachi)
Government of Pakistan: *Pakistan Economic Survey*
(Various issues, Islamabad).
Government of Pakistan: *Five Year Plans*
(First, second, third, fourth, fifth and sixth) (Planning Commission, Islamabad).
Government of Pakistan: *Twenty five years of Pakistan in Statistics*
(1972, Statistics Division, Islamabad).
Government of Pakistan: *Taxation Structure of Pakistan*
(1981, Islamabad).
Government of Pakistan: *White Paper on the Performance of the Bhutto Regime: Misuse of the Instruments of State Power*
(1979, Islamabad).
Government of Pakistan: *White Paper on the Performance of the Bhutto Regime: The Economy*
(1979, Islamabad).
Government of Pakistan: *Report of the Farm Mechanisation Committee*
(1970, Ministry of Agriculture and Works, Islamabad).
Government of Pakistan: Four Studies in Basic Democracies.
(1964, Bureau of National Construction, Islamabad).
Government of Pakistan: *Pakistan Legal Decisions*
(1963, Islamabad).
Griffin and Khan (eds): *Growth and Inequality in Pakistan*
(1973, Macmillan, U.K.).
Guisinger and Hicks: "Long Term Trends in Income Distribution in Pakistan"; *World Development*
(1978).
Guisinger, Hicks and Pilvin: "Wages and Relative Factor Prices in Pakistan". mimeograph, (September 1977,World Bank, U.S.A.).
Habib, H.: *Babus, Brahmins and Bureaucrats*
(1973, People's Publishing House, Pakistan).
Harrison, S. S.:"Nightmare in Baluchistan" *Foreign Policy*, (Fall 1978).
Harrison, S S: *In Afghanistan's Shadow*
(1981, Carnegie, Washington U.S.A.).
Haq, M.: *The Strategy of Economic Planning*
(1967, Oxford University Press, U.K.).
Herring, R. J.: "Zulfiqar Ali Bhutto and the 'eradication of feudalism' in Pakistan". *Economic and Political Weekly*
(22 March, 1980, India).
Hodgkin, T.: "The Revolutionary Tradition in Islam" *Race and Class*,

(1980, XXI, 3, U.K.).
Holloway and Picciotto: *State and Capital*
(1978, Verso, U.K.).
Huntington, S.: *Political Order in Changing Societies*
(1968, Yale University, U.S.A.).
Hussain, A.: *Elite Politics in an Ideological State*
(1979, Dawson, U.K.).
Huttenback, R. A.: *Racism and Empire*
(1976, Cornell University Press, U.S.A.).
I.B.R.D.: Industrial Development of Pakistan
(1966, U.S.A.).
Ionescu, G.: *The Politics of the European Communist States*
(1967, Macmillan Press, U.K.).
Islam, N.: *Foreign Trade and Economic Controls in Development*
(1970, Pakistan Institute of Development) Economics, Islamabad.
Jahan, R.: *Pakistan, Failure in National Integration*
(1972, Columbia University Press, U.S.A.).
Jahan, R.: *Bangladesh Politics*
(1980, Dacca University Press, Bangladesh).
Jalal, A.: *Jinnah: the Sole Spokesman*
(1985, Cambridge University Press, U.K.).
Jang: Urdu daily newspaper
(Various issues, Karachi).
Janowitz, M.: *The Military in the Political Development of New Nations*
(1964, University of Chicago Press, U.S.A.).
Jeffalyn Johnson and Associates: *A Review of U.S. Assistance to Pakistan*
(1982, U.S.A. Agency for International Development).
Johnson, J.: *The Role of the Military in Underdeveloped Countries*
(1962, Stanford University Press, U.S.A.).
Jones, P. E.: *South Asian Politics and Religion*
(1972, Princeton University Press, U.S.A.).
Jones, P. J.: *The Pakistan People's Party*
(1979, Unpublished Ph.D. thesis, Fletcher School of Law and Diplomacy, U.S.A.).
Kamal, K. L.: *Pakistan, the Garrison State*
(1983, Vanguard, Pakistan).
Kelsen, H.: *General Theory of Law and State*
(1968, University of California Press, U.S.A.).
Khan, A. A.: *The Jamaat-e-Islami of Pakistan*
(1962, Jamaat-e-Islami, Pakistan).
Khan, A. R.: "What has been happening to real wages in Pakistan?", *Pakistan Development Review*
(Autumn 1967, Pakistan).
Khan, A.:*Generals and Politics*

(1982, Vanguard, Pakistan).
Khan, A.(ed.): *Islam, Politics and the State*
(1975, Zed Publications, U.K.).
Khan, I.(ed.): *Fresh Perspectives on India and Pakistan*
(1985, Bougainvillea Books, U.K.).
Khan, M. H.: *Underdevelopment and Agrarian Structure in Pakistan*
(1981, Vanguard, Pakistan).
Khan, M. I.: "Industrial Labour in Karachi"; *Pakistan Development Review*
(Winter 1963, Pakistan).
Khan, T. M. (ed.): *Studies on National Income and its Distribution*
(1970, P.I.D.E., Pakistan).
Korson, J.: Contemporary Problems of Pakistan. (1974, E. J. Brill, Leiden, Holland).
Laclau, E.: *Politics and Ideology in Marxist Theory*
(1977, New Left Books, U.K.).
La Porte, R.: "Pakistan in 1972: Picking up the Pieces", *Asian Survey*, (February 1973).
Lewis, B.(ed.): *Islam*
(1974, Harper and Row, U.S.A.).
Lewis, S. R.: *Pakistan: Industrialisation and Trade Policies*
(1970, OECD, France).
Leys, C.: "The Overdeveloped Post-Colonial State: a Re-evaluation", *Review of African Political Economy*
(1976).
Little, Scitovsky and Scott: *Industry and Trade in Developing Countries*
(1970, OECD, France).
Lodhi, M.: *The Pakistan People's Party*
(1979, Unpublished Ph.D. thesis, London School of Economics).
Macaulay: *Critical, Historical and Miscellaneous Essays*
(Oxford University Press, U.K.).
Mahmood, Z.: *Income Inequality in Pakistan*
(1984, Paper presented at conference of the Pakistan Society of Development Economists, Islamabad).
Majumdar, Raychaudhuri and Datta: *An Advanced History of India*
(1967, Macmillan, U.S.A.).
Malik, H.: "Martial law and political development in Pakistan", *Defence Journal*
(1972, Karachi University, Pakistan).
Maron, S.: "Regional Tensions in East Bengal", *Pacific Affairs*
(June 1955).
Marx and Engels: *On Colonialism*
(1961, Foreign Languages Publishing House, U.S.S.R.).
Mascaranhas, A.: *Bangladesh: Legacy of Blood*
(1986, Hodder and Stoughton, U.K.).

Masud, M.: *Hari Report: Note of Dissent*
   (1948, Hari Publications, Pakistan).
Maududi, A. A.: *Islamic Law and Constitution*
   (1960, Jamaat-e-Islami, Pakistan).
Maududi, A. A.: *The Process of Islamic Revolution*
   (1955, Jamaat-e-Islami, Pakistan).
McIntyre, W. D.: *Colonies into Commonwealth*
   (1966, Blandford Press, U.K.).
Moody, P.: *Zulfi My Friend*
   (1973, Thomson Press, India).
Morning News: Daily newspaper
   (Various issues, Karachi).
Mukerjee, D.: *Zulfiqar Ali Bhutto: Quest for Power*
   (1972, Vikas Publishing House, India).
Munir, K.: *From Jinnah to Zia*
   (1979, Vanguard, Pakistan).
Mustafa, S.: *Pakistan: A Study in Underdevelopment*
   (Research Monograph, University of the Punjab, n.d.)
Naseem, S. M.: *Underdevelopment, Poverty and Inequality in Pakistan*
   (1980, Vanguard, Pakistan).
Nazeer, M.: *The Islamic Economic System*
   (1981, P.I.D.E., Islamabad).
Naqvi et al: *Principles of Islamic Economic Reform*
   (1984, P.I.D.E., Islamabad).
Nehru, J.: *The Discovery of India*
   (1946, John Day Company, U.S.A.).
Noman, A.: *Industrialisation in Pakistan: Social Costs and Private Benefits*
   (1972, B.Phil. thesis, University of Oxford, U.K.).
O'Connor, J.: *The Fiscal Crisis of the State*
   (1973, New York, U.S.A.).
Omvedt and Patankar, "The State in post-colonial social formation";
   Economic and Political Weekly
   (November 1979, India).
Oren, S.: "Sikhs, Congress and Unionists in British Punjab"; *Modern Asian Studies*
   (1974, Cambridge University Press, U.K.).
Papanek, G.: *Pakistan's Development: Social Goals and Private Incentives*
   (1967, Harvard University Press, U.S.A.).
Pasha, H. A.: "Measurement of the Contribution of different factors to inflation in Pakistan"; *P.I.D.E. Discussion Paper.*
Peiris, D.: "Bhutto's Rise to Power"; *Far Eastern Economic Review*
   (July 1977, Tokyo, Japan).
Phillips and Wainwright: *The Partition of India*
   (1970, Allen and Unwin, U.K.).

Polanski, Arensberg and Pearson: *Trade and Markets in the Early Empires*
(1968, History Book Club, U.K.).
Quarterly Economic Review of Pakistan, Bangladesh, Afghanistan
(Economist, London, Various Issues).
Qureishy, M. L.: *Planning and Development in Pakistan*
(1984, Vanguard, Pakistan).
Qureshi, I. H.: *Pakistan: An Islamic Democracy*
(1959, Ferozesons, Pakistan).
Rashid, J.: "Economic Causes of Political Crises in Pakistan"; *Developing Economies*
(June 1978, Tokyo, Japan).
Rashid, J.: "Pakistan in the Debt Trap: A Mortgaged Economy",
Viewpoint, (Pakistan)
(10, 17, 24 December 1976).
Richter & Gustafson: "Pakistan 1979 Back to square one"; *Asian Survey*
(February 1980).
Rizvi, H. A.: *PPP — The First Phase, 1969-71*
(1972, Progressive Publications).
Rizvi, H. A.: *The Military and Politics in Pakistan*
(1974, Progressive Publishers, Pakistan).
Roll, E.: *History of Economic Thought*
(1938, Faber and Faber, U.K.).
Salek, S.: *Witness to Surrender*
(1977, Oxford University Press, Pakistan).
Sarmad, K.: *Pakistan's Economy through the Seventies*
(1983, P.I.D.E., Islamabad).
Saul, J.: "The State in Post-Colonial Societies", *Social Register*
(1974, Merlin Press, U.K.).
Sayeed, K. B.: *Pakistan: The Formative Phase*
(1968, Oxford University Press, U.K.).
Sayeed, K. B.: *The Political System of Pakistan*
(1967, Houghton Mifflin, U.S.A.).
Sayeed, K. B.: *The Nature and Direction of Political Change in Pakistan*
(1980, Praeger, U.S.A.).
Sayeed, K. B.: "The role of the Military in Pakistan" in Van Dorn (ed.),
Armed Forces and Society
(1966, Moulton, U.S.A.).
Seal, A.: *The Emergence of Indian Nationalism*
(1968, Cambridge University Press, U.K.).
Sen, S.: *Muslim Politics in Bengal 1937-47*
(1976, Oxford University Press, India).
Shapiro, L.: *Totalitarianism*
(1972, Hutchinson, U.K.).
Sharif, M: "Dialectical Monadism" *Contemporary Indian Philosophy*

(1952, Institute of Islamic Culture, Pakistan).
Sharif, M.: *About Iqbal and his Thought*
(1964, Institute of Islamic Culture).
Sharif-ul-Mujahid: *Jinnah*
(1984, University of Karachi, Pakistan).
Siddiqi, K.: *Conflict, Crisis and War in Pakistan*
(1972, Macmillan, U.K.).
Siddiqi, M.: "Socialistic trends in Islam". *IQBAL*
(1952, Volume 1, No. 1. Pakistan).
Siddiqi, M.: *What is Islam?* (1954, Ranpur, Pakistan).
Singhal, D.: *Pakistan*
(1972, Prentice Hall, Australia).
Smith, V. A.: *The Oxford History of India*
(1920, U.K.).
Smith, W. C.: *Modern Islam in India*
(1957, Princeton University Press, U.S.A.).
Soligo and Stern: "Tariff protection, Import substitution and Investment efficency"; *Pakistan Development Review;*
(Summer 1965).
State of Bank of Pakistan: *Annual Reports*
(Various years).
Stepanyants, M. T.: *Pakistan: Philosophy and Sociology*
(1971, Nauka Publishing House, U.S.S.R.).
Sudama, T.: "Analysis of classes by Mao Tse Tung 1923-39"; *Journal of Contemporary Asia*
(Fall, 1978).
Syed, A. H.: *Islam, Politics and National Solidarity*
(1983, Praeger, U.S.A.).
Syed, A. H.: "Pakistan in 1976: business as usual"; *Asian Survey*,
(February, 1977).
Taher-Kheli, S.: *The U.S. — Pakistan relationship*
(1983, Washington, U.S.A.).
Taseer, S.: *Bhutto; a political biography*
(1980, Ithaca Press, U.K.).
Tawney, R. H.: *Religion and the Rise of Capitalism*
(1977, Penguin Books, U.K.).
United States Government: Report of the President's Committee to Study the United States Military Assistance Programme
(1959, Washington D.C., U.S.A.).
Usman, M.: *Islamic Socialism*
(1970, Progressive Publishers).
Venkataramani, S.: *The U.S. Role in Pakistan*
(1982, Vanguard, Pakistan).
Vorys, K. V.: *Political Development in Pakistan*

(1965, Princeton University Press, U.S.A.).
Wheeler, R.: "Pakistan in 1975; the hydra of opposition": *Asian Survey*
(February 1976).
Wolf-Phillips, L.: *Constitutional Legitimacy*
(1979, Third World, U.K.).
Wolpert, S.: *Jinnah of Pakistan*
(1984, Oxford University Press, U.S.A.).
World Bank: *World Development Reports 1979-85*
(Washington D.C., U.S.A.).
World Bank: *Industrialisation of Pakistan*
(1970, Washington D.C., U.S.A.).
World Bank: *Country Reports on Pakistan*
(Various issues).
World Bank: Education Sector Working Paper
(1974, Washington D.C., U.S.A.).
World Bank: *Pakistan; Development Issues and Policies*
(1978, Washington D.C., U.S.A.).
World Bank: *Public Sector Resource Mobilisation*
(1978, Washington D.C., U.S.A.).
Ziring, L.: *The Ayub Khan era*
(1971, Syracuse University Press, U.S.A.).
Ziring, L. (ed.): *Pakistan — the long view*
(1977, Duke University Press, U.S.A.).
Ziring, L.: *Pakistan — the enigma of political development*
(1980, Duke University Press, U.S.A.).
Ziring, L.: "The Pakistan Bureaucracy: Administrative Reforms"; *Asian Survey*
(December, 1974).

Index

Adult literacy rate, ix.
Afghanistan; Soviet invasion of, 120-1.
Agricultural sector; between 1947-1958, 16; under Ayub, 36; under Bhutto, 93; under Zia, 163; land reforms, 93; 'green revolution', 39.
Aid, 168; Aid to Pakistan Consortium, 38.
Army, 117; political role, 199; crackdown in East Pakistan, 46.
Awami League, 32; six-points demand, 31. (*see also* Mujib).
Ayub Khan, 27; political developments under, 28; economic policies, 35; attitude to Islam, 33; downfall, 43.

Balance of payments, 160; impact of devaluation on, 76.
Baluchistan, 13; conflict in the sixties, 32; '70 election result in; armed insurrection against PPP regime, 64.
Bangladesh, 47.
Basic democracy programme, 27.
Basic economic indicators, ix.
Bengal, language riots, 14; poor representation in army, 13; deprivation of political power, 30; secessionist movement in, 47.
Bhutto, Z. A., 57; rise of, 101; political structure under, 57; economic policies, 74; foreign policy, 109; Islamic socialism, 108; populist appeal, 101; execution, 120.
Board of industrial management, 80.
Bonus voucher scheme, 38.
British; legacy, 4.
Bureaucracy; political dominance of, 12; administrative reforms, 61; colonial legacy, 11.
Burki, S. J., 97.

Cabinet Mission Plan of 1946, 5.
Caliphate, 6.
Capital intensive industrialisation, 39; industrial capital, 16.
CENTO, 14.
China, 48.
Communism, 144.
Congress Party, 4.

Constitution; of 1956, 10; of 1962, 28; of 1973, 58; constitutional amendments, 69; problems, 68.
Consumer goods industrialisation, 16.
Courts, 122; Supreme Court, 123; High Court, 193.

Debt burden, 161.
Defence expenditure, 175.
Deficit financing, 167.
Democracy; failure of, 13, 69.
Denationalisation; 172.
Devaluation; in the fifties, 15, in 1972, 76.
Distribution of income, ix; regional, 41; class, 42.
Doctrine of functional inequality, 40.

East Pakistan, 9; role in Partition, 5; political demands of, 31; economic grievances, 41; Ayub's attitude towards, 30; National Assembly elections in, 45 (*see also* Bengal).
Economic policies; in the fifties, 15; in the sixties, 35; in the seventies, 74; in the eighties, 157.
Education; poor allocation for, 173.
Elections; indirect, 27; of 1954, 14; of 1964, xi; of 1970, 45; of 1977, 69; of 1984, 126. (*also see* basic democracy programme).
Employment; poor employment generation by industrial sector, 160; migration to Gulf, 157.
Exports; incentives, 38.

Family laws ordinance, 34.
Farm mechanisation, 39.
Fiscal policy, 171.
Five-year plans; first, 18; second, 36; third, 36; fourth, 84; fifth, 167; sixth, 169.
Foreign aid, 168.
Foreign policy, 14, 48, 109.
Free list, 37.
Federal Security Force, 59.

Gandhi, 5.
Ghulam Mohammad, 8, 11.
Government of India Act (1935), 11.
Green revolution, 36, 39.
Gross National Product; per capita, ix.

Hadith, 141.
Hamza, Alavi, 199.
Haq, Mahbub, 40, 166.
Harrison, S., 72.
Health facilities, 174.
Hinduism, 30.
Huntington, S., 48.

215

IBRD, 37, 90.
IMF, 39.
Iftikharuddin, Mian, 26.
Import controls, 16.
Incomes; distribution of, 94; inequalities in, 41; per capita, ix.
India; partition of, 13; relations with Pakistan, 48.
Indirect taxes, 82.
Industrial development, 16; industrial investment schedule, 15; industrial relations, 95.
Infant mortality rate, ix.
Inflation, 88.
Inter-regional disparity, 31.
Interest-free economy; proposals and implementation, 145.
Iran; Shah of, 67.
Iskander Mirza, 12.
Islam; official attitudes towards, 7; two-nation theory, 3; debate over theocracy, 140.
Islamic laws, 146.

Jagirdari, 65.
Jamaat-e-Islami, 141.
Jinnah, M. A., 3.
Judiciary, 123.
Junejo, M., 130.

Kashmir, 43.
Karachi, industrial concentration in, 20.
Kasuri, Ahmed Reza, 135.
Khan, Asghar, 114, 118.
Khan, Liaquat Ali, 7.
Khan, Mairaj Mohammed, 102.
Khan, Qayyum, 44.
Korean boom, 16.

Labour; role of in mass protests, 43; laws, 95; migration, 157.
Lahore resolution, 4.
Land reforms; in 1959, 39; in 1972, 93.
Large-scale manufacturing, 38.
Legislature; in the fifties, 9; under Ayub, 47; under Bhutto, 63; under Zia, 127; elections to, 126.

Manufacturing sector, 85.
Market mechanism; reliance on, 39.
Martial law, 122.
Maududi (Maudoodi), A. A., 3, 6-7, 141, 143.
Mechanisation; in agriculture, 39; in industry, 160.
Merchant capital, 20.
Middle class; benefits under Ayub, 42; role in anti-Bhutto movement, 87.
Middle East; Pakistani workers in, 157; army in, 109.

Mohammed, the Prophet, 108.
Monetary policy, 88.
Mudaraba, 145.
Mujib (*see also* Awami League), 31.
Mullahs, 142.
Multiple exchange rate system, 38.
Muslim League, 4; role in Pakistan movement, 5; disintegration of, 9.

National Assembly elections; in 1970, 47; rigging of elections in 1977, 110.
National identity, 13; strains on national integration, 46.
Nationalisation, 77; denationalisation, 172.
Nehru, J., 5.
Niazi, K., 108.
NDVP, 84.
NWFP, 186.
Nuclear power, 121.

Objectives Resolution, 7.
Oil prices, 97; effects of, 88.
Omar, Caliph, 153.
One-unit scheme, 10.

Pakistan Industrial Development Corporation, 81.
Pakistan Institute of Development Economics, 159.
Pakistan Resolution, 4.
PPP; formation, 104; relationship with . . . army, 58 . . . bureaucracy, 61; . . . opposition, 64; economic policy of, 74; civil service reforms, 61; attitude towards Islam, 107; attitude towards socialism, 108; role of Bhutto, 105; downfall of government, 69; suppression under Zia, 119.
People's Work Programme, 84.
Parliamentary system (*see* Legislature).
Pathans, 186; representation in government, 187.
Peerzada, A. H., 99.
Planning commission, 169.
Political power, 199; uneven distribution of, 200.
Population, ix; growth rate, ix.
Press, 69; control of, 124;
Private sector; role of, 37; attacks on, 77.
PRODA Act, 12.
Profit and loss sharing scheme, 145.
Public sector, 79.
Punjab; importance of, 119; dominance of civil service & army, 182.

Qadianis, 7; persecution of, 109.
Quaid-e-Azam *see* Jinnah.
Quran, 141.

Rahim, J. A., 103.

Rahman, Sheikh Mujib *see* Mujib.
Rana, Mukhtar, 102.
Rashid, Sheikh, 103.
Real wages, 158.
Regionalism; in East Pakistan, 31; in Baluchistan, 64; in Sind, 181; in NWFP, 186.
Religion *see* Islam.
Remittances, 157.
Republican Party, 12.
Riba, 145.
Round Table Conference, 43.

    Saudi Arabia, 109; influence of, 151.
Savings, 146.
SEATO, 14.
Secularisation, 8.
Shariah, 141.
Sind, 181.
Socialism, 108.
Social sectors, 173; neglect of, 174.
State Bank of Pakistan, 166.
Steel mill, 82.
Supreme Court verdict on Bhutto, 123.

    Tariff policy, 16.
Tashkent agreement, 101.
Twenty-two families, 41.
Two-nation theory, 3.

    Ulema, 6.
United States, 121.
Urdu, 14.
Ushr, 146.

    Wavell Viceroy, 4.
West Pakistan; merged into one unit, 10; dominance of military and bureaucracy, 20; tension with East Pakistan, 44.
Women, 142; laws of evidence against, 142.
World Bank, 37, 90.

    Yahya Khan; assumption of power, 43; elections under, 44; military crackdown under, 46.

    Zakat, 167.
Zia-ul-Haq; coup 117; Islam under, 140; economy under, 157, regionalism under, 180.